MASTERING CRYPTO

From Basics to Advanced

By

Budhil Vyas

Published by:

Invincible Publication Pvt. Ltd.

For permissions, contact:
Invincible Publication Pvt. Ltd.
Office No. 1103-A, 11th Floor
SAS Tower, Sector 38, Gurugram Haryana - 122003
Email: Sales@i-publish.in
www.invinciblepublishers.com

Sales Office: - 4760-61/23, Basement, Pratap Street,
Ansari Road, Daryaganj, New Delhi - 110002
Email: invinciblepublishers@gmail.com

Title: Mastering Crypto

Author: Budhil Vyas

ISBN: 978-93-5886-532-5

Printed in India
First Edition: 2024

Table of Contents

Dedication:

I dedicate this book to Marudhar Bhagwat Bhaskar and my late grandfather, Pandit Mohanlal Vyas. The lessons they taught me during my early years have stayed with me and shaped my future.

My grandfather's unique and loving approach was unlike anyone else's, and although I didn't always understand it at the time, I now see how his guidance laid the foundation for my success. I wish every grandchild could have a mentor like him—one who offers sheer love and guidance, helping them envision and strive toward a bright future from a young age.

Acknowledgements:

I respectfully pay homage to my esteemed grandfather, Pandit Mohanlal Vyas, for inspiring me to write this book. My heartfelt thanks go to my family, friends and teachers for their unwavering support and encouragement. I am also grateful to the Crypto Talks family for their trust and support through challenging times.

I look forward to continuing to grow our social media community together with our audience's ongoing love and support.

Thank you!

Preface

The cryptocurrency market appears quite attractive from a distance. We often hear stories of people earning life-changing amounts of money almost overnight. It's tempting to think we can jump in and do the same. But once you step into the world of crypto trading, it quickly becomes clear that it's not as straightforward as it seems. You may start asking yourself: How are others making money in this market? Will I be able to do it too? Is there something I'm missing?

The truth is, cryptocurrency trading requires more than just enthusiasm—it takes knowledge, patience, and a willingness to learn from both successes and failures. That's exactly what this book aims to provide. I've been in your shoes, wondering how to make sense of this complex world of digital currencies. My journey began when I was still an engineering student in Bangalore. It was during a machine learning course that I first encountered Bitcoin, and though I couldn't afford to invest back then, I knew this new form of currency was something special.

After entering the world of data science and working with stock market data, my path took a new direction during the COVID-19 lockdown. That was when I met people who were actively trading cryptocurrencies. Intrigued by the possibilities, I started my own crypto trading journey, and it wasn't long before I began sharing my experiences and predictions with others.

But my passion for crypto wasn't born just from excitement about technology. It was driven by something deeper: the desire to create a better life for myself and my family. Coming from humble beginnings, where we relied on Below Poverty Line (BPL) government schemes for food, I understood the importance of financial security in a way that goes beyond just making quick profits. For me, crypto trading became a way to build a stable and prosperous future, and that's what I hope to help you achieve with this book.

I didn't want to keep what I learned to myself, so I created a YouTube channel, Crypto Talks, where I share my insights with thousands of followers. But unlike many who promise fast and easy money, I focus on the importance of patience and long-term success. As I always say, "Quick money never guarantees long-term success. Slow and steady is the key to sustainable growth." This philosophy is at the core of everything I teach.

In this book, I'll walk you through my journey and provide you with practical ways to go about the crypto market. I won't just talk about profits and predictions, but also about the risks, the challenges, and the strategies that can help you build a lasting success. Whether you're completely new to crypto or have already dabbled in trading, I want this book to be your companion, helping you understand the market and develop the skills you need to thrive.

The world of cryptocurrency is constantly evolving, and I truly believe it offers incredible opportunities for those willing to learn and adapt. This book is your guide to unlocking those opportunities. Let's embark on this journey together—I promise you'll come out the other side with a clearer understanding of the market and the knowledge needed to make informed decisions in this exciting space.

Yours sincerely,

Budhil Vyas

Important to Understand Before you Enter in Market:

Although these types of sections usually go at the end of the book, I kept it right at the beginning. The purpose is that you may keep these points in mind as you begin your crypto journey, and once you finally finish the book and truly understand the value of these below points, you may revisit this section every once in a while once.

Why Are Investors Missing Out on Potential Profits in Crypto?

1. **Buying at the Wrong Times -** Many investors and traders tend to buy when prices are high and sell when they're low, leading to significant losses.

2. **Poor Profit Booking Decisions -** Often Investors and traders often hesitate to book profits or cut losses, waiting for dips that may never come.

3. **Waiting for Dips Instead of Accumulating -** Many panic-driven traders miss opportunities to accumulate during market corrections. A strategic dollar-cost averaging (DCA) approach can help you navigate through volatility.

4. **Greedy Traders -** Overconfidence can lead traders to

neglect stop-loss orders. Even if they set them, they often fail to trail them, assuming the market will follow their predictions—this is a risky mindset in the unpredictable crypto landscape.

5. **Greedy Investors** - While aware of the risks, many investors refuse to book profits. A key strategy is to safeguard your principal amount by taking profits when your investment doubles. This allows you to secure your initial amount while still enjoying potential gains.

6. **Panic Retailers** - Many retail investors act on impulse, missing profitable opportunities by waiting for ideal conditions. For example, those who hesitated recently might have missed out on coins that have surged, achieving 2X or 3X returns.

How Should Investors Approach the Market?

- **40% in Large Caps** (e.g., Bitcoin, Ethereum) – A safe bet.
- **30% in Mid Caps and Small Caps** (e.g., BNB, Solana, Jupiter, Near, Arbitrum, Ocean) – A balanced risk-reward profile.
- **20% in Emerging Trends** (e.g., AI, gaming, RWA, DEPIN) – Investing in new coins can yield high returns.
- **10% in Futures or Options** – For those looking to take calculated risks.

By diversifying wisely, you can maximize their potential in the crypto market. Remember not to let fear and greed dictate your decisions—stay informed and stay strategic.

Chapter 1:

The Journey From Currency To Cryptocurrency

Concept and Genesis

The first Cryptocurrency, short for encrypted currency, was introduced in 2009, following a financial crisis in 2007-2008. The innovations around the concept were progressing over the years, but the final result of this simple concept in 2009 disturbed the financial systems and all the beliefs around currency. Hence, cryptocurrency attracted a lot of media coverage, commentaries, research papers, and books throughout the years. But despite the media coverage and the hype, it still remains one of the most misunderstood concepts. People remain unaware of why and how crypto came into being even today. Some still believe that it is just an alternative to stocks and that is the first mistake people usually make when starting to invest in it.

This encrypted form of currency is a type of digital money. Now, money can be defined as a property of a particular person or a community and every unit of it has some value in the market. In ancient times, things like honey, grains, or fruits would be used to buy or barter things. Over time, humanity switched to coins, which were accepted by all sellers and buyers. These coins were a widely accepted unit of currency, holding a certain value, meaning that you would accordingly get something in return for it. Today, we can see several currencies such as Dollars, Euro, Yen, and Rupee, and they all have a certain value attached to them, which keeps increasing or decreasing over time based on various factors.

As we know, not just any piece of coin or a note has a value unless it is real i.e. a proper authority has created it, and society has completely accepted it as a currency to buy and sell things. In modern societies, this authority to create money is with the government or the central banks. They regulate the amount of money going into the market, and they also determine its value. But all money is possible to abuse. Fake coins and notes are still produced. Even though we now have electronic or digital records of our money, some still manage to commit fraud by duplicating these records or committing double-spending. As an alternative to a currency that is controlled by an authority and can be faked, a cryptocurrency was created by Satoshi Nakamoto in 2009. He wanted to create a fair, borderless, and secure currency that could be safely used anywhere with anyone.

Nakamoto took the help of a simple concept known as Blockchain technology. Blockchain simply means a chain of digital blocks that permanently records each and every transaction. Somewhat similar to your finance guy maintaining a ledger, but the only difference is that information recorded in blockchain cannot be changed once it is created.

Blockchain Technology and How It Led to Cryptocurrency

Blockchain technology can be defined as a public digital ledger that stores data in blocks linked together in a chain. These blocks are continuously formed and linked together using unique codes. The data stored in these blocks is permanent and almost impossible to delete or duplicate. This technology came back in 1991 when some scientists wanted a solution for creating and storing digital documents or data that cannot be copied or wrongly dated.

They used cryptography to create the blocks of the data, which is rooted in advanced computer science, mathematics, and algorithms. Cryptography is a way of protecting the data by uniquely coding it so that access to information only remains with the sender and receiver. It is widely used in encrypting messages, banking systems, VPNs, cell phones, websites, etc. To describe it in a simple manner, let's say you and I created a separate language that only we knew. Now any information that we may share, will not be understood by others, and the information will seem secure or coded to them.

The use of cryptography and blockchain technology evolved over the years. It was in 2004, that Hal Finney introduced a concept of digital cash known as "Reusable Proof of Work". This concept was a game-changer that helped in solving the issue of double-spending (using the same currency unit to make multiple transactions) by registering the ownership of the currency unit to a trusted server. Because of this concept, every transaction of the currency could be tracked effortlessly. With such innovations over time, the concept of cryptocurrency was evolving only to culminate into something known as Bitcoin.

The Birth of the First Cryptocurrency: Bitcoin

In 2007-2008, the world experienced a major financial crisis. It was one of the worst financial crises that led to a loss of more than $2 trillion from the global economy. One of the reasons for this crisis was the decision of the US Federal Reserve System to print and push $60 Billion into the global economy every month, to help the post-war economy. This move resulted in a crisis and loss of trust in the financial systems.

It was because of this "need of the moment" that the concept of Bitcoin arose; to overcome the monopoly of financial authorities in regulating money. In 2008, a private currency known as Bitcoin was introduced by Satoshi Nakamoto. A paper was published on the internet explaining the cryptocurrency mechanism behind "Bitcoin". It was on 9th January 2009, that Nakamoto released the first version of Bitcoin, and worked on the same till 2010.

Who is exactly Satoshi Nakamoto? No one knows. There is a theory that it is a person or a group of people that launched Bitcoin under the name of Satoshi Nakamoto. Over the years, people have made their guesses and gone to extreme lengths to identify him but with no luck. It is said that he finally gave all of Bitcoin's system control to Gavin Andresen and other prominent members of the Bitcoin community. But to this date, no one knows of the true existence of the legendary Satoshi Nakamoto.

What Happened Thereafter?

Until the introduction of Bitcoin, the concept of cryptocurrency was not as popular amongst people as it is today. One of the reasons for that is people's resistance to something new and a bias for something more familiar. In his introductory paper, Nakamoto described it as a "fully-fledged version of electronic money, based on peer-to-peer network communication models, allowing online payments to be sent from one entity to another without the need for transactions to flow through financial institutions". This meant that Bitcoin would function without interference from any third party or intermediary such as a bank & their transaction system, yet it was so secure. And this reminds me of an incident that took place with James Howells who was involved in the mining of bitcoin in 2009. He had spent $17000 on it and stopped working on it thereafter. He sold his laptop but shifted the data related to his Bitcoin to a hard drive so that he could work on it later. In 2013, he accidentally threw his hard drive while cleaning his home. It is said that bitcoins owned by him were worth $4 million when he lost the drive. Today their value is estimated to be around $200 million. But the only problem is that he never found that drive and all this money remains unclaimed in the bitcoin system. That's how secure Bitcoin's system is.

Within a few years, authorities began to consider it as real-time money as people became more interested in cryptocurrency. Even though there was reluctance from the side of authorities, they could no longer ignore it. It was in 2012 that the European Central Bank officially introduced a definition of virtual money, and laid out certain schemes for it. Consequently, other institutions followed and cryptocurrency started gaining a massive acceptance in the society.

People were quick to introduce other coins after Bitcoin's debut. These new coins were known as Altcoins, short for 'Alternative Coins for Bitcoin'. There are almost 18000 plus cryptocurrencies in existence today. Bitcoin still remains one of the most popular ones, followed by another currency known as Ethereum, which has grown massively in recent years.

Importance of Understanding Cryptocurrencies

The financial landscape has been evolving ever so quickly.

Innovations like cryptocurrency not only represent an improvement in technology but also in society's financial outlook. There was a time when people were unaware and doubtful of using digital methods of money. Now, digital apps to transfer money are used by people at all levels, whether an organization at large or a single vegetable seller. Such changes have happened over the years but are extremely powerful. If you know how to ride such waves of changes in the society, you can easily benefit from the same. Cryptocurrency is one such innovation that has taken over the world. Hence, the importance of understanding cryptocurrencies cannot be overstated. It brought a shift in how we think about money, finance, and technology, but most importantly, it brought endless opportunities for people to make money.

Potential Benefits

One of the biggest reasons for the boom in popularity of crypto has been its 'high potential' for giving returns. Early investors of Bitcoin, Ethereum, and other currencies experienced massive growth in returns, and still steadily continue to gain. This is mainly because cryptocurrency is a relatively new market. It still has a lot of scope to grow, to be adopted completely by the world.

The second important benefit or attraction of cryptocurrencies is their decentralized nature. The currencies work on a decentralized network; meaning that they are not controlled by any one entity like a government, bank, or corporation. This gives the owner of such currency a certain control over their finances by allowing transactions with anyone in the world without a third party in between.

Now, one may question the security of such currencies that are free from government or bank oversight. But that is not so. Cryptocurrencies are secured by cryptographic techniques, actually making them immune to fraud, duplicity, or unauthorized access. The nature of blockchain technology ensures utmost transparency and traceability.

Unlike the stock market, the cryptocurrency market operates 24/7 and does not have fixed open or close timings. This availability allows the traders to react timely and manage trades. In a world, where prices fall upon a news article, or because a celebrity moves away a cold drink bottle, it is a significant advantage to be able to access the market any time and not wait for the next day for it to open.

Another charming factor of crypto is its default global nature. Investing and trading in crypto is not confined to any specific region or country. This allows the trading of crypto against a wide variety of traditional currencies and digital assets, leading to various other opportunities.

Potential Risks

Just as there are charms of trading in the stock market and crypto, there are also a few risks involved. Being a relatively new phenomenon, cryptocurrencies are quite volatile (the ability of prices to extremely increase or decrease). Prices can fluctuate wildly in short spans of time, sometimes within minutes or hours. This volatile nature can lead to good profits, but also losses if the market moves against the traders. This volatility depends on various factors such as market sentiments, news events, social media trends, or opinions expressed by certain individuals. Hence, it requires actively observing and following the market.

While people may have accepted crypto, governments, and banks are surely taking their time. There is a regulatory uncertainty around cryptocurrencies. This means that there are hardly any rules or regulations around this market, as we do in the stock market. Even though some governments around the world have legalized the currency, some have even banned it entirely. This poses trouble for crypto, as the government's acceptance or ban on crypto may lead to sharp declines.

Another factor we must consider is that even though cryptocurrencies ensure enhanced safety through their blockchain technology, they are still not immune to risks. The platform being used for trading and storing funds can be prone to hacking or cyber-attacks. There are certain risks including fraud, phishing, and scams. We shall go into the details in the coming chapters.

Future Prospects

One of the most significant trends in the future of cryptocurrency trading is its acceptance by institutions. In recent times, major institutions such as governments and banks have accepted cryptocurrency as a legitimate asset class. Moreover, institutions like hedge funds, companies, and other entities have begun to invest in crypto. This shift in perception is likely to go forward and expand. With increasing acceptance, the crypto market is expected to mature, stabilize, and grow further. Increased investments shall also lead to new products, instruments, and facilities over time, giving a wide range of choices to traders and investors.

The acceptance of crypto and its technology will also lead to its normalization. It is expected that blockchain technology will also be adopted by various financial institutions for operations, security, and reducing costs. It shall also be used for efficient cross-border transactions, enabling cheaper and faster transactions. The landscape of rules and regulations is also expected to evolve with time. This will not only lead to stability in the crypto market but also investor safety shall become better.

As I said earlier, crypto is relatively new and its market is not yet saturated. There a huge scope for its growth. I believe that in the coming years, crypto will play a major role in shaping the global economy in a unique manner. Its decentralized nature is yet to be entirely understood and dealt with accordingly if the governments and banks wish to normalize it further.

Overall, we can say that the concept and scope of crypto is vast and multifaceted. Even though there are challenges to be overcome, there is tremendous potential for the ones who understand how it works. As the market continues to evolve, traders who stay informed and actively make sound decisions will be able to take advantage of the opportunities that lie ahead in this dynamic and ever-changing space.

Chapter 2:

Understanding the Crypto Market

Cryptocurrency

Now that we have understood the concept and story behind cryptocurrency, let's establish the definition.

Cryptocurrency can be defined as a form of digital currency that is used as a digital medium of exchange without the intervention of any central authority. The ownership of every coin as well as transactions are stored in a digital ledger, which is secured by using strong cryptographic codes. This ledger created by using blockchain technology also controls the creation of additional coins and also verifies the transfer of ownership of these coins.

Characteristics of Crypto

To understand the definition further, let's understand the fundamental characteristics of cryptocurrency. These characteristics will help you understand how cryptocurrencies fundamentally differ from financial assets like stocks.

1. **Decentralization:** As you read earlier, cryptocurrencies operate without the intervention of a central authority, this means that they are not controlled or regulated by any authority such as the government or bank. Instead, the cryptocurrency relies on a distributed ledger system (Blockchain technology), where each and every transaction is recorded and validated by a network of nodes (computers). Hence, we can say that cryptocurrencies are free of any interference or regularization. Whereas, stocks are centralized in nature - they are issued by companies and regulated by government authorities, such as SEC in

the US, or SEBI in India. The stock transactions are then processed through centralized exchanges such as NSE or BSE in India.

2. **Security:** Cryptocurrencies are secured using cryptographic techniques, which ensure the integrity, confidentiality, and authenticity of transactions. Public and private keys are used to control ownership of the coins, and digital signatures verify that transactions are authorized by the rightful owner. Moreover, the blockchain also adds another layer of protection by making it impossible for someone to mess with the transaction history. Once recorded, it cannot be changed. Unlike crypto, where the security is embedded in the technology, stocks rely on central authorities that regulate them to prevent any fraud and maintain the integrity of transactions.

3. **Privacy and Anonymity:** Even though all transactions of cryptocurrency are recorded on a public ledger, the identities of the parties involved is not directly revealed. Instead, the transactions are linked to cryptographic addresses, providing a level of anonymity. Some cryptocurrencies like Monero and Zeash offer enhanced privacy features, which makes it difficult to trace transactions back to individuals. But when it comes to stocks, this is not the case. Your identity is known to the broker and the exchange, plus your transactions are recorded with your personal information for regulatory purposes.

4. **Unchangeability:** Once a transaction is recorded and confirmed, this information is almost impossible to alter

or reverse. This is how blockchain ensures its integrity and prevents any kind of fraud. Meanwhile, in the case of stocks, final transactions are still subject to change or correction in situations of error, fraud, or authority interference. Centralized exchanges and authorities have the authority to halt trading, cancel orders, and reverse trades to protect investors and maintain the stock market integrity.

5. **Limited Supply:** Many cryptocurrencies have a limited supply which means there is a cap or a limit to the total number of coins or tokens that will ever be created. Bitcoin has a maximum supply of 21 million bitcoins, which will be reached around the year 2140. Now unlike crypto, stocks do not have a fixed supply. Companies can issue more shares by way of secondary offerings or splitting the stocks. This practice generally dilutes the value of existing shares. Hence, we can say that the supply of stocks is more flexible and can be adjusted by the companies based on the market conditions.

6. **Portability and Divisibility:** portability refers to the ability to transfer or carry a currency from one place to another. Whereas, divisibility refers to the ability to divide a currency into smaller units. Crypto, being more digitally advanced in nature has better portability and divisibility. It can easily transferred quickly across the globe. The divisibility of crypto allows breaking it into very small units, which helps in making microtransactions. Similar to how we can break down the Rupee into paisas, Bitcoin can be divided into 100 million smaller units called satoshis. But stocks are completely different. Although

they can be bought and sold on global exchanges, they are not as divisible as cryptocurrencies. Lately, fractional shares have become popular. Generally, the stocks are still bought and sold in whole units. Moreover, the existence of intermediaries like brokers and stock exchanges can cause a delay and require a fee.

7. **Volatility:** This is one of the most significant characteristics of cryptocurrency because it can be both positive and negative. As explained earlier, volatility means that the price of the asset can quickly decrease or increase unexpectedly, and Cryptocurrencies are especially known for this price volatility. This volatility is driven by factors like market sentiment, regulatory news, technological advancements, or any changes in demand and supply. Now, stocks are also volatile, but compared to stocks, they can be considered stable. This is primarily because the stock market is way older than crypto. Hence, stock market has had a lot of time to form a proper system, and mature over the years, and also because it has been regulated by authorities since decades, that's why stocks are considered less riskier than cryptocurrency.

Types of Cryptocurrencies

As of March 2024, there are approximately 13,200 cryptocurrencies in existence, along with 420 million users, and new currencies are being started every day. They all rely on the same technology as explained above, but there are several types of currencies being created for different purposes. The most popular ones are listed below, from which you can choose your favorite:

1. **Payment Cryptocurrency:** this is the first major category, and the well-known example is Bitcoin. There are other currencies as well. Bitcoin and similar currencies were designed specifically for the purpose of digital payments. As the name of the category suggests, the payment cryptocurrency serves as a medium of exchange and is a general-purpose currency. Such currencies have a capped supply, meaning that there are only a limited number of coins that can be created. A few examples of this type of currency are Bitcoin, Bitcoin Cash, Litecoin, and Monero.

2. **Alt Coins:** this term refers to any cryptocurrency other than Bitcoin. This term was coined in the initial days when new currencies were introduced after Bitcoin. Although based on the same technology, these coins may differ in their purpose, mechanism, and functioning. Currently, there are thousands of altcoins and some of the most popular ones are Ethereum (ETH), Ripple (XRP), Cardano (ADA), and more.

3. **Stable Coins:** these are the ones specifically designed for the purpose of maintaining a stable value by being linked to a set of assets - like traditional currency or a commodity (such as USD or EUR, or a commodity like gold). This nature of the stablecoins makes them useful for transactions and saving money in a market where prices are changing a lot. Currently, there are several stablecoins such as Tether (USDT), USD Coin (USDC), and Dai (DAI).

4. **Privacy Coins:** These currencies are designed with the specific goal of protecting the users' identities and

transaction details. Whereas most of the currencies have a transparent transaction history (that anyone can view), privacy coins use a much more complex cryptographic method to hide this information. These coins are preferred by individuals who wish to keep their financial activities confidential for various reasons. The popular example of these types of coins is Monero or Zcash.

5. **Meme Coins:** yes, memes reached here as well. These types of coins were created as a joke or for fun, inspired by an internet meme or a trend. Besides their funny origin, some coins immediately gained huge popularity and attracted large communities of fans who traded them. These coins do not have a specific purpose or any innovation behind them, and their value mostly depends on the people who support them, through social media, memes, or viral content. Similar to memes, these coins are very volatile, meaning that their value can rapidly rise and then suddenly dip because of any quick change in trend. The most popular example is Dogecoin, created in 2013, based on thc shiba dog with funny expressions, which is still popular on social media.

6. **Utility tokens:** these tokens can be described as a subcoin that is used on a specific cryptocurrency's blockchain network. Suppose a currency has its own platform and several products, services, or features on it, and to buy or access these, you need to pay via tokens. In this way, a currency becomes a system in itself. For example, the Ethereum network has tokens named 'Ether'. These types of tokens do have a limit, meaning they can be created in any number. On this network, you have to use Ether

for purposes like paying transaction fees, or building and purchasing products on DApps (Website, or a platform app created on a blockchain network).

7. **Security Tokens:** these tokens are like digital versions of traditional assets like stocks, real estate, or loans. When you own a security token, you own a piece of something valuable like a share in a company. Another example can be - instead of buying a whole building, you can buy a security token that represents a fraction of the ownership in that building. These tokens make investing more accessible to people. Since these tokens are considered securities, they are regulated by financial authorities. Examples of security tokens include Polymath, tZero, Harbor, and many more.

8. **Governance tokens:** these tokens are like voting tickets that allow holders to have a say in the governance or decision-making on a currency's platform. People who own such tokens on the platform can vote on important decisions such as technical updates, how the platform operates, how the funds are spent, or any change in fees. The more tokens someone has, the more influence they hold on the voting process. This type of system ensures that the platform evolves in a way that benefits the users. Uniswap, Aave, and Maker are a few examples of governance tokens.

9. **Non-Fungible Tokens (NFTs):** you must have heard about a digital picture of a cool/hippy monkey character, which was sold for millions, and after which the Internet went crazy. That's how NFTs became popular. NFTs are a type of cryptocurrency that represents ownership of rare or

unique digital items - like a piece of art, a photo, a video, or a song. When you buy an NFT, it means you are buying a certificate of ownership of that rare item. This token immediately became popular, because it provided new opportunities for artists, musicians, and creators to monetize their work. In fact, you can also create an NFT and upload it on the blockchain platform, and if someone likes it, they can buy the same.

Cryptocurrency Exchanges and How They Work

To simplify, an exchange is a marketplace, which can be accessed through your desktop or mobile. These exchanges offer a wide range of trading and investing tools that help users to manage their digital assets. Beyond basic buying and selling, crypto exchanges also help with advanced trading. This feature caters to both newcomers as well as advanced traders through the same platform.

In the last 5-6 years, the Crypto market experienced explosive growth, crossing a valuation of 1 trillion dollars. This was mainly possible because of easy accessibility to the market. This accessibility was made possible by the exchanges in the market. Earlier, it was very difficult for people to buy crypto. The process back then was complex and less accessible. Investors were only able to obtain cryptocurrency by either mining or arranging a transaction on online or offline forums. Hence, we can say crypto exchanges play an important role in facilitating the buying, selling, and trading of digital assets. Today, there are hundreds of exchanges operating globally.

To provide services to the users on the platform, exchanges also charge a fee on transactions made. The fees differ from exchange to exchange and also depend on the number of types of transactions being made. For example, some exchanges may charge higher fees for margin trades as compared to general buying and selling. There are two types of exchanges that you must know about.

Types of Cryptocurrency Exchanges

There are two types of cryptocurrency exchanges namely: centralized exchanges (CEX) and decentralized exchanges (DEX). Each has its unique advantages, features, as well as challenges. In order to understand which exchange to choose from, let's take a look at the types.

1. Centralized Exchanges (CEX)

These are the most common types of exchanges. They function similarly to traditional stock exchanges or brokerage firms. Here, being 'centralized' means that the exchange is being controlled or regulated by one single entity. This entity can be a government authority, bank, or company. The central authority or entity that runs the exchange looks after user accounts, transactions, security, and customer service. The centralized exchanges generally hold your funds in custodial wallets. This essentially means that they have control over the private keys or access codes to your wallet where the crypto is stored. This setup is convenient because it is easier, and it's also the responsibility of keeping your assets safe lies on the exchange.

One of the major advantages of the centralized exchange is its higher liquidity. In simple words, liquidity means how easily you can cash in your asset. The centralized exchanges quickly process the buy and sell orders. They are also designed to be user-friendly and easy-to-navigate interfaces. Such exchanges also offer educational tools, customer support, and advanced trading features. Moreover, these exchanges also have insurance covers or reserved funds to cover any losses that may happen because of any security issues.

However, centralized exchanges also have some downsides. Although they are more secure, the exchange can be still a target for hackers because they store large amounts of funds as well as data. Also, the exchanges can freeze or limit your access to funds at their will. But these exchanges are also bound by government regulations and can face legal issues if they do not follow the law.

The most popular examples of centralized exchanges are Binance and Coinbase. Binance is the largest and most popular exchange worldwide. It is known for its wide range of cryptocurrencies and low fees. Whereas, Coinbase is known for its easy and user-friendly design. Coinbase is based in the US, and it is considered one of the most secure and respected exchanges in the crypto industry.

2. Decentralized Exchanges (DEX)

Decentralized exchanges (DEXs) are the second type of exchange platform. As the name suggests, these exchanges are not centralized - meaning that they are not controlled by any one single entity. These exchanges use blockchain technology and allow the users on the platform to directly trade with one another. There is no middleman as in the case of centralized exchanges. This is done with the help of a feature called smart contracts, which can be described as automated agreements, which are coded into the blockchain. These contracts are already regulated by certain rules, hence, there is no need for a third party to see or verify each transaction.

Another important feature of DEXs is that they do not hold the user's funds through a custodial wallet. Instead, you get to have complete control of your wallet which holds the crypto. The control of the private keys to the wallet is managed by the user only. This means that the crypto is stored in private wallets, and not on the exchange platform. This helps protect the user's fund from being hacked or mismanaged by the exchange.

Compared to CEXs, decentralized exchanges also offer more privacy. These exchanges do not require the users to go through the KYC process, which means that you do not have to share personal information to trade. But there are some downsides to these exchanges too.

DEXs may have fewer trading volumes at times (number of trades made for a specific currency over a period of time). This can lead to frequent price changes when users buying or selling. This is also known as price slippage. It is mostly noticeable with less popular or small currencies.

Moreover, DEXs can be more complicated to use than centralized exchange platforms. Their design may not be so simple for beginners to use and there is an added responsibility of managing the private keys to their wallet. Also, these exchanges usually do not have the advanced features you get on centralized exchanges such as margin trading or detailed charts and tools.

Some popular examples of DEXs are Uniswap and PancakeSwap. Uniswap exists on the Ethereum blockchain. Whereas, PancakeSwap functions on the Binance Smart Chain. These two are quite popular because of their efficient and cost-effective trading options.

Difference between Crypto Exchange and Crypto Wallet

Crypto exchange and wallet are part of the same ecosystem but they have different functions. People who are new to the world of crypto may confuse the two. While exchanges only allow you to buy, sell, or trade, the wallets are only to store your assets. The two can be linked accordingly. As you read above, centralized exchange have their own wallets in which you can store your crypto assets. In decentralized ones, you can create a wallet separately through platforms like Metamask, Ledger, Trezor, etc., and then link it with your trading account on the exchange.

For example, you can create a wallet on Metamask and link it with your account on Opensea, which is a marketplace for buying and selling NFTs. NFTs are bought and sold on the Ethereum blockchain with a currency called Ether.

Now, there are two types of wallets namely Hot and Cold wallets. They offer different levels of security and convenience. Hot Wallets are connected to the internet and they can be accessed through your mobile, desktop, etc. These are convenient for everyday or frequent transactions. Exodus, Trust Wallet, and Metamask are a few examples of this. Whereas, Cold wallets are offline-based wallets, such as Hardware wallets or paper wallets. These offer a higher level of security by keeping the private keys away from the internet. These types of wallets are more useful for long-term storage of crypto instead of everyday transactions. Ledger or Trezor are popular examples of hardware wallets.

How to Choose and Exchange and Create an Account

You can begin by exploring the various crypto exchanges mentioned above. Make sure to consider factors like security features, available crypto on these exchanges, and user reviews. Accordingly, find a platform that you trust and is easy for you to use. Once you have selected an exchange, you can go ahead with creating an account by providing all the details that the platform asks for. You'll have to complete a KYC process, which includes submitting identity proofs.

Once the above is done, you can fund your account or crypto wallet by depositing your currency such as Rupee or INR. Thereafter, you can use this money to buy cryptocurrencies. Let's say you wish to buy Bitcoin worth INR 5,000 - you can select the currency, and follow the instructions to initiate and complete the transaction. Make sure to review the details before confirming the purchase.

Once the purchase is made, check your account or wallet to ensure that the purchase was successful and the cryptocurrency is credited to your account. In case you face issues with making accounts on exchanges or creating wallets, you can always refer to my YouTube videos that explain the process in an easy manner.

Market Participants

The world of crypto is a dynamic place, meaning that it is forever changing, growing, and evolving. This market is formed by various types of participants, who play different roles in the market's operation. The entire crypto ecosystem is huge and has a variety of people doing a variety of things to earn money and keep the crypto world functioning. Let's take a brief look at these participants.

1. **Investors:** Investors are the ones who play the long game. They have a long-term perspective. Such individuals buy and hold an asset for a long time - months, years, or decades; and wait for the value of the asset to rise over time. Investors usually conduct heavy research into the technology behind the crypto that they wish to invest in. It is important to understand a business or a currency before you purchase the same. This research includes understanding the technology, progress, market demand, or popularity of the currency. We shall learn about carrying out this type of research in the upcoming chapters.

2. **Traders:** Traders are more active participants in the market than investors. These individuals make profits from short-term price movements. Their focus is to buy and sell crypto frequently to generate profit instead

of holding them for a long time. This is done through different types of strategies. Moreover, there are various types of trading and strategies that one can use in the market. Traders rely on fundamental as well as technical analysis, charts, indicators, and patterns to make trading decisions. We will learn about these concepts in detail in the upcoming chapters.

3. **Miners:** Now these individuals are crucial for the operation of blockchain networks. Miners are the ones who validate and record transactions, which is done by solving cryptographic puzzles - this process is known as mining. Miners solve these cryptographic puzzles to create new blocks and add them to the blockchain, which in turn creates more units of the currency. The first miner to solve these puzzles is rewarded with newly minted currency and transaction fees from the transactions included in the blockchain. Moreover, the miners also play an important role in the decentralization of the currency networks, so that no single entity is in control of the entire system.

4. **Developers:** Developers are the architects or the builders of the cryptocurrency and blockchain ecosystem. These individuals are responsible for designing, implementing, and maintaining the software behind a currency. Different developers work on different aspects. For example- core developers work on blockchains, some developers work on creating and running decentralized apps (Dapps), and some work on smart contracts that take place during transactions between individuals. Therefore, we can say that different types of developers are running the grand show of crypto.

5. **Regulators:** Regulators or market regulators refer to the governmental or non-governmental bodies that make sure the crypto market complies with the legal and ethical standards. Regulators basically develop and enforce rules or regulations on different activities of the market, such as market conduct, investor protection, or financial stability. It is the regulators that implement anti-money laundering and KYC requirements to prevent illegal activities. The main purpose is consumer protection, meaning to protect the investors or traders from fraud, manipulation, or other risks.

6. **Media and Analysts:** Media has played an important role in the growth of the crypto world and continues to do so. The media is an important part since it helps in shaping an opinion and understanding of the crypto market. Outlets like newspapers, websites, blogs, and social media platforms - provide a lot of information, updates, and developments happening in the crypto market. As we know, media also holds the power to influence price movement and affect market sentiment as well as investor behavior. Media consists of various types of analysts and experts that conduct a lot of research and give their insights about the market situations, therefore guiding investors and traders.

Chapter 3

Ways to Earn Money in Crypto

The rise of cryptocurrency clearly transformed the landscape of finance and investing. With its rise, it brought limitless opportunities for individuals as well as institutions. These opportunities are only growing further and gaining more and more attraction worldwide. Every participant in the market has figured out a way to earn, be it through investing, trading, or mining. But is this all? Investing, Trading, and Mining? No, there are other paths as well, and each path gets further divided too, out of which you can choose your favorite to apply and earn from the market. Let's take a brief look at all of these.

1. Long-Term Investing (a.k.a Crypto Hodling)

Long-term investing in crypto means buying and holding the assets with an expectation that their value will highly increase over a long period of time. This strategy is also known as 'Hodling' - to Hodl or 'hold on for dear life'. This slang originated in 2013 when someone misspelled 'holding' and it became popular. The ones who hold crypto for long periods of time also call themselves 'Hodlers'.

Now, long-term investing or hodling requires research. Similar to how you check the fundamentals of stocks in the stock market, one needs to check for the fundamentals of the currency that they wish to invest in. Checking fundamentals of currency includes evaluating its concept, technology, uses, adoption rate, popularity, market potential, etc. Upcoming chapters will explain in detail how you can carry out thorough research or fundamental analysis. But is it worth waiting so long to get the rewards? Yes, it is, and the greatest example is

Bitcoin itself. Let's map the rollercoaster trajectory of Bitcoin and see what's the hype about long-term investing.

Launched in 2009, Bitcoin's value was so low that it was nearly worthless. The first transaction was valued at $0.0009. By 2010 it rose to $0.30. The first major spike in its price was then observed in 2011 reaching $30, before it fell again. The same coin was then valued at $4 in 2018. Investors had almost lost all hope. But then, the price reached an all-time high of $7,000. After a drop in March of 2020 to $4,000, Bitcoin saw an unbelievable hype of $29,000 by the end of the year.

Within a year, Bitcoin had reached new heights, peaking at $69,000, and then once again dropping to $32,000. It was a classic case of 'What goes up, must come down'. The price continued to be up and down in 2022, and at the end of the year the price had fallen to $20,000 because of economic issues. Thereafter, it was revived again in 2023, surfing between $16,000 and $42,000. It finally reached its all-time high of $73,750 in March of 2024. Currently, at the time of writing this book, the price is $62,840, equivalent to INR 52,70,946. Hence, the Bitcoin story is enough to understand the power and importance of long-term investing.

2. Mining

This is another way to earn good money in the crypto world. As you read earlier, mining refers to the process of minting new coins in the cryptocurrency blockchain. Miners are the ones who mint new coins by validating and adding new transactions to the blockchain by solving complex puzzles. Accordingly, they are rewarded with new cryptocurrency and transaction fees for their work. There are two ways or concepts in mining, namely Proof-of-Work (PoW) and Proof-of-Stake (PoS).

In PoW, the miners use powerful computers to solve mathematical problems. The first miner to solve the problem adds a new block to the blockchain and earns new cryptocurrency and fees. Whereas, in PoS, instead of solving puzzles, the miners lock up a certain amount of cryptocurrency in a wallet to help validate a transaction.

3. Participating in ICO

You may have heard of IPOs (Initial Public Offerings) in the stock, now let me present to you - ICOs, known as Initial Coin Offerings in the crypto world. The ICOs are like events where new crypto projects raise money by selling tokens to inventors. This can be a chance for early investment in projects that have the potential to grow. But before joining an ICO right away, it is important to research it thoroughly - or do a fundamental analysis. This helps the investors in spotting any risks or opportunities.

Similar to IPOs, initial coin offerings also start at a lower price than their expected value. Sometimes, investors even get bonus tokens, coins, or other rewards for investing early or large amounts of money. How these coins are allocated and distributed, is usually explained in an ICO's terms and conditions. Moreover, specific instructions for investors to follow are also given in ICO projects. This can involve sending funds to a particular address or using a special platform to buy tokens. It's important to use secure methods and make sure that the ICO is legitimate to avoid any scams or fraud. After investing in an ICO, it is also important to keep track of the progress and stay updated on any news or changes.

4. Trading

Finally on to trading, the main subject of this book. Now, compared to long-term investing in crypto, trading is completely different. It's an everyday job. Trading is a much more dynamic and fast-paced activity that revolves around the continuous buying and selling of assets to generate profit. It's not a new concept or business, it's been there since the first societies and markets evolved, where people bought things at lower prices and later sold them at higher prices to gain profit.

When it comes to trading in cryptocurrency, the aim is to benefit from the everyday fluctuations in the prices. Many assume trading and investing are all about making random gambles, but I assure you it's not. One has to make as informed decisions as they make in any other business or profession. People engaging in trading have to know a range of strategies and master them. The skill of trading also involves technical analysis using different tools, indicators, chart patterns, etc. By studying all this, a trader identifies when he has to buy, and at what point he must sell and exit the market.

One thing about trading is that it can become a full-time profession for the ones who are not interested in 9-5 traditional jobs. Choosing to trade as a full-time income source has its perks such as flexibility of time, complete freedom of decision-making, the flexibility of working space, etc. Once you learn the ways and dedicate enough time, you're good to go with it.

Types of trading in crypto

As the popularity and accessibility to crypto grew, ways to invest and trade in the crypto market also got better with time. Like the stock market, you can also carry out spot trading, margin trading, futures trading, options trading, etc. in the crypto market. Each type of trading has a different level of difficulty or complexity, as well as rewards. You can opt for any trading method based upon the market conditions, individual goals, and considering the experience at hand. Let's understand the basic concepts behind the types of trading practices, and you can decide which one you feel drawn to. We shall discuss the strategies for these types in detail in the later chapters of the book.

1. **Spot Trading:** Spot trading refers to the purchase and sale of crypto for immediate delivery and settlement, meaning that it takes place 'on the spot'. Here the transfer of ownership of crypto and exchange of funds occur instantly at the market price. It's a simple or straightforward form of trading that involves direct buying and selling of assets. To simplify it further, suppose you went to buy a chocolate at the store, you saw a chocolate bar that you liked and immediately bought it on the spot. You paid the store, and the store gave you the chocolate. After a day, let's say the price of the chocolate increased - now you can go back to the store and sell it, and therefore, make more money than you originally spent. Spot trading in crypto works the same way. Hence, the simplicity and transparency of spot trading make it an attractive option.

2. **Margin Trading :** This type of trading is a bit more complex. It basically allows traders to borrow funds to take larger positions than their budget or capital would allow. In this practice, you borrow money to leverage or amplify potential returns. Let's understand this with the help of chocolates again. Now, imagine you went to the candy store with INR 100 in your pocket. Since you wish to buy more candy than you can afford, the store owner decides to lend you another INR 100 to buy more chocolate. You bought INR 200 worth of chocolate. Now after a day, the price of chocolate increased to INR 250. So you went back to the store and sold it. You received INR 250, out of which you gave INR 100 back to the store owner that he had given to you. As a result, you made a profit worth INR 50.

   To begin with margin trading, one has to create a margin account on the exchange or the trading platform. After which, traders have to deposit an initial margin of the total trade size. This margin acts as collateral or security. To put it in a simple manner, suppose you use 5:1 leverage, which means that you'll be able to trade $5000 worth of crypto with only $1000 of your own money. Thereafter, you can begin trading with the borrowed funds, and after closing a trade, you repay the borrowed money.

3. **Futures Trading:** This type of trading involves buying and selling 'futures contracts' to speculate on future price movements of a cryptocurrency. A futures contract is like an agreement between two parties to buy or sell crypto on

a future date at an already decided price. This allows you to earn a profit if the price goes up or down, depending on how you bet. Unlike buying and selling crypto on the spot, futures trading is about predicting what will happen later.

Here too, one has to deposit an initial margin, which is a percentage of the total contract value. Similar to margin trading, the trader can use leverage as they prefer, let's say 10:1, this means that the trader will be able to take a position worth $10,000 with just $1000 of their own capital. This is how leverage magnifies both potential gains and losses.

4. **Options Trading:** Options Trading involves the buying and selling of option contracts. These contracts are a type of agreement that give the trader the right to buy or sell crypto at a set price before a specific date. This allows you to bet on whether the price of crypto will go up and come down. To understand the concept better, suppose you think the price of Bitcoin will increase from $30,000. Here you can buy the Bitcoin option, and when the price does go up, you can still buy the Bitcoin at $30,000 and profit accordingly. In another instance, let's say you believed that the price would go below $25,000, and hence bought the Bitcoin option at the fixed price of $25,000. Now if the price does go down, you still have the right to sell Bitcoin at $25,000 and make a profit.

Chapter 4

Basics of Crypto Trading

Understanding Trading Pairs

In Cryptocurrency, trading pairs are important for understanding how different assets are traded against each other. A trading pair shows the value relationship between the assets, by comparison. For example, if you trade Bitcoin (BTC) in exchange with Ethereum (ETH), you are looking at a BTC/ETH trading pair. This pair helps to see the value of Bitcoin in terms of Ethereum and vice versa.

Each trading pair is made up of two parts, namely base currency and quote currency. The base currency is the one that is written first and it is also the one being bought or sold, and the one written after is quote currency, and shows how much of it is needed to buy one unit of the base currency. Let's take another example; BTC/USD. In this Bitcoin is the base currency and US Dollars is the quote currency, hence, the pair shows much of the US dollar is required to buy one unit of Bitcoin. If the value of the pair BTC/USD is $25,000, it means Bitcoin is currently worth $25000. On the other hand, you can also take a trading pair like USD/BTC. If the price of this pair is 0.00004, it means that one US dollar is worth 0.00004 Bitcoin.

Traders use this information from trading pairs to make decisions about buying or selling. They observe how the base currency may perform compared to the quote currency. If they think the base currency might increase in value, they buy it and vice versa, if they suppose the value will decrease, they may sell it. This concept comes in handy in certain strategies and helps to manage risk.

Types of Pairs

There are two types of trading pairs namely direct and indirect pairs. It is important to understand how to choose between them according to your trading needs. The first one, direct pairs involve one cryptocurrency directly against another cryptocurrency. In such pairs, both currencies are digital assets. For example, BTC/ETH (Bitcoin and Ethereum). Direct pairs are useful when you want to trade one cryptocurrency for another without using traditional money.

On the other hand, indirect pairs involve at least one traditional currency, usually it is the US dollar or Euro. For example, BTC/USD (Bitcoin and US dollar). Such types of pairs are useful when you want to convert cryptocurrencies into traditional money or vice versa. Also, this helps you to understand how a cryptocurrency is performing compared to traditional currency, like how we compare the value of the Rupee to the US Dollar or Euro.

Selccting Trading Pairs

It is crucial to be thorough while selecting trading pairs for efficient trading. In order to do it wisely, you can keep several factors in mind. Liquidity is one of the first important factors. It refers to how easily a cryptocurrency can be bought or sold without causing too many price changes. BTC/USD or similar pairs are considered to be more stable and have more liquidity. They are convenient to trade, as they allow easier and less risky transactions, especially for people who wish to trade quickly.

Another factor that can be considered is volatility. Different pairs experience different levels of price fluctuations. Accordingly, if you are okay with taking higher risks and aiming for higher gains, you can opt for volatile pairs. But, if you prefer more stability in your profits, then choosing stable pairs is the way to go. This solely depends on your comfort and ability to take risks.

Other than volatility, market trends also play an important role in selecting trading pairs. Certain events or news have the ability to affect the value of trading pairs, it can be positive or negative. If you stay updated on the trends and calculate the possible impact, you can use such opportunities to make significant profits.

Important Terms Related to Trading

Trading is significantly different from investing. In long-term investing, you simply buy and forget about the asset for a long period of time. Whereas, in trading, you buy and sell every day on a platform. The procedures can be different, there are steps involved in trading, hence, certain terms come when we go about trading every day, such as - market orders, bid price, ask price, volume, percent in point and so on. It is important to know and understand these terms to create a smooth trading system for yourself. Knowing what is what, where, and how it is done, makes your trading more efficient and less confusing. Let's take a look at a few of these terms.

Order Types

In crypto trading, there are various order types. Order simply means your request to buy an asset. Since there are several types of orders, each type has a specific purpose and allows you to control how and when the trades are executed. There are different types of orders such as - market orders, limit orders, stop orders, stop-loss orders, stop-limit orders, and trailing stop orders.

1. **Market Orders:** it is the simplest type of order and it is executed at the immediate market price at that moment. It is for traders who wish to trade immediately and are less concerned about the price they receive. If you place a market order for Bitcoin, the exchange will fulfill it at the current market price.

2. **Limit Orders:** these types of orders allow you to specify the exact price at which you want to buy or sell a cryptocurrency. When you place a limit order, you can set a price limit, and the order is completed only when the crypto's current price reaches the one that you have set. Although this gives you control over the price at which you want to buy or sell, but there is still no guarantee that the price will reach that set limit. For instance, let's say you want to buy Bitcoin at $25000 and the current price of Bitcoin is $26000. Hence, you place a limit order with a price set of $25000. Now, if the price reaches the set limit, you'll receive Bitcoin at the set price.

3. **Stop-loss orders:** this type of order is used to limit potential losses on a trade, and help in managing risk in a volatile market space. The price limit is set at a lower price than the current market price for buying purposes, and conversely, you can set it at a higher price for selling

purposes. If the crypto's price reaches the set limit, the order is executed. For example, suppose you bought Bitcoin at $26000, and want to limit your loss, so you set a stop-loss order at $24000. Now if the price falls to $24000, the order will be executed to save you from further loss.

4. **Stop-Limit Orders:** this type of order combines the elements of both stop orders and limit orders. This means that when you place this type of order, you specify two prices - the stop price and the limit price. When the stop price is reached, the order becomes a limit order to buy or sell at the limit price. For example, let's say you want to sell Bitcoin and accordingly you set a stop-limit order with a stop price of $24,000 and a limit price of $23,500, then the order will trigger when the current price reaches $24,000. But it will be only executed if the current price then reaches $23,500 or better. Therefore, we can say this type of order gives you better control over the execution price, but it may not be filled if the current market price moves too quickly or does not reach the limit price.

5. **Trailing Stop Orders:** this order type is designed to protect profits by setting a stop price that gets adjusted if the market price moves in your favor. Basically, the stop price trails the ongoing market price by a specified amount or percentage. When the market price is going in the direction that you want, the set limit of the stop price follows along and accordingly, it locks the gains. If the direction of the price changes, and it hits the limit that was following it, the order immediately becomes a market order and is executed. To understand it better, suppose you have a trailing stop order, set with a trailing

amount of $500. Now, if Bitcoin's price rises from $25,000 to $26,500, the stop price will adjust accordingly, moving up to $26,000. In case, Bitcoin's price then falls to $26,000, the trailing stop order will be triggered and Bitcoin will be sold at the ongoing market price. This is how trailing stop orders help traders to lock in profits.

Bid Price

The bid price is the highest price the buyer is willing to pay for a cryptocurrency at a specific time. In the trading market, buyers make offers called bids, which are gathered on one side of the order book. For example, if the top bid price for Bitcoin is $25000, it means that the buyers are willing to pay up to $25000 for it. This gives the traders an idea about the demand in the market.

Ask Price

The ask price or offer price is the lowest amount that a seller is willing to accept for a cryptocurrency at a specific time. Sellers choose this price based on the minimum that they are ready to accept. The ask price shows the supply side of the market. For example, if the lowest ask price for Bitcoin is $25,500, this means sellers are willing to sell Bitcoin for at least $25,500.

Bid-Ask Spread

This bid-ask refers to the difference between the highest price a buyer is willing to pay (bid price) and the lowest price a seller is ready to accept (ask price). This difference between the two prices shows the cost of making a trade, and how easily an asset can be bought or sold in the market. A smaller spread or lesser difference between the bid and ask price means that the market is more active. Whereas, a larger spread or difference between the two prices implies that the market is less active and trading costs are higher. For example, if the bid price for Bitcoin is $25,000 and the ask price is $25,500, then the spread is $500. Hence, traders should pay attention to the spread because it affects how much they pay to trade.

Order Book

The order book is a digital ledger that shows all the buy and sell orders for a specific cryptocurrency. It displays the current bid and ask prices, along with the amounts of trades happening. The order book is important for traders to understand how much of a cryptocurrency is being bought or sold and at what prices. This helps them sense the market's mood and identify where the price where buying or selling might increase.

Liquidity

As I have mentioned before, liquidity refers to how easily you can buy or sell an asset without changing its price much. High liquidity means there are plenty of buy and sell orders at different prices, which makes it easier to trade quickly and at the prices you want. Low liquidity implies there are fewer orders, which can cause bigger price changes when you trade.

Slippage

Slippage happens when the price at which your trade is carried out is different from the price that you expected. This generally happens in fast-moving markets or when there is not enough liquidity. For instance, if you place an order to buy Bitcoin at

$25,000 but the trade goes through at $25,200 because of a very quick price change at the moment. This difference of $200 in this situation will be considered as slippage. Slippage can affect how much you pay or receive in a trade, hence, traders need to be careful during times of such high market volatility.

Percentage in Point (PIP)

PIP is a unit that measures any change in the value of an asset. In crypto, PIPs usually show the smallest possible price movement in the trading pair. For most cryptocurrencies, one PIP is the change in the fourth decimal place (example, 0.0001). For instance, if Bitcoin's price moves from $25,000.0000 to $25,000.0001, that's a movement of one PIP. The PIP usually helps traders to measure price changes and understand it affects their trades and profits.

Chapter 5

Fundamental Analysis

In the world of crypto trading, dealing with so many digital assets and blockchain projects can be both exciting and confusing at the same time. Having to choose an asset to invest in can feel like a major task. People often tend to avoid this task assuming it's quite difficult. Moreover, people also look up to other individuals for some insights on what they should invest in, and more often than not, they are not able to make a confident choice. This usually happens because we avoid doing the much-needed homework, which is 'analysis'. Shying away from this task always leads to making uninformed decisions, which also leads to losses that could have been avoided. But is analysis that difficult? I assure you it's not. If you wish to become a full-time trader, or a part-time one, one thing you must make sure to do is to understand what you're investing in. I'm not going to ask you to learn the coding behind a cryptocurrency, but we can surely try to understand the intention and purpose of currencies that you wish to buy, and how it can serve you in achieving your financial goals. In order to use crypto efficiently at your disposal, you'll have to know its uses as well as its potential. This is achieved by fundamental analysis.

Now, fundamental analysis is similar to studying a company's financial health by looking at its earnings, balance sheets and future business plans. For crypto, this means studying the crypto project's goals, technology, real-world use and the team behind it. The basic aim of fundamental analysis is to find out what makes a project valuable and worth the investment. By understanding various fundamental aspects, you can not only make smart decisions but also avoid mistakes and spot really good opportunities in the crypto market. Let's find out how you can easily carry out fundamental analysis and evaluate crypto projects.

Evaluating Cryptocurrency Projects

Fundamental analysis is a crucial part of this evaluation because it helps you determine the intrinsic value of the cryptocurrency and its potential beyond the market price. This involves assessing the factors that can determine the success and sustainability of a cryptocurrency. In this particular section, I am going to share how you can analyze a project's vision and mission, the team and advisors, technology and innovation, use case and market need, and lastly, community and ecosystem.

1. **Project Vision and Mission:** The vision and mission of any crypto project define its goals and objectives. The vision specifically outlines the long-term goals and aspirations, describing how they want to achieve them and how they wish to impact the industry or society. The purpose of checking the vision and mission of any asset is to see if they align with the market trends and needs. If the vision and mission are well-defined, it indicates a strong sense of direction and purpose, which is quite important for guiding a project's development. For instance, A project with a vision to improve cross-border payments should have a mission that can solve certain challenges in the current payment systems.

2. **Team and Advisors:** The team and advisors are the life force behind the crypto project's success. Evaluating the team that's running a crypto project involves studying

their qualifications, experience and track record in the cryptocurrency world. The team that has relevant technical skills, industry experience and a good history of projects, has a better chance of making a project successful. The top team should consist of experts that can provide guidance on tech, finance, regulations as well as business development.

3. **Technology and Innovation:** The technology and innovation lay the foundation for a project's success. One must evaluate a project's unlying technology such as blockchain protocol, consensus mechanism, and scalability solutions, and consider what kind of innovations are being introduced, or what kind of problems are being solved. You can also assess the project's development roadmap. The development roadmap of a project shows that it is committed to improving, expanding, and adapting further to the market conditions. For instance, a project that has a unique consensus mechanism or advances privacy features may have a competitive edge over others in the market.

4. **Use Case and Market Need:** Use case and market need refers to what type problems are being solved by the project or is there a market need for certain features that are being offered by the project. Moreover, you can also analyze the market need, the size of the market and the level of competition in that sphere. The bigger the market needs with lesser competition, the more there is space for a project to grow easily.

5. **Community and Ecosystem:** Once a crypto project takes off, it starts to create its own community or an

ecosystem of users. This community can be crucial in the further improvement of the project. You can evaluate this community and the impression of the cryptocurrency project on them, through various social media channels, experts, platforms, news, etc.

Understanding Whitepapers

A whitepaper is a document that provides an in-depth view of the cryptocurrency project. It helps the users, investors, traders and stakeholders to detail the project's goals, technology and implementation plan. The following section will break down the key components of a whitepaper and explain what to look for in each section.

1. **Project Introduction:** This sets the stage for understanding cryptocurrency. It generally includes a small introduction of the problem that the project aims to solve and the goal it wants to achieve. Project introduction can include - the purpose of crypto, the market it wants to target, the background of the founders, the inspiration behind the project and how it intends to align itself with the market etc.

2. **Executive Summary:** This summary gives you a concise view of the entire white paper. It highlights the important aspects of the project such as - mission, key features, value proposition, as well as the problem being addressed, proposed solution, market opportunity and overall approach towards its success.

3. **Technology Description:** This section provides a detailed explanation of the technology behind cryptocurrency. It

includes - underlying blockchain technology, protocols and algorithms. It may also include information about how the technology works, its scalability, security features, unique aspects etc. You should look for clarity and detail in this section to ensure that the technology is robust and well-thought-out.

5. **Token Utility:** This section describes the role and the purpose of the project's token currency. It explains how the token is used, its functionality and its benefits to users. There are common uses for tokens such as payments, access to features, governance rights or staking. The utility section of a token should be very clear and well defined, explain how it can add a lot of value to the crypto ecosystem and also explain why someone should invest in it.

6. **Token Distribution:** This section details how the project's tokens are distributed among different stakeholders. It includes information on initial distribution, allocations for team/ advisors/ partners and for future development. You should look for a reasonable distribution plan to ensure that the project is interested in long-term success and not just short-term gains.

7. **Development Roadmap:** This section of the white paper outlines the project's timelines in regard to the key milestones that the team aims to achieve. It includes planned phases of technical development, such as beta releases and full product launches. Analyzing this roadmap helps to understand the feasibility and the team's track record of meeting deadlines.

8. **Past Achievements:** This section is quite important. Everyone can talk about what they are going to do in the future, but it is important to talk about what they have already done, and how is their track record. The past achievement section consists of how much development has taken place, how well were the plans executed and what were the results. You should look for concrete examples and evidence to get an idea of the project's capabilities.

9. **Identifying Risks:** this section covers various risks or challenges that a project may face, such as technical challenges, market competition, regulatory issues, and financial problems. Moreover, it's important to note if such problems do arise, how do they plan to solve or mitigate them. Hence, you should carry out a thorough risk assessment before diving into a cryptocurrency with your money.

Key Metrics

Other than studying the cryptocurrency project and its whitepaper, there are a few metrics that you can keep your eye on to understand how a currency is doing in the market. It is possible that big ideas and promises in the whitepaper are not doing so well in the real world. Hence, it becomes crucial to see how the currency is doing in the market. This analysis includes taking a look at metrics such as market capitalization, circulating supply, ongoing volume and liquidity, development, adoption and real-world usage.

1. **Market Capitalization:** It is a fundamental metric that reflects the total value of the cryptocurrency in the market. A currency's capitalization is calculated by multiplying the current price with its total circulating supply. For example, if the current price of a cryptocurrency is at $50, and there are 10 million coins in circulation, then its market capitalization or market cap would be $500 million. Market cap is also used in categorizing the currency into different groups such as large-cap, mid-cap, and small-cap. Similar to stocks, currencies with higher market caps are considered more stable and less volatile as compared to mid-cap or small-cap currencies. But one interesting thing to note is that it is the mid-cap and small-cap currencies that have more scope to grow faster and give more gains as compared to large-cap currencies since their growth has slowed down or gotten saturated after enough expansion.

2. **Circulating Supply:** Circulating supply refers to the number of coins being bought and sold in the market. Circulating supply helps to understand the availability of crypto, which impacts its price and liquidity. Now the circulating supply is different from the total supply. Total supply refers to the number of coins that will ever be created. Suppose a currency has a total supply of 21 million coins, but only 18 million are in the market being traded, then we can say the circulation supply is 18 million. If the supply of crypto is less than its total supply and there's a scarcity, it can potentially increase the price of the currency. Whereas, if the circulating supply is higher than the demand of the currency in the market, then the price or the value can decrease.

4. **Network Activity:** Analyzing this activity gives you an idea about the usage and engagement on the cryptocurrency's blockchain. To properly analyze this, firstly, you can take a look at the number of transactions happening in the crypto's blockchain. A higher number of transactions indicates a strong usage and adoption by the people. Another metric you can check out is active addresses, which shows you how many new addresses (of users) are involved in transactions. A growing number of active addresses can be a sign of increasing usage.

5. **Development Activity:** This metric reflects the ongoing work and progress being made by the development team of a cryptocurrency. It is measured by various factors. The first factor is regular updates and improvements in the codebase. Secondly - how many developers and contributors are functioning to drive a project to success. The third factor is the activity taking place on development platforms like Github. Analyzing the above can give you a significant idea of what the team behind a crypto project is doing.

6. **Adoption and Real-World Usage:** This metric is about how widely a cryptocurrency is being used and accepted in practical scenarios. To observe adoption and usage, you can check out how many strategic partnerships do they have with established companies, how many platforms is the cryptocurrency available on, how many businesses accept the currency as payment, and how much is the user base expanding over time.

Chapter 6

Technical Analysis

I refer to 'technical analysis' as reading the market's mood. It is used to predict price movements of assets like stocks or crypto by looking at charts, past prices and volumes, etc. The term 'technical analysis' is misunderstood by people, they assume since the word 'technical' is there, technical analysis must be a very complex task. Let me assure you, it is not so. Carrying out technical analysis is equal to being a financial detective but instead of magnifying glass, you need to use market data.

Whereas, fundamental analysis gives you a broader view of the project and economic situation, technical analysis helps you understand and predict price movements with the help of a few tools. By being able to predict the price movement, a trader can know when to enter or exit a trade; meaning when to buy and when to sell to make a profit.

How does one even figure out where the price is going to go? This was answered by Charles H. Dow, who gave a theory for the purpose of carrying out market analysis - whether fundamental or technical. His theory consisted of several principles that stand true even today.

The DOW Theory

The first rule of the famous theory is that the '**market moves in trends**'. It means that an asset's price does not zig zag aimlessly - it moves in trends due to various reasons. A trend is a general direction in which the price is moving. The price can move upward, downward or sideways. Traders generally use tools and indicators to identify which trend is being followed by the price. By identifying a trend, a trader can understand when to buy in and take a position in the market.

The second rule says '**history tends to repeat itself**'. The principle behind this rule is that human behavior often repeats. Patterns formed in the charts of a price of asset, form patterns and reoccur over time. If these recurring patterns are caught timely, you can make profitable trades.

The third rule talks about how the '**market discounts everything**'. It means that all available information such as economic data, political events, and market sentiment - is already factored into the current price of a currency. In other words, the current price not only reflects the fundamental factors but also the emotions, perceptions, and expectations of the people. For example, if a new regulation or a law is expected to have some effect on a particular currency, then this will already be reflected by the movements in the price, way before the regulation even comes.

Over time, these above principles took shape and resulted in different types, methods, and tools for analysis. **Therefore, technical analysis can be broken down further into**:

1. Trend Analysis

2. Pattern Analysis

3. Volume Analysis

4. Other Technical Indicators

Trend Analysis

This is the key component of technical analysis. This involves identifying the general direction in which a price may go. In the price graphs that we see for any asset like stock or crypto, we can see that the price does not move in a straight line instead, it creates fluctuations and moves in a zig-zag manner touching higher and lower points, seeming to go in a certain direction. There are three general directions in this regard namely - uptrend, downtrend, and sideways.

1. **Uptrend:** an uptrend is observed when the price is moving in a series of higher highs and higher lows. It indicates that the market is moving upwards. This trend is also known as a bullish trend. What are higher highs and higher lows? As the graph moves up in a zig-zag pattern, it creates points called higher highs and higher lows. As long as the graph keeps making higher highs, we know the trend is going up. If we draw a straight line through all the higher lows, we can see how steep the trend is. This line is called the support line or axis.

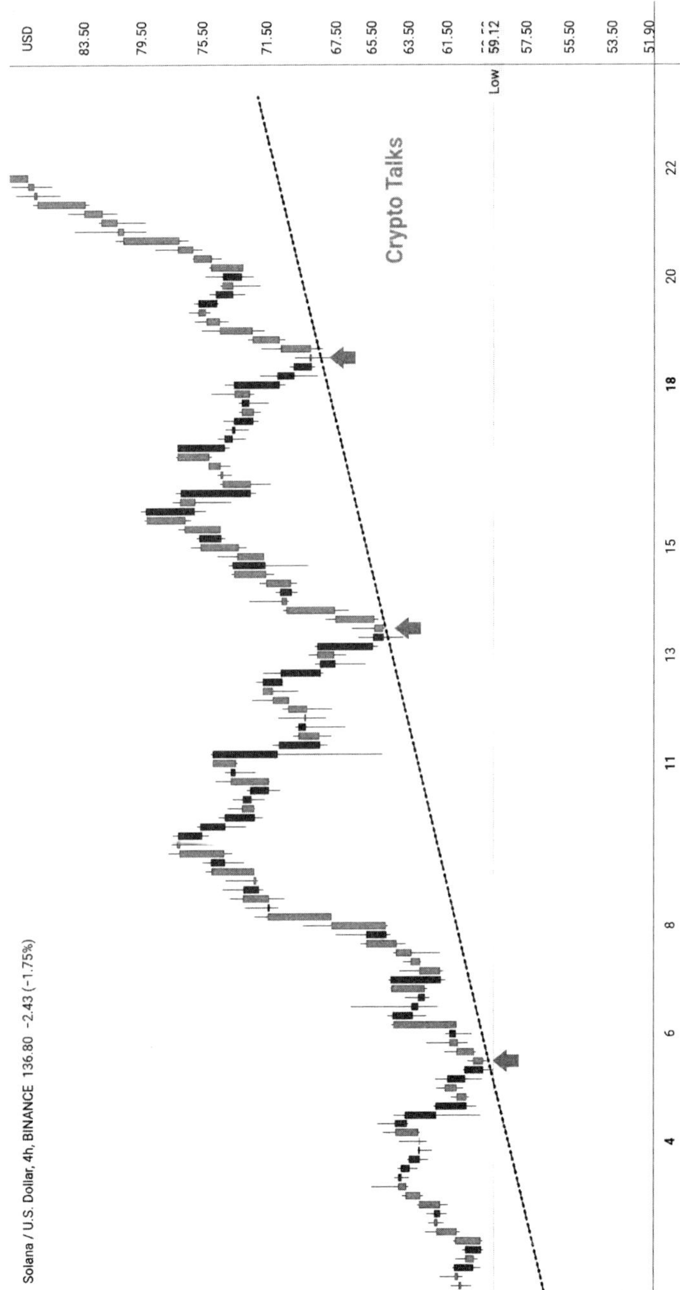
Solana / U.S. Dollar, 4h, BINANCE 136.80 −2.43 (−1.75%)
Crypto Talks
USD
83.50
79.50
75.50
71.50
67.50
65.50
63.50
61.50
59.12
57.50
55.50
53.50
51.90
Low
22
20
18
15
13
11
8
6
4

2. **Downtrend:** a downtrend is observed when the prices are moving downwards. This trend is also known as the bearish trend. When the graph moves down in a zig-zag way, it reaches points called lower highs and lower lows. Connecting the lower highs shows the trend is going down. But if the graph goes above the last lower high and starts going up, making higher highs, it might mean the trend is changing direction.

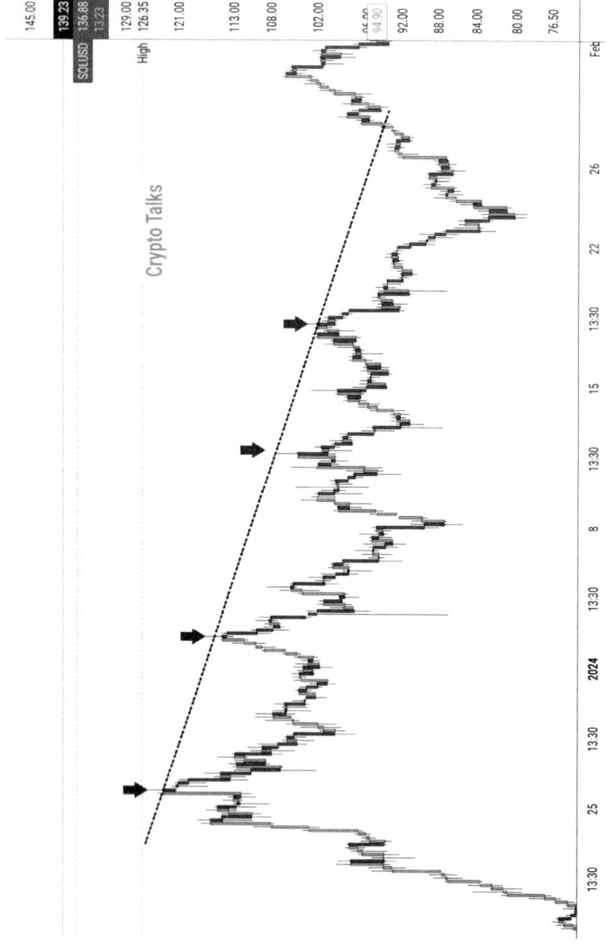

3. **Sideways trend:** If the graph shows highs and lows at about the same levels and these levels run side by side, it means the market is moving sideways. This means the price isn't going up or down much and it is staying pretty steady, as shown below. Traders often watch for the price to move out of this range to spot new trends.

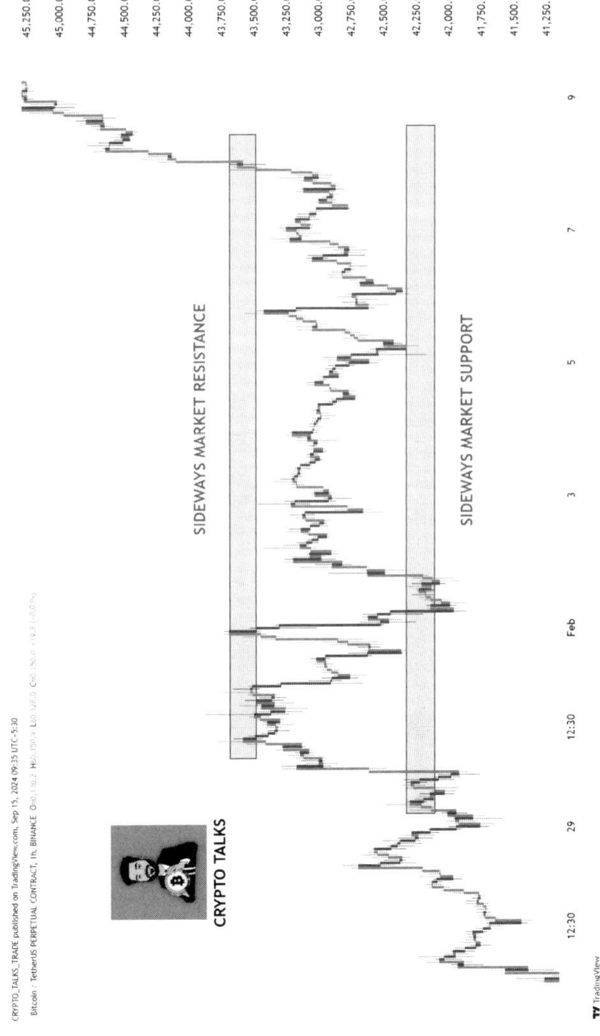

Support and Resistance

These two terms are another crucial part of trend analysis. As mentioned above, Support is like a floor for the price. The support is formed when we connect all the higher highs made by the price graph. When the price of a cryptocurrency drops and keeps stopping at a certain level before going back up, we call that level 'support'. It shows where people are willing to buy and push the price higher. As long as the price stays above this level, it means the trend is likely going up.

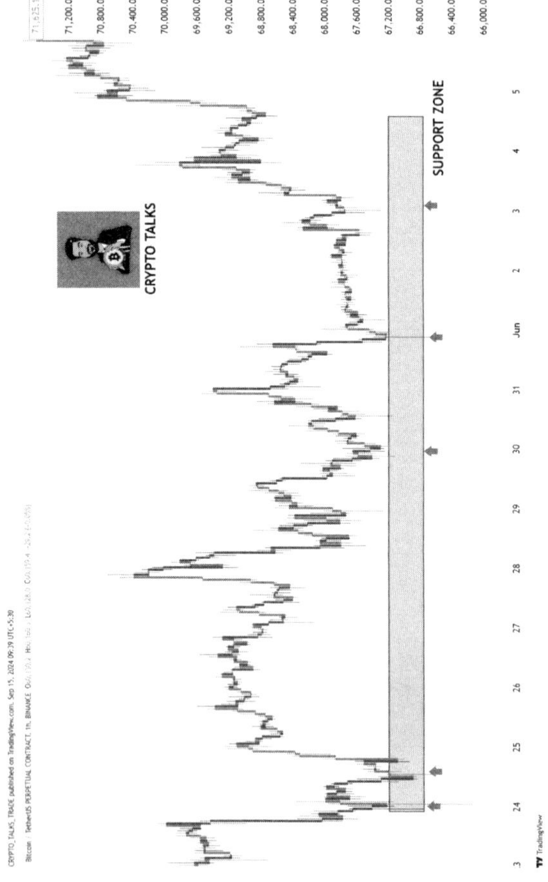

Resistance is like a ceiling for the price. When the price rises and keeps hitting a certain level before dropping back down, we call that level 'resistance'. It shows where people are selling their asset more and stopping the price from going higher.

When the price is stuck between support (the floor) and resistance (the ceiling), it means the market isn't really going up or down—it's moving sideways. Traders look at these levels to guess what might happen next. If the price goes above resistance, it might keep going up. If it falls below support, it might keep going down.

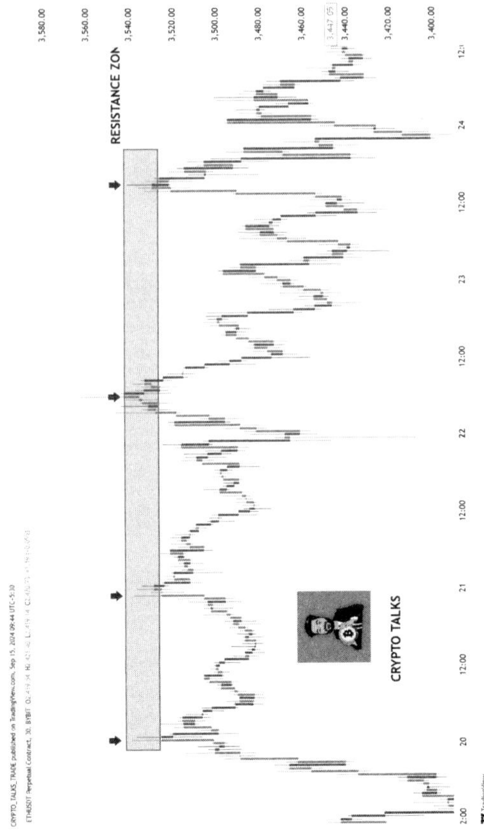

Moreover, how you look at trends depends on your trading style. If you're a long-term investor, you can watch the trends over several years or at least six months. But if you're a short-term trader, like a swing trader, you'll have to focus on trends over a day or a week, or even on an hourly basis. To make spotting these trends easier, you can pick a cryptocurrency's chart and check its chart to draw the trend lines yourself. If you don't want to do this by hand, you can use the supertrend tool, which shows the trend lines automatically, making it simple to follow.

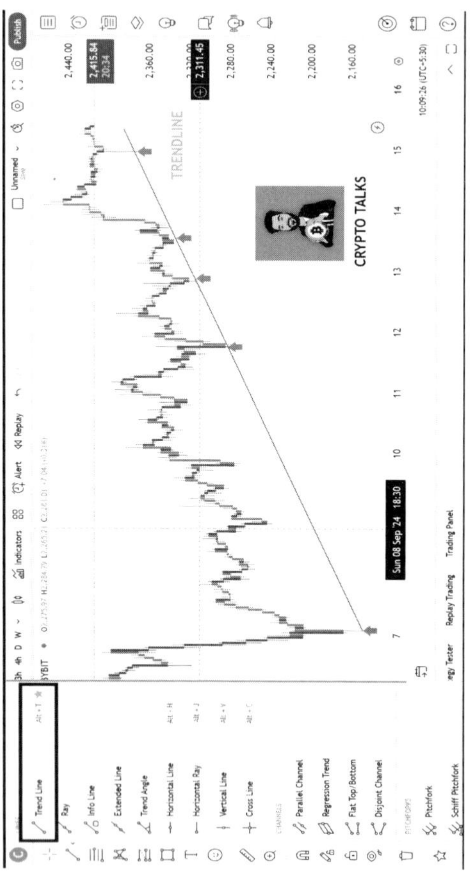

Pattern Analysis

In trading, patterns are formed by the arrangement of candlesticks on a price chart. Each candlestick represents a specific time period, like a day, an hour, or even a minute, depending on the chart's settings. By looking at how these candlesticks are arranged and how they relate to each other, traders can spot patterns that give clues about what the market might do next. These patterns are like a visual language that helps traders understand what the market might do next.

To understand how candlestick patterns are formed, it's essential to first understand the structure of a candlestick itself. Each candlestick is made up of a **body** and **wicks** (sometimes called shadows). At times these candlesticks appear one after another in different sizes, making a certain pattern. These patterns then signify in which direction the price can go. The candlestick patterns can be simple as well as complex, which must be understood well. Hence, the next chapter is dedicated to it in detail.

Volume analysis

Volume analysis is all about looking at how many shares, contracts, or units of an asset are being traded during a specific time period. Volume is a crucial piece of information because it tells us how much interest there is in a particular asset. When a lot of people are buying or selling an asset, the volume is high, showing strong participation in the market. Volume analysis is important because it gives traders an extra layer of insight into the market. Prices alone don't tell the whole story—volume shows how much conviction there is behind a price movement. When combined with other tools and analysis, understanding volume can help traders make better decisions about when to enter or exit a trade.

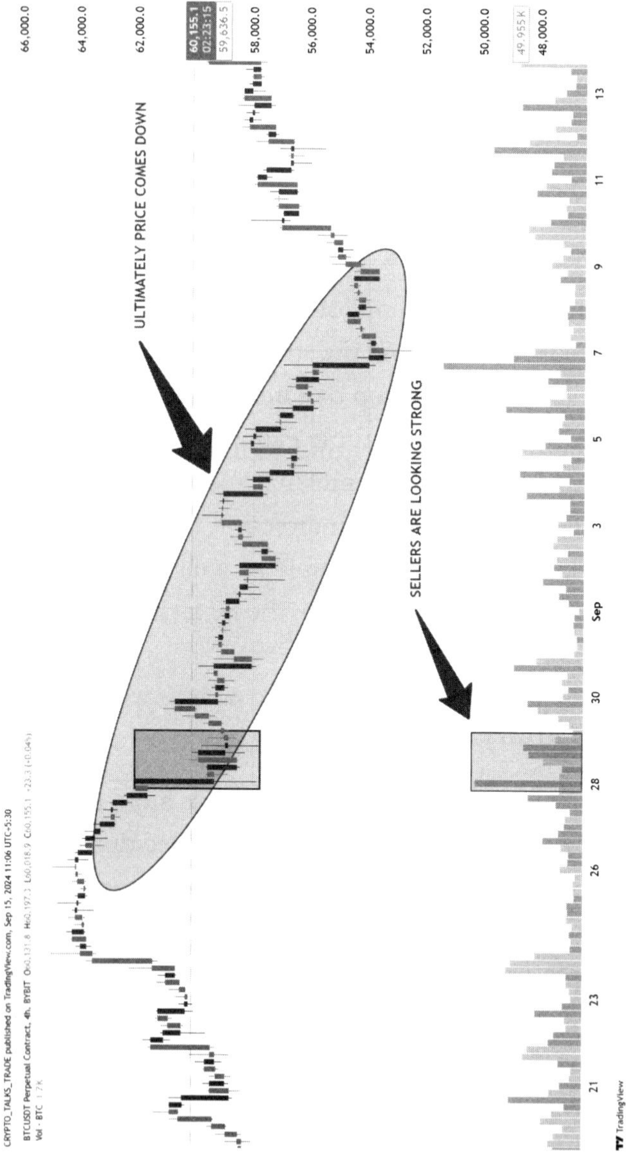

Volume Confirms Trends: In an **uptrend** (when prices are going up), rising volume is a good sign. It means that more people are buying, which supports the continuation of the uptrend. In a **downtrend** (when prices are going down), if the volume is also increasing, it suggests that many people are selling, confirming that the downtrend is likely to continue.

Volume Comes Before Price: Often, changes in volume happen before we see a change in price. For example, if there has been very little trading activity and suddenly there's a big spike in volume, it could be a sign that a new trend is about to start. Traders watch for these spikes in volume as early indicators of what might happen next with the price.

Divergence Between Price and Volume: Divergence is when the price and volume are not moving in sync. For example, if the price of an asset is going up but the volume is going down, it could be a warning sign. This situation might indicate that the buying interest is weakening, even though the price is rising and a trend reversal could be on the way.

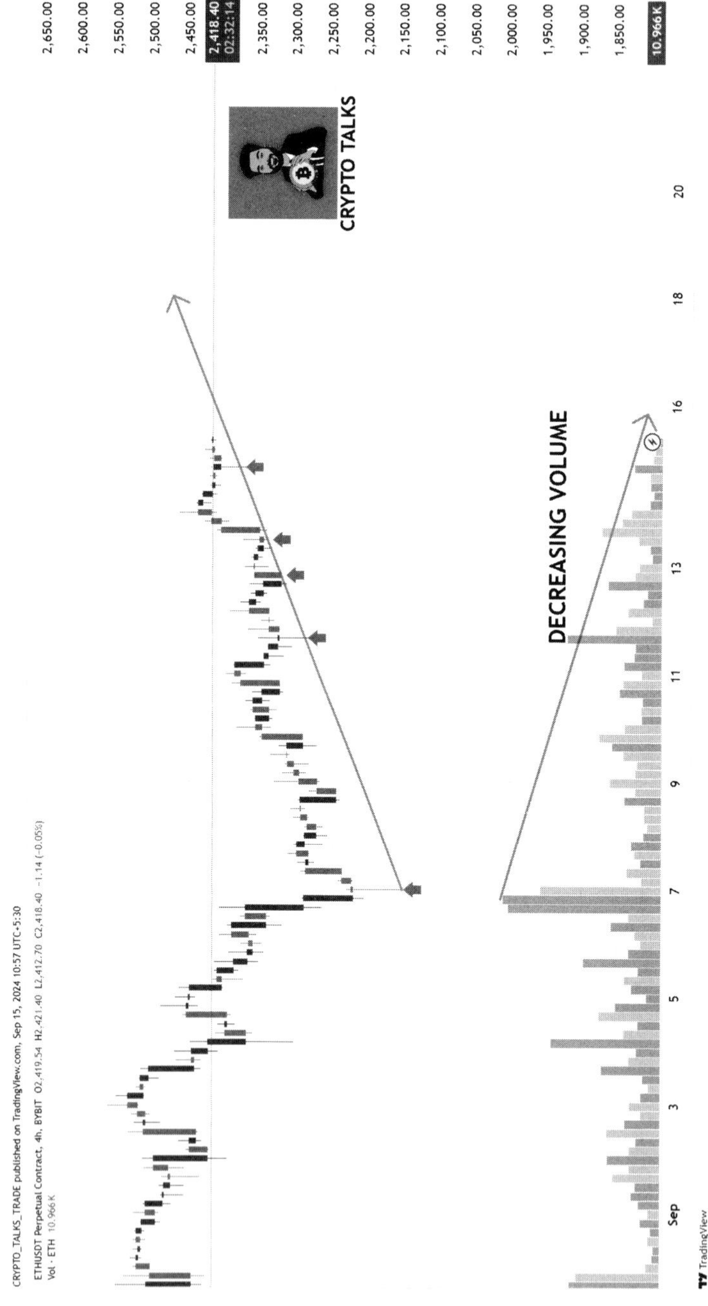
CRYPTO_TALKS_TRADE published on TradingView.com, Sep 15, 2024 10:57 UTC+5:30
ETHUSDT Perpetual Contract, 4h, BYBIT O2,419.54 H2,421.40 L2,412.70 C2,418.40 −1.14 (−0.05%)
Vol · ETH 10.966K
CRYPTO TALKS
DECREASING VOLUME
2,650.00
2,600.00
2,550.00
2,500.00
2,450.00
2,418.40
02:32:14
2,350.00
2,300.00
2,250.00
2,200.00
2,150.00
2,100.00
2,050.00
2,000.00
1,950.00
1,900.00
1,850.00
10.966K
Sep
3
5
7
9
11
13
16
18
20
TradingView

Indicators or Tools for Different Types of Analysis

In trading, just looking at price charts isn't always enough to understand market movements and make smart decisions. Traders use different indicators and tools to help them analyze trends, patterns and volume. Each of these tools has its own strengths, and they can be combined to get a clearer picture of what's happening in the market.

The important thing is to know how these tools work and to use them in the right way, depending on your trading strategy and what the market is doing. Whether you're trying to see if a trend will continue, or spot a possible reversal, or gauge the market's interest, there's an indicator or tool that can help you make better trading choices.

Let's take a closer look at some of these tools and indicators, how they work and how you can use them for different types of analysis.

Trend Analysis Indicators

Trend analysis is all about identifying the direction in which the market is moving. Is it going up, down or moving sideways? To answer these questions, traders use various tools and indicators mentioned below:

1. Moving Averages: Moving Averages (MAs) are fundamental tools in crypto trading that help smooth out price data to identify trends over a specific period. A Moving Average is a calculation that takes the average price of an asset over a certain number of time periods. It helps to filter out "noise" from random price fluctuations and gives a clearer view of the overall trend.

- **Simple Moving Average (SMA):** This is the most basic type. It's calculated by adding the closing prices over a specified number of periods and dividing by that number. For example, a 10-day SMA adds up the closing prices of the last 10 days and divides by 10.
- **Exponential Moving Average (EMA):** This type gives more weight to recent prices, making it more responsive to new information. This can be more useful in fast-moving markets like crypto.

If the price is above the moving average, it generally indicates an upward trend. If the price is below the moving average, it suggests a downward trend.

Bullish Crossover: When a shorter-term moving average (like the 10-day SMA) crosses above a longer-term moving average (like the 50-day SMA), it's often seen as a signal to buy because it indicates increasing upward momentum.

Bearish Crossover: When the shorter-term moving average crosses below the longer-term moving average, it signals a potential sell opportunity, indicating downward momentum.

Moving averages can act as dynamic support or resistance levels. For example, if the price approaches a moving average and bounces back, it may act as support. Conversely, if the price hits a moving average and falls, it can act as resistance.

Let's say you're looking at a cryptocurrency like Ethereum. You calculate the 20-day SMA and notice that the price has consistently stayed above this average. This suggests that Ethereum is in an upward trend. Later, the 10-day SMA crosses above the 50-day SMA. This could be a signal to consider buying, as it indicates a stronger upward momentum.

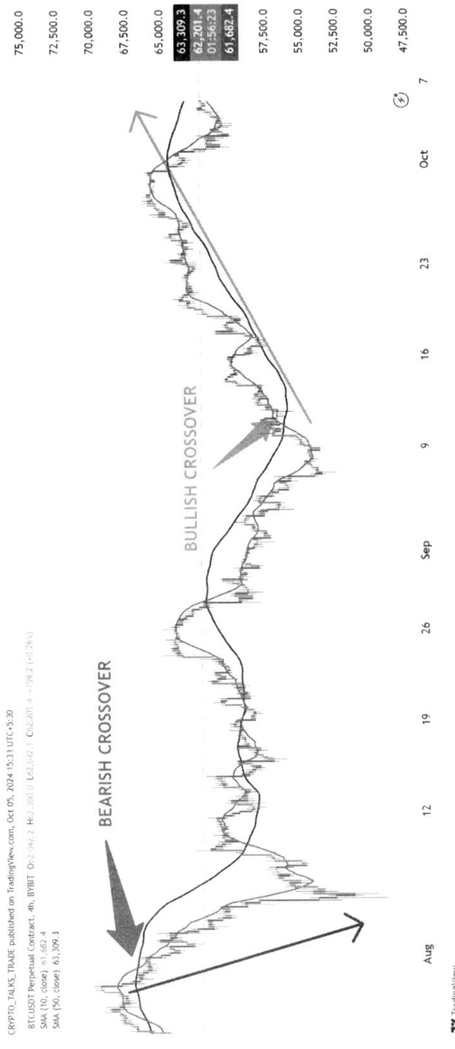

2. Moving Average Convergence Divergence (MACD): The MACD, or Moving Average Convergence Divergence, is a popular technical analysis tool used in trading to help identify potential buy and sell signals. Here's a breakdown of how it works:

The MACD consists of three main components:

MACD Line: This is the difference between two exponential moving averages (EMAs)—typically, the 12-day EMA and the 26-day EMA. The MACD line shows the momentum of the asset.

Signal Line: This is usually a 9-day EMA of the MACD line. It smooths out the MACD line and helps traders spot trends.

Histogram: This represents the difference between the MACD line and the signal line. It helps visualize the strength of the momentum.

When the MACD line crosses above the signal line, it may indicate that the price is starting to rise, signaling a potential buy opportunity. Conversely, when the MACD line crosses below the signal line, it may suggest that the price is starting to fall, signaling a potential sell opportunity.

If the price of a cryptocurrency is making lower lows, but the MACD is making higher lows, this can indicate that the price may reverse and start to rise. If the price is making higher highs, but the MACD is making lower highs, this can indicate that the price may reverse and start to fall.

A growing histogram (bars getting taller) indicates increasing momentum in the direction of the MACD line. A shrinking histogram (bars getting shorter) suggests that the momentum is decreasing, and a reversal could be near.

Let's say you're analyzing a cryptocurrency like Bitcoin. You notice: The MACD line crosses above the signal line. This could be a signal to consider buying because it suggests upward momentum. After some time, you see that the MACD line has crossed below the signal line. This might be a signal to sell, indicating that the price could be going down.

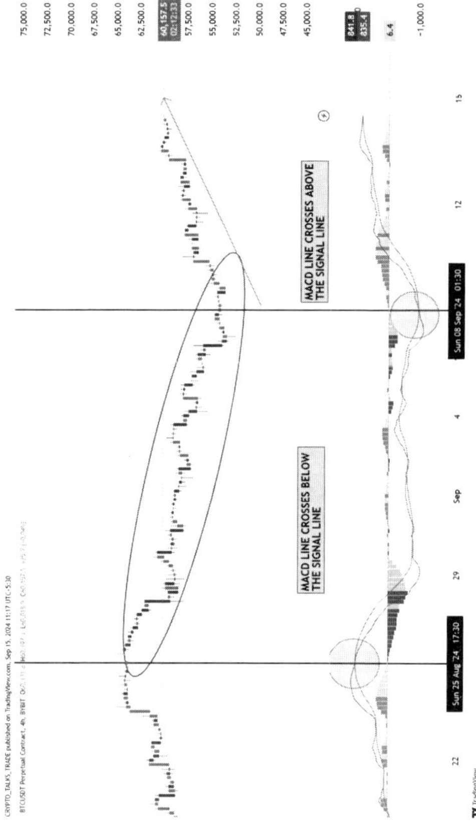

3. Average Directional Index (ADX): The Average Directional Index (ADX) is used to measure the strength of a trend in the market, whether it's an uptrend or a downtrend. It doesn't tell you if the price is going up or down—it just tells you how strong the current trend is.

The ADX is a line that moves between 0 and 100. It's calculated using the differences between upward and downward price movements over a set period (usually 14 days). The ADX is usually shown with two other lines:

- **+DI (Positive Directional Indicator):** This measures the strength of the upward movement.
- **-DI (Negative Directional Indicator):** This measures the strength of the downward movement.

Together, these lines help traders determine the direction of the trend, while the ADX line tells you the strength of the trend. When the ADX is above 25, it signals that the market is in a strong trend. The higher the ADX, the stronger the trend. For example, if the ADX is at 40, the market is in a very strong trend, and it's likely that the trend will continue.

If the ADX is below 25, the market is not in a clear trend, and it may be moving sideways. If the ADX starts to rise above 25, it may indicate that a new trend is starting, whether it's up or down. If the ADX starts to fall from a high level, it may suggest that the trend is weakening and could reverse soon.

When the +DI line crosses above the -DI line, it indicates an uptrend, and when the -DI line crosses above the +DI line, it indicates a downtrend. Traders often look for these crosses to confirm the trend's direction and then check the ADX to see how strong the trend is.

Let's say you are looking at Ethereum, and you notice that the +DI line is above the -DI line, signaling an uptrend. You check the ADX, and it's reading 30, which means the uptrend is strong. This could be a good time to follow the trend and go long (buy Ethereum). On the other hand, if the -DI line is above the +DI line (indicating a downtrend), and the ADX is at 40, it signals that the downtrend is strong, and it may be a good time to sell or short the asset.

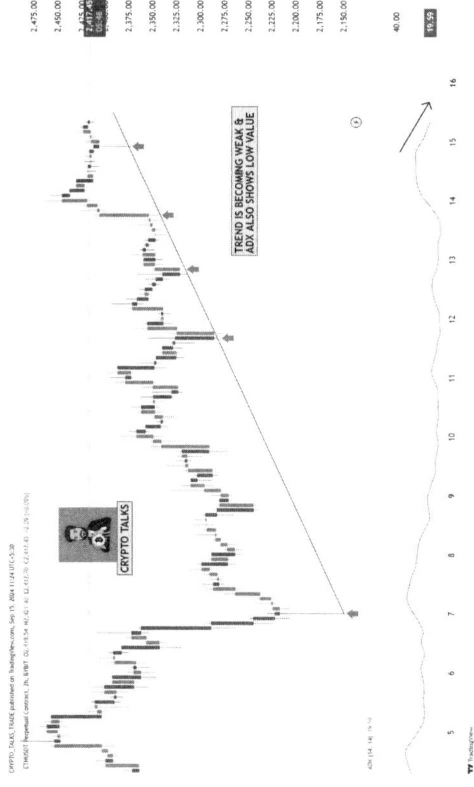

4. Fibonacci Retracements: Fibonacci retracement is a used to find key levels where the price of an asset (like a stock or cryptocurrency) might reverse direction or take a break during a trend. It's based on numbers from a mathematical sequence called the Fibonacci sequence. Traders use this to predict how much the price could pull back (or retrace) before continuing its trend. The Fibonacci sequence is a series of numbers where each number is the sum of the two before it. It looks like this: 0, 1, 1, 2, 3, 5, 8, 13, 21, 34, and so on. When you divide certain numbers in this sequence, you get ratios like 23.6%, 38.2%, 50%, 61.8%, and 78.6%. These ratios are important because they show up in nature, and in the charts as well.

While using this tool, look for a clear upward or downward trend in the price of the asset. If the price has been moving up, you'll draw the Fibonacci retracement from the lowest point (start of the move) to the highest point (end of the move). If the price has been moving down, you draw it from the highest point (start of the move) to the lowest point (end of the move). When you apply the Fibonacci retracement tool, it will automatically draw horizontal lines at the key Fibonacci levels: 23.6%, 38.2%, 50%, 61.8%, and 78.6%. These lines show you where the price might stop falling (in an uptrend) or stop rising (in a downtrend) before continuing the trend.

Fibonacci levels often act like invisible barriers in the market. For example, in an uptrend, a pullback might hit the 38.2% level and bounce back up, meaning this level acts as support. In a downtrend, the price might rise temporarily, hit the 61.8% level, and then start falling again, meaning this level acts as resistance.

Key Levels to Watch: These levels help traders figure out where the price might reverse. Many traders look closely at the 38.2% and 61.8% levels because price often bounces back or changes direction around these points.

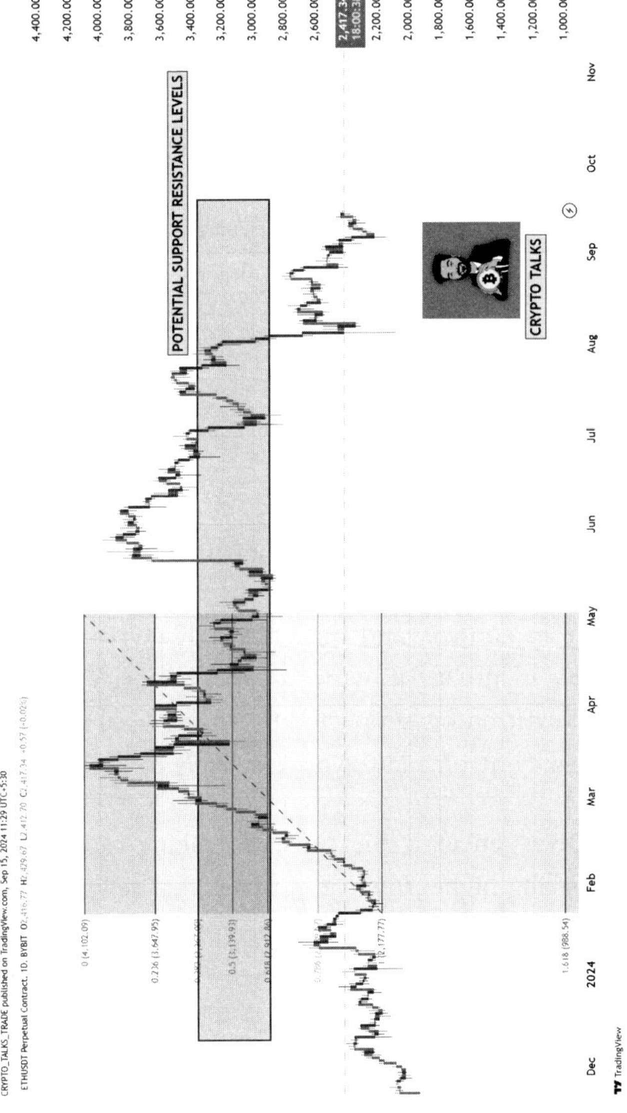

Volume Analysis Indicators

Volume analysis focuses on the number of shares, contracts or units traded during a specific time period. Here are some tools that help in volume analysis:

1. **On-Balance Volume (OBV):** On-Balance Volume (OBV) is a tool used to measure the flow of volume (buying and selling) in a market. It helps to understand whether volume is supporting a price trend, which can give clues about whether the price will continue to move up or down.

The basic idea behind OBV is that volume precedes price. This means if a lot of volume (trading activity) is happening, the price is likely to follow in that direction. OBV is shown as a single line that goes up or down based on whether the volume is being added or subtracted.

When OBV is moving upward along with the price, it confirms that the uptrend is supported by strong volume, meaning buyers are in control, and the price is likely to keep rising. When OBV is moving downward with the price, it confirms that the downtrend is supported by strong volume, meaning sellers are in control, and the price is likely to keep falling.

Bullish Divergence: If the price is making new lows, but OBV is making higher lows, it indicates that selling volume is weakening, and a price reversal to the upside may happen soon.

Bearish Divergence: If the price is making new highs, but OBV is making lower highs, it shows that buying volume is weakening, and the price may reverse downward soon.

If the OBV is steadily rising while the price is moving sideways, it can signal that a breakout to the upside is coming, as buying volume is increasing. Similarly, if OBV is falling while the price is moving sideways, it could indicate a breakout to the downside, as selling volume is increasing.

Let's say Bitcoin is trading at $30,000. The price has been moving up, and the OBV line is also rising. This suggests that the uptrend is being supported by strong buying volume, so the price is likely to continue rising. Now, if the price of Bitcoin reaches $35,000 but the OBV starts to fall, this could be a sign that the uptrend is losing strength, and a downward reversal might happen soon.

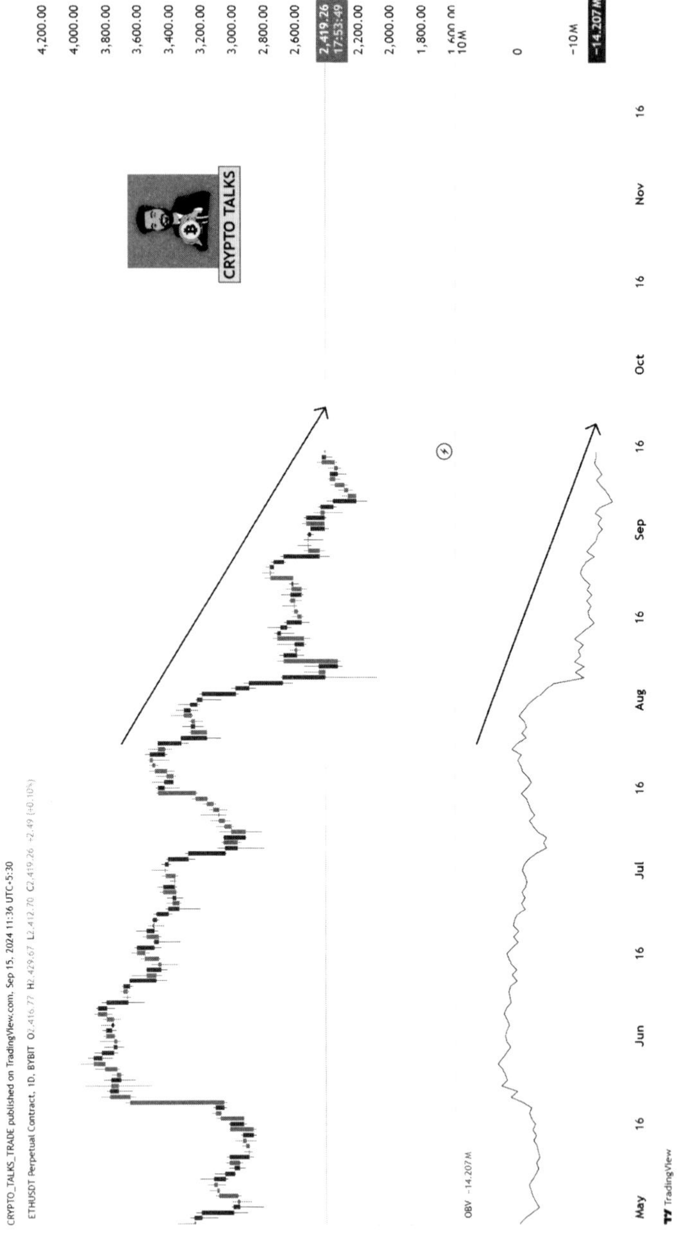

CRYPTO_TALKS_TRADE published on TradingView.com, Sep 15, 2024 11:36 UTC+5:30
ETHUSDT Perpetual Contract, 1D, BYBIT
CRYPTO TALKS
4,200.00
4,000.00
3,800.00
3,600.00
3,400.00
3,200.00
3,000.00
2,800.00
2,600.00
2,419.26
17:53:49
2,200.00
2,000.00
1,800.00
10M
0
−10M
−14.207M
OBV −14.207M
May
16
Jun
16
Jul
16
Aug
16
Sep
16
Oct
16
Nov
16
TradingView

2. Volume Weighted Average Price (VWAP): The Volume Weighted Average Price (VWAP) is used to figure out the average price of an asset, but with a twist: it considers both the price and volume of trades. VWAP helps to understand if the current price is higher or lower than the average price buyers and sellers have been trading at, based on the volume of trades.

VWAP calculates the average price of an asset over a specific time period, but it gives more importance (or "weight") to prices with higher trading volume. This means that prices with more trades have a bigger impact on the VWAP than prices with fewer trades. VWAP is plotted as a line on a price chart, and it changes throughout the day as new trades happen.

When the price is below VWAP and starts moving upwards toward the VWAP line, it might be a good buying opportunity, indicating the price could rise. When the price is above VWAP and starts moving downwards toward the VWAP line, it might be a signal to sell, as the price could fall.

VWAP can also be used to confirm trends. In an uptrend, the price will generally stay above the VWAP line, showing that buyers are in control. In a downtrend, the price will stay below the VWAP line, indicating that sellers are in control. VWAP can act like a support level when the price is above it, and a resistance level when the price is below it. This means the price may "bounce" off the VWAP line, either moving up from it (support) or down from it (resistance).

Let's say Bitcoin is currently trading at $30,000. The VWAP

for the day is calculated at $28,000. If the current price is above $28,000, it means Bitcoin is trading at a premium compared to its volume-weighted average price, indicating buying pressure.

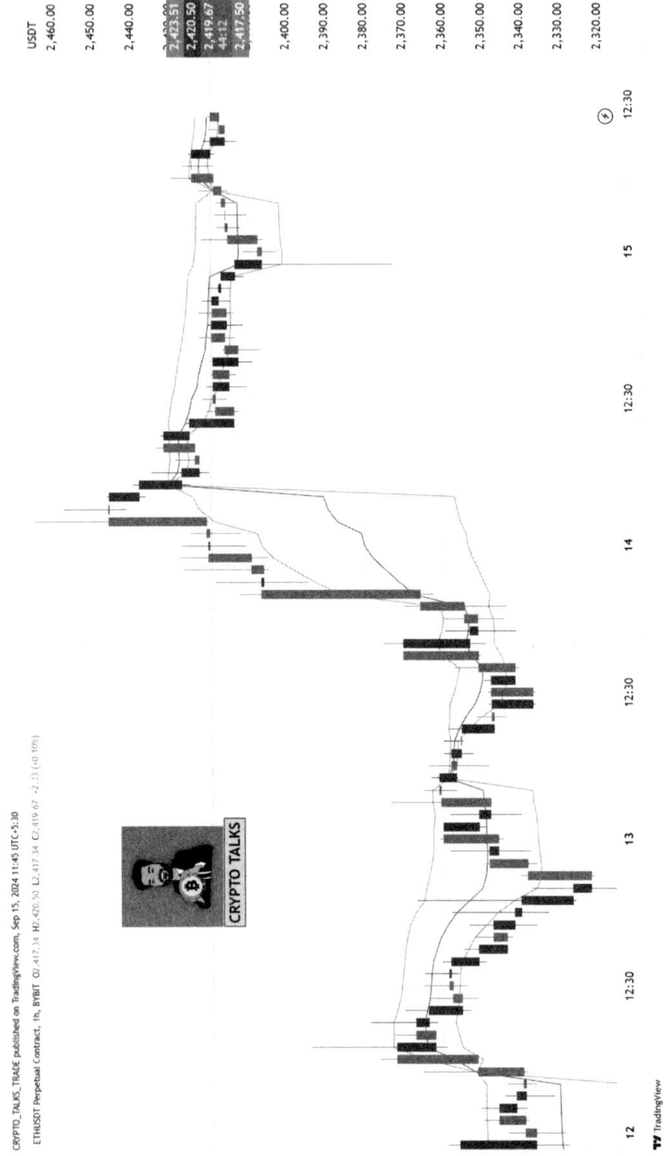

3. Volume Oscillator: The Volume Oscillator is a tool used by traders to analyze the strength or weakness of a price movement based on the volume of trades. It compares two different moving averages of trading volume to help you understand whether the current volume is high or low relative to past activity.

The Volume Oscillator calculates the difference between two moving averages of volume: a short-term and a long-term moving average.

- **Short-Term Moving Average:** Tracks the recent volume over a shorter period (e.g., 5 days).
- **Long-Term Moving Average:** Tracks the volume over a longer period (e.g., 20 days).

The oscillator is plotted on a chart, usually as a line that moves above or below zero. When the Volume Oscillator moves above zero, it signals that the recent trading volume is higher than usual, which could indicate the start or continuation of a strong trend. When the Volume Oscillator moves below zero, it signals that the recent trading volume is lower than usual, which may suggest a weakening trend or lack of interest.

If the price of a cryptocurrency is going up, and the Volume Oscillator is above zero, it confirms that the uptrend is strong because it's backed by high volume. If the price is going up but the Volume Oscillator is below zero, it suggests that the uptrend might be weak and could reverse because there's not much trading activity to support it. The same logic applies for downtrends. If prices are falling and the Volume Oscillator is high, the downtrend is strong. If prices are falling but the oscillator is low, the downtrend might be weak. When the Volume Oscillator moves sharply above zero, it can indicate a potential breakout, where the price is likely to make a big move (up or down) due to increasing volume. This is a sign that more traders are entering the market, which can cause a price spike.

Let's say Ethereum is trading at $2,000, and you notice a sudden increase in volume. The Volume Oscillator moves above zero, showing that the recent trading activity is higher than usual. This could suggest that the price may keep rising because the uptrend is supported by strong volume. On the other hand, if the price of Ethereum is going up but the Volume Oscillator stays below zero, it might be a sign that the uptrend is weak and could reverse soon because there isn't enough volume to support it.

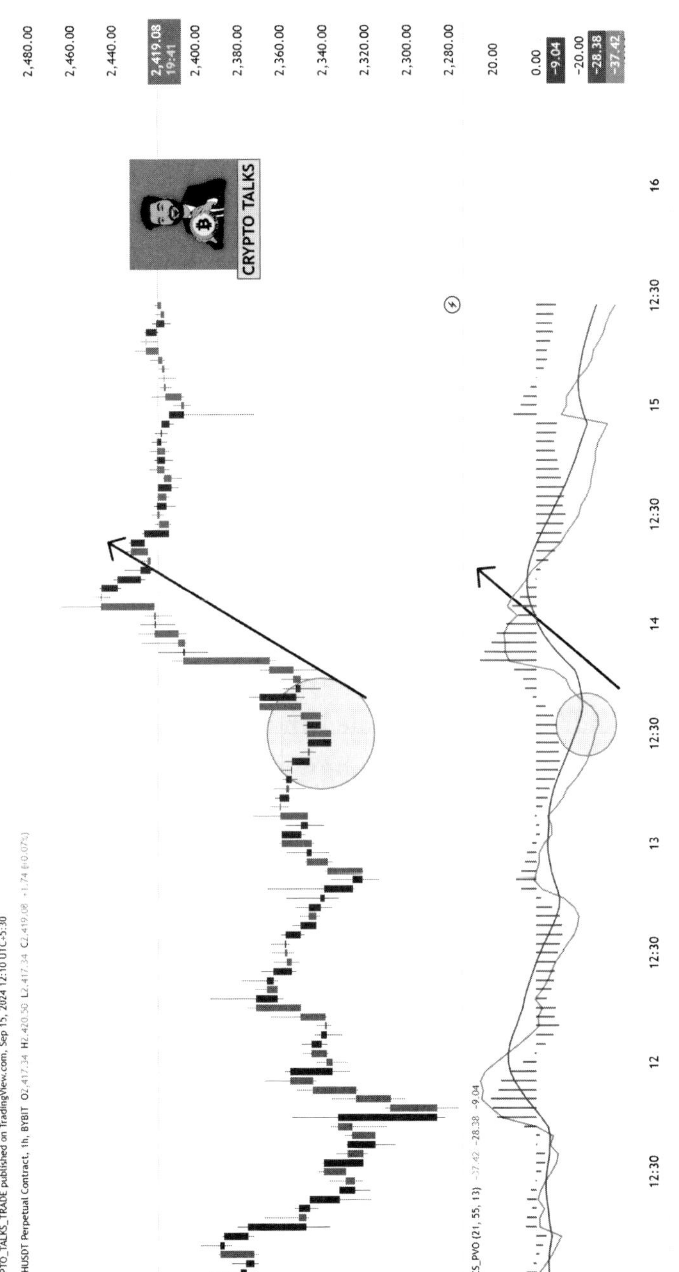
CRYPTO_TALKS_TRADE published on TradingView.com, Sep 15, 2024 12:10 UTC+5:30
ETHUSDT Perpetual Contract, 1h, BYBIT O2,417.34 H2,420.50 L2,417.34 C2,419.08 +1.74 (+0.07%)
UCS_PVO (21, 55, 13) -37.42 -28.38 -9.04
CRYPTO TALKS
2,480.00
2,460.00
2,440.00
2,419.08
19:41
2,400.00
2,380.00
2,360.00
2,340.00
2,320.00
2,300.00
2,280.00
20.00
0.00
-9.04
-20.00
-28.38
-37.42
11
12:30
12
12:30
13
12:30
14
12:30
15
12:30
16
TradingView

Other Popular Indicators and Tools

Beyond trend, pattern, and volume analysis, there are other powerful tools that you can use to enhance your market analysis:

1. **Bollinger Bands:** Bollinger Bands can be used to measure market volatility—how much the price of an asset is moving up or down. They consist of three lines (or "bands") that are plotted on a price chart. These bands expand (move apart) and contract (move closer) based on the volatility of the market.

Middle Band: This is a simple moving average (usually a 20-period moving average). A moving average is just the average price of an asset over a set number of days. In this case, it's the average price over the past 20 days.

Upper Band: This is the middle band + 2 standard deviations. Standard deviation measures how spread out the prices are from the average. If prices are more volatile, this band moves higher.

Lower Band: This is the middle band - 2 standard deviations. When prices are more volatile, this band moves lower.

Bollinger Bands help traders see when an asset is likely overbought or oversold—in other words, when the price is too high or too low compared to its recent average. When the price touches or moves above the upper band, it could mean the asset is overbought, and the price might drop soon. When the price touches or moves below the lower band, it could mean the asset is oversold, and the price might rise soon.

When the bands expand (move apart), it means the market is volatile—prices are moving a lot. When the bands contract (come closer together), it means the market is less volatile—prices are not moving much. If the price moves towards the upper band, it might be overbought, meaning the price has gone up too much and could fall soon. If the price moves towards the lower band, it might be oversold, meaning the price has dropped too much and could rise soon.

When the bands are narrow (close together), it's called a "squeeze." This suggests that the market might soon experience a breakout—either a strong upward or downward move. Imagine a coin is trading at $50, and the middle band (the 20-day moving average) is also around $50. The upper band might be at $55, and the lower band at $45, depending on the market's volatility. If the coin moves to $55 and touches the upper band, it might be considered overbought, suggesting the price could fall back down. If the coin drops to $45 and touches the lower band, it might be considered oversold, suggesting the price could rise.

Prices can "walk the bands," meaning they can stay near the upper or lower band for a while before reversing. This is why traders often use Bollinger Bands with other tools, like support and resistance levels, moving averages, or candlestick patterns, to make better decisions.

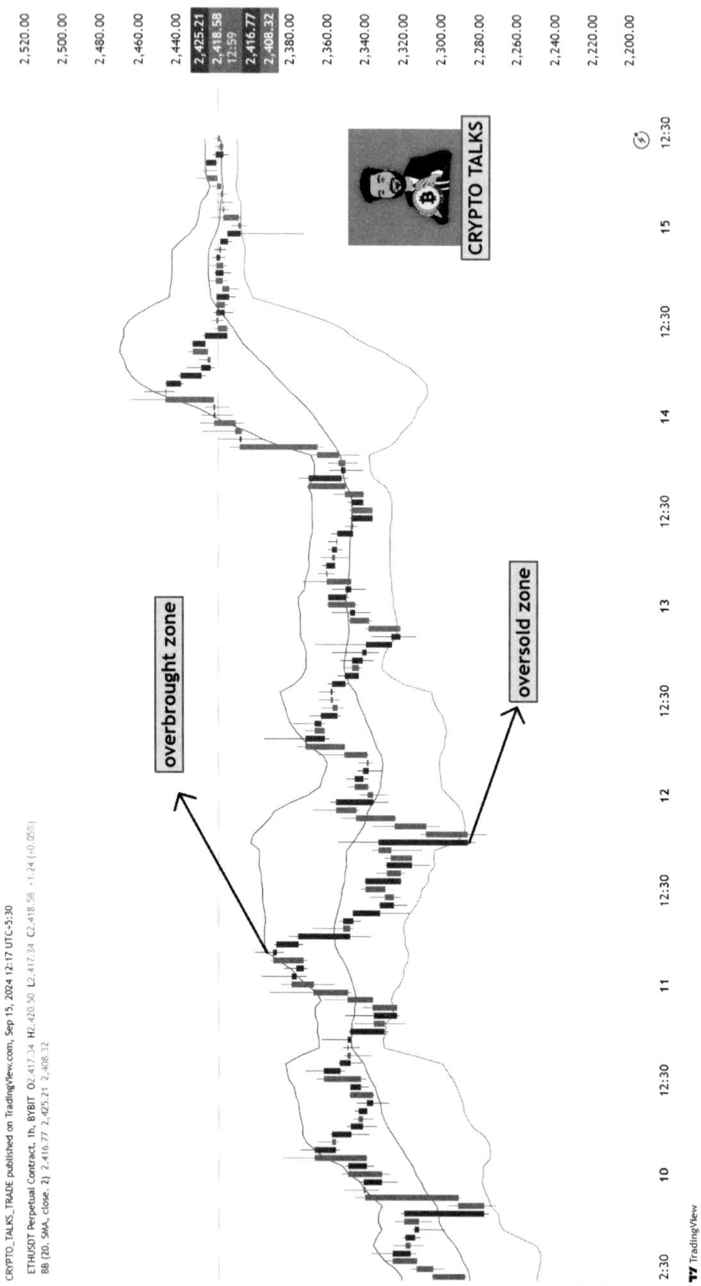
CRYPTO_TALKS_TRADE published on TradingView.com, Sep 15, 2024 12:17 UTC+5:30
overbrought zone
oversold zone
CRYPTO TALKS
TradingView

2. Relative Strength Index (RSI): TThe Relative Strength Index (RSI) is a popular tool used to measure the strength and momentum of a price movement. It helps traders figure out if a cryptocurrency (or any asset) is overbought (too high in price) or oversold (too low in price), which can suggest whether the price is likely to reverse direction soon.

RSI is shown as a number between 0 and 100 and is usually calculated over a 14-day period. The basic idea is to compare the size of recent gains to recent losses to see if the price is moving too far in one direction.

RSI Above 70: This usually indicates that the asset is overbought. In other words, the price has risen too fast, and it might be due for a pullback or drop.

RSI Below 30: This usually indicates that the asset is oversold. The price has fallen too fast, and it might be due for a bounce back up.

In an uptrend, the RSI tends to stay above 30 and often moves between 40 and 80. In a downtrend, the RSI tends to stay below 70 and often moves between 20 and 60.

Bullish Divergence: This happens when the price of the cryptocurrency makes a lower low, but the RSI makes a higher low. This suggests that momentum is building up for a possible price rise.

Bearish Divergence: This happens when the price makes a higher high, but the RSI makes a lower high. This suggests that momentum is weakening, and the price might drop.

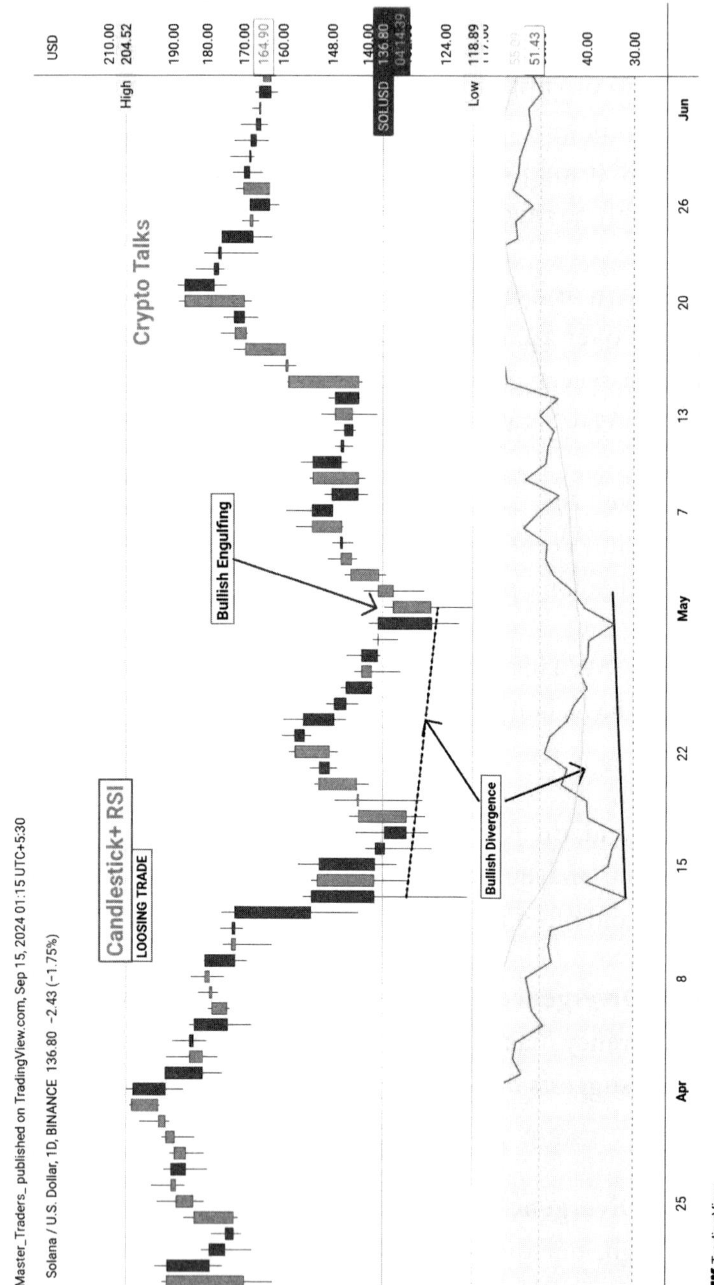
Master_Traders_ published on TradingView.com, Sep 15, 2024 01:15 UTC+5:30
Solana / U.S. Dollar, 1D, BINANCE 136.80 −2.43 (−1.75%)
Candlestick+ RSI
LOOSING TRADE
Crypto Talks
Bullish Engulfing
Bullish Divergence
High
Low
SOLUSD
USD
TradingView

Let's say Bitcoin's RSI is at 80, which is above the overbought level of 70. This could indicate that Bitcoin has been going up too quickly, and there might be a pullback soon. On the other hand, if Bitcoin's RSI is at 25, which is below the oversold level of 30, it might be a signal that Bitcoin has dropped too much and could bounce back up soon.

3. Stochastic Oscillator: The Stochastic Oscillator is used to figure out whether a cryptocurrency (or any asset) is overbought (too high in price) or oversold (too low in price). Like the RSI, it helps to predict potential price reversals by comparing the current price to the price range over a certain period.

The Stochastic Oscillator moves between 0 and 100 and is made up of two lines:

%K Line: This shows the current price's position relative to the high-low range over a set period (usually 14 days).

%D Line: This is a moving average of the %K line, usually calculated over 3 days, and acts as a signal line.

The key idea is that prices tend to close near their highs in uptrends and near their lows in downtrends. The Stochastic Oscillator helps spot these patterns. When the Stochastic Oscillator goes above 80, it signals that the cryptocurrency may be overbought, and the price could drop soon. When the Stochastic Oscillator goes below 20, it signals that the cryptocurrency may be oversold, and the price could rise soon.

When the %K line crosses above the %D line in the oversold region (below 20), it can be a buy signal. This means the price might go up soon. When the %K line crosses below the %D line in the overbought region (above 80), it can be a sell signal. This means the price might go down soon.

Bullish Divergence: If the price makes a lower low, but the Stochastic Oscillator makes a higher low, it can signal that momentum is building up for a price rise.

Bearish Divergence: If the price makes a higher high, but the Stochastic Oscillator makes a lower high, it suggests that momentum is weakening, and the price might fall.

Let's say Bitcoin is currently trading at $20,000, and the Stochastic Oscillator shows a reading of 85. Since it's above 80, this might suggest that Bitcoin is overbought and could be due for a pullback. If the %K line crosses below the %D line, it could signal that it's time to consider selling. On the other hand, if Bitcoin is at $15,000, and the Stochastic Oscillator shows a reading of 15, it might be considered oversold. If the %K line crosses above the %D line, it could be a signal to buy, as the price might rise soon.

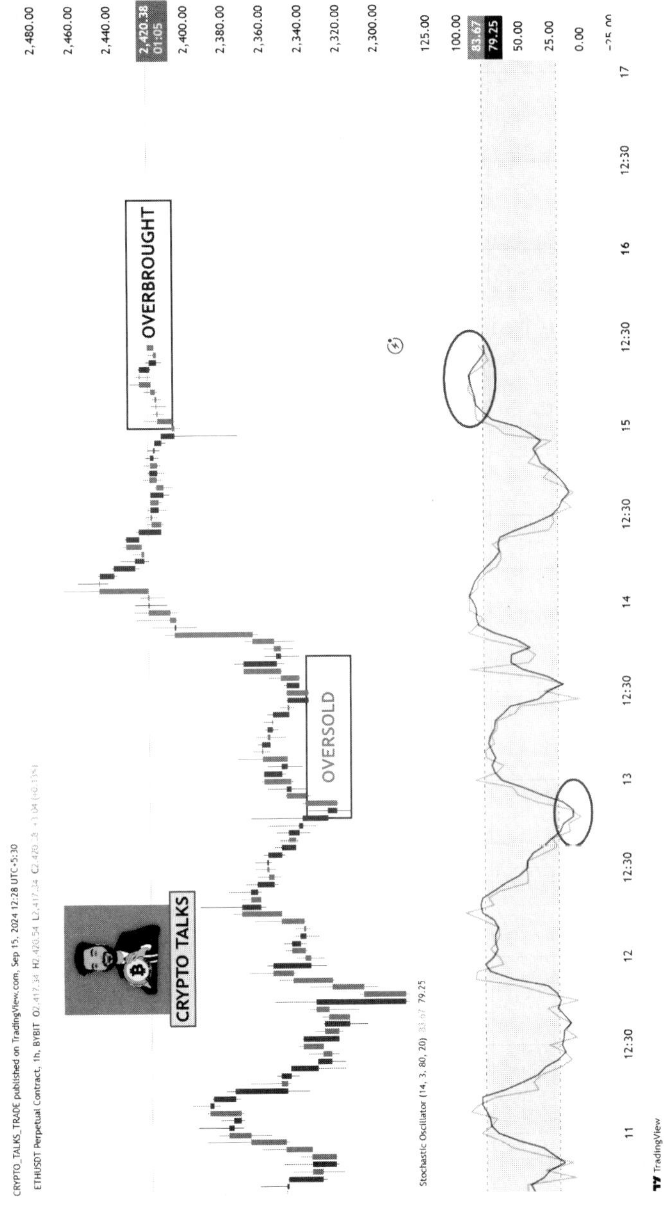
CRYPTO_TALKS_TRADE published on TradingView.com, Sep 15, 2024 12:28 UTC+5:30
ETHUSDT Perpetual Contract, 1h, BYBIT
CRYPTO TALKS
OVERSOLD
OVERBROUGHT
Stochastic Oscillator (14, 3, 80, 20)
2,480.00
2,460.00
2,440.00
2,420.38
01:05
2,400.00
2,380.00
2,360.00
2,340.00
2,320.00
2,300.00
125.00
100.00
83.67
79.25
50.00
25.00
0.00
11
12:30
12
12:30
13
12:30
14
12:30
15
12:30
16
12:30
17
TradingView

Chapter 7

Candlestick Patterns

Candlestick patterns have been used for centuries to help traders understand and predict market movements. They originated in Japan in the 18th century, when a rice trader named Munehisa Homma first developed them. Homma discovered that, by observing the patterns of price movements, he could predict future price changes more accurately. These early candlestick charts became a powerful tool for traders in Japan and eventually spread to the rest of the world. Today, candlestick patterns are a key part of technical analysis and are used by traders all over the globe. The Candlestick is made of two parts, namely the body and the wicks as shown below.

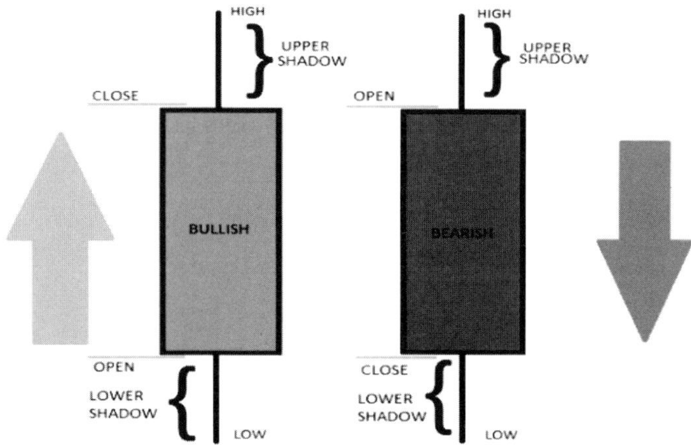

The Body: The body of the candlestick shows the opening and closing prices of the asset during the chosen time period. If the closing price is higher than the opening price, the body is usually colored green or white indicating a bullish movement (price went up). If the closing price is lower than the opening price, the body is usually red or black indicating a bearish movement (the price went down).

The Wicks: The lines extending above and below the body are called wicks. The top wick shows the highest price reached during that time period, while the bottom wick shows the lowest price. If there are no wicks, it means the price didn't go higher or lower than the opening or closing prices.

Candlestick patterns continue to be important because they provide valuable information about market trends and potential price movements. Each candlestick on a chart shows four key pieces of information for a specific period: the opening price, the closing price, the highest price and the lowest price as shown above. By looking at the shape and position of candlesticks on a chart, traders can identify patterns that indicate whether the price is likely to go up or down. These patterns help traders make informed decisions about when to buy or sell, which can lead to more successful trades.

For example, a certain pattern might indicate that the price of a cryptocurrency is about to rise, signaling a good time to buy. Another pattern might suggest that the price is likely to fall, indicating that it might be time to sell. Now, there are several types of patterns. It starts with single, double or triple candlestick patterns but they get more complex as we go ahead. Understanding these patterns can give you an edge in the market, helping you to anticipate price movements and make profitable trades.

Single Candlestick Patterns

Single candlestick patterns are essential tools in technical analysis, helping traders understand potential market movements with just one candlestick on a chart. Each pattern provides valuable insights into what might happen next with an asset's price.

1. Doji

A Doji candlestick is a pattern that looks like a cross or a plus sign on a chart because the opening and closing prices are almost the same. This means that during the time period, the price moved up and down but ended up closing right around where it started. The Doji pattern indicates that there's indecision in the market—neither buyers nor sellers were able to gain control. This often suggests that the current trend might be losing strength and a change could be coming. However, on its own a Doji doesn't tell us which direction the market will go next, so it's often used with other indicators to confirm a potential reversal or continuation of a trend.

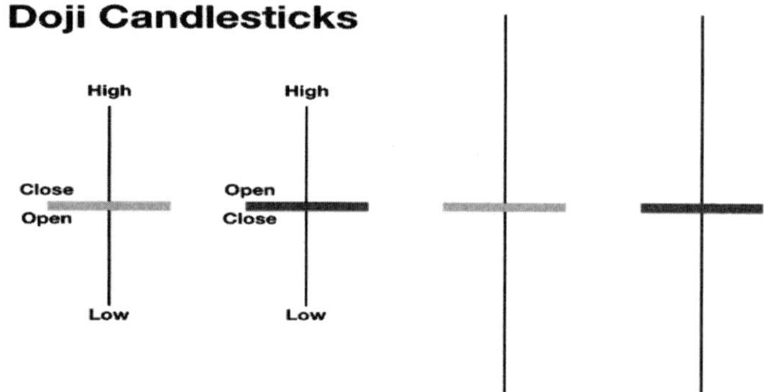

2. Hammer and Hanging Man

The Hammer and Hanging Man candlesticks look very similar but they appear in different contexts and tell us different things. A Hammer candlestick has a small body at the top with a long lower wick and it usually shows up after a downtrend. The long wick indicates that sellers pushed the price down during the period but buyers stepped in and pushed it back up, suggesting that the market might be ready to start moving upwards. On the other hand, the Hanging Man looks just like the hammer but appears after an uptrend. It signals that while buyers were still able to push the price up, the selling pressure is starting to build, which could mean that the market is about to turn downwards.

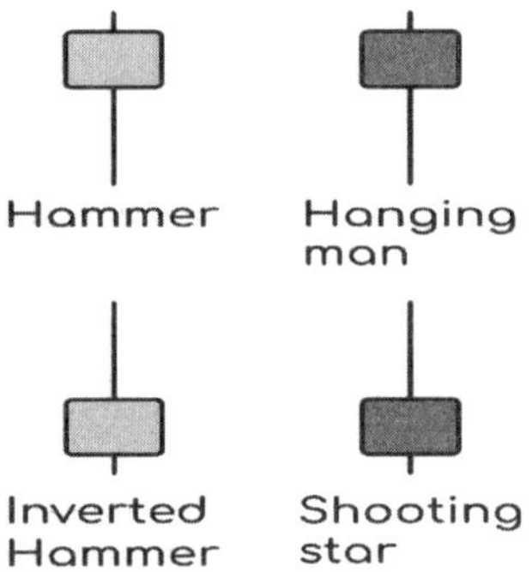

3. Spinning Top

The Spinning Top candlestick pattern shows indecision in the market. It has a small body, meaning the opening and closing prices are almost the same, and long wicks above and below, which means the price moved up and down a lot during that time. However, neither buyers nor sellers could take control, so the price stayed near the opening level. There are two types of Spinning Tops. A Bullish Spinning Top happens during a downtrend and suggests that sellers are losing power, so the price could start going up soon. A Bearish Spinning Top occurs during an uptrend and shows that buyers are struggling, meaning the price could start falling. This pattern alone doesn't tell you where the market will go, but it signals that a change might be coming, and traders should look at the next candlestick for a clearer direction.

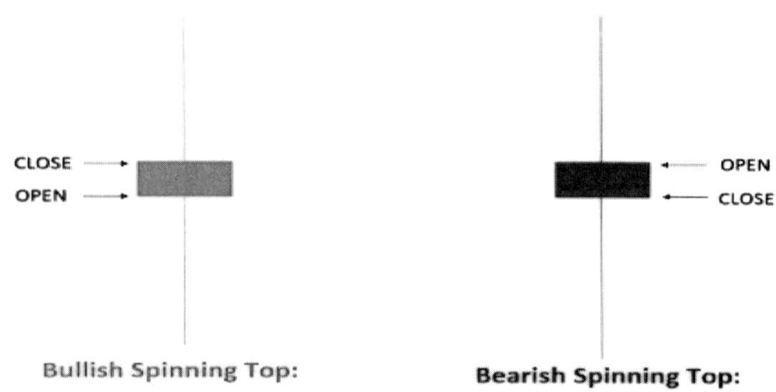

4. Marubozu

A Marubozu candlestick is a strong indicator of market direction because it has no wicks or shadows—just a solid body. This means that the price opened and kept moving in one direction throughout the entire time period, without any significant pullback. There are two types of Marubozu candles:

Bullish Marubozu: This candle has no wicks, and the opening price is the lowest, while the closing price is the highest. It shows strong buying pressure, indicating that buyers were in control from start to finish. This often signals that the price may keep going up.

Bearish Marubozu: This candle also has no wicks, but in this case, the opening price is the highest, and the closing price is the lowest. It shows strong selling pressure, meaning sellers dominated the session. This usually suggests that the price might continue to drop.

A Marubozu candle shows confidence in the direction, either up or down, without hesitation from the market. Traders often see this as a strong signal for continuing the trend.

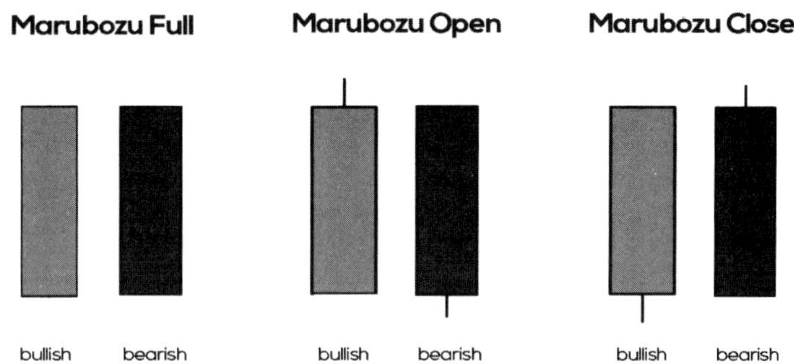

Double Candlestick Patterns

1. Bullish and Bearish Engulfing

Bullish Engulfing: This pattern appears during a downtrend and consists of two candles. The first candle is a smaller bearish (red) candle, showing that sellers are still in control. The second candle is a larger bullish (green) candle that completely "engulfs" the previous one. This means the second candle's body opens lower and closes higher than the first one, showing that buyers have stepped in strongly, taking control. It's often seen as a sign that the price could start moving upward.

Bearish Engulfing: This pattern shows up during an uptrend and is also made up of two candles. The first is a smaller bullish (green) candle, indicating that buyers are still pushing the price higher. The second is a much larger bearish (red) candle that completely "engulfs" the first one. This suggests that sellers have overpowered the buyers, and the market might start to fall.

In both patterns, the larger second candle signals a strong shift in momentum—either from sellers to buyers (Bullish Engulfing) or from buyers to sellers (Bearish Engulfing). These patterns are usually seen as important reversal signals.

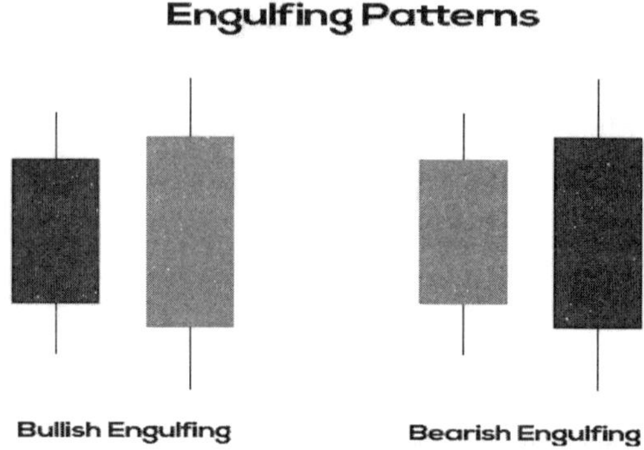

2. Piercing Line and Dark Cloud Cover

Piercing Line: This is a bullish reversal pattern that appears during a downtrend. It consists of two candles. The first candle is a long bearish (red) candle, showing strong selling pressure. The second candle is a bullish (green) candle that opens lower but then closes more than halfway up the body of the first red candle. This indicates that buyers are starting to take control, suggesting that the price might reverse and start moving upward.

Dark Cloud Cover: This is a bearish reversal pattern that occurs during an uptrend. Like the Piercing Line, it has two candles. The first candle is a long bullish (green) candle, showing strong buying pressure. The second candle is a bearish (red) candle that opens higher but closes more than halfway down the body of the first green candle. This shows that sellers have stepped in strongly, and the price could start to fall.

Both patterns show a strong shift in momentum. The Piercing Line suggests a possible upward reversal after a downtrend, while the Dark Cloud Cover hints at a downward reversal after an uptrend. Traders watch these patterns for signs of a change in market direction.

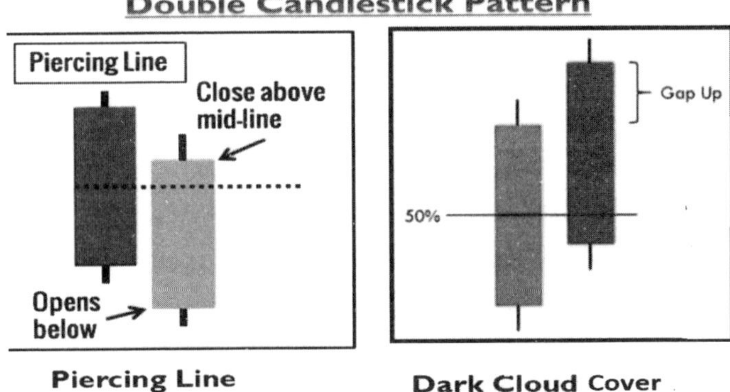

Piercing Line

Dark Cloud Cover

3. Tweezer Tops and Bottoms

Tweezer Tops: This is a bearish reversal pattern that appears at the end of an uptrend. It consists of two candles, often with similar highs. The first candle is usually a bullish (green) candle, showing strong buying pressure. The second candle is bearish (red) and opens at or near the high of the first candle but fails to push the price higher. This pattern shows that buyers couldn't continue the rally, and sellers have stepped in, signaling that the price might start falling.

Tweezer Bottoms: This is a bullish reversal pattern that occurs at the end of a downtrend. It also consists of two candles with similar lows. The first candle is usually bearish (red), showing selling pressure. The second candle is bullish (green) and opens at or near the low of the first candle but then pushes the price higher. This signals that sellers are losing strength, and buyers are gaining control, suggesting the price could start to rise.

Both Tweezer Tops and Tweezer Bottoms indicate that the market is struggling to break past a certain level, making them strong reversal signals for traders.

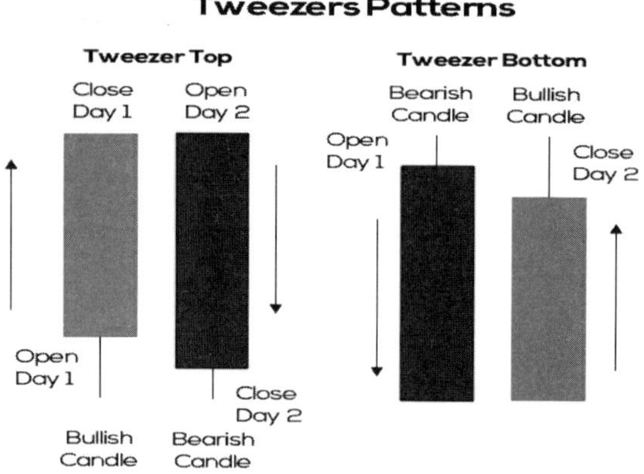

4. Harami Pattern

The Harami pattern is a candlestick pattern that signals a possible change in the market's direction. "Harami" means "pregnant" in Japanese, and the pattern resembles a smaller candle inside a larger one.

Bullish Harami: This pattern appears during a downtrend and suggests a potential upward reversal. It consists of two candles. The first is a long bearish (red) candle, showing that sellers are in control. The second candle is a small bullish (green) candle that forms completely within the body of the first red candle. This shows that selling pressure is weakening, and buyers might be stepping in, hinting that the price could start moving up.

Bearish Harami: This pattern shows up during an uptrend and signals a possible downward reversal. The first candle is a long bullish (green) one, indicating strong buying pressure. The second is a small bearish (red) candle that forms within the body of the first green candle. This suggests that the buying momentum is slowing down, and sellers might take control, causing the price to fall.

The Harami pattern is a sign that the market might be preparing to change direction. In both cases, the small second candle shows hesitation in the market, signaling that a reversal could be on the way. Traders look for confirmation in the following candles before making decisions.

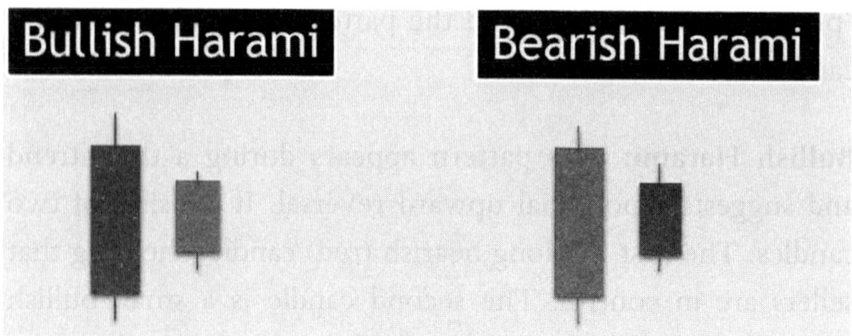

Understanding Complex Chart Patterns

Reading chart patterns is like following a map—it helps you figure out where the market might go next. The road of the map is made of candlesticks and each candlestick represents a specific time period and provides information about price movements. When you see the graph or the map as a whole, these candlesticks form patterns that you can use to predict the price behavior. The complexity of these patterns increases—starting from simple single candlestick patterns to more difficult chart patterns like flags, pennants, cup-handle patterns. As you will read on, you'll find that the patterns can become quite complex, requiring a sharper eye and a deeper understanding. Whether you're trying to catch a trend before it happens or avoid a sudden drop, understanding these complex patterns will give you quite an advantage in trading.

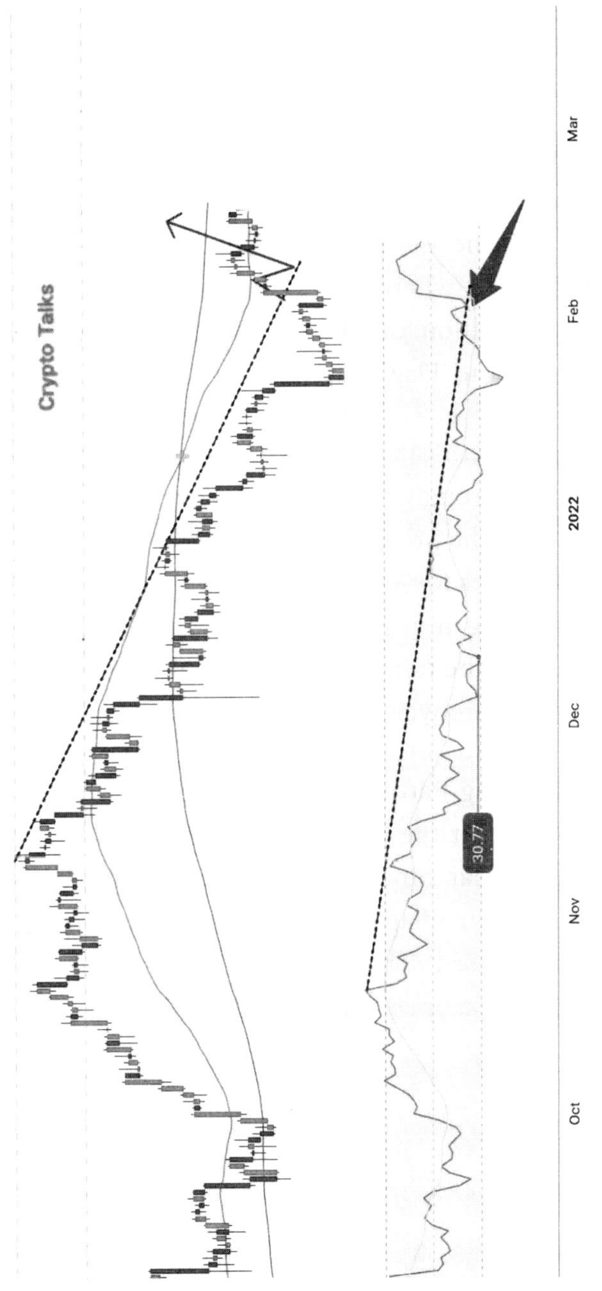
Master_Traders_ published on TradingView.com, Sep 14, 2024 20:31 UTC+5:30
Bitcoin / TetherUS, 1D, BINANCE 59,892.00 −606.00 (−1.00%)
Crypto Talks
30.77
Oct
Nov
Dec
2022
Feb
Mar
TradingView

Some Important Chart Patterns

Flag

A 'Flag' is a chart pattern that traders look for after the price has made a strong move in any one direction—either up or down. Imagine the market takes a quick water break after this big move, where prices move sideways or slightly in the opposite direction for a short time. This pause in the market is what forms the 'Flag' pattern.

The flag pattern can tell us two things, firstly if the price was moving up strongly before the flag formed, the pattern might suggest that the price will continue to rise once the flag ends. The same goes for a downward move; if the price was falling before the flag, it might keep falling after. Secondly, a flag can indicate that the trend might change direction after the flag is complete. Moreover, flags are of two types:

1. **Bullish Flag Pattern:** When a bullish flag pattern appears, it indicates that the bullish trend will continue. In this case, we need a clear continuation of the uptrend, represented by the flagpole. In a flag pattern, there are two parallel lines that slope downward. This forms a consolidation area within a downtrend of a price pattern as shown below.

2. Bearish Flag Pattern: When a bearish flag pattern is observed, it indicates that the downtrend is in a consolidation phase and that the downward momentum in the market is likely to continue. The flagpole in a bearish flag pattern is formed by the continuation of the downtrend, while the flag itself forms when there is a brief consolidation or slight upward movement in the price. Therefore, the flag forms when the price action shows a slight upward movement within a channel and is in the opposite direction of a bullish flag. Generally, in this case, the direction is downward as shown below.

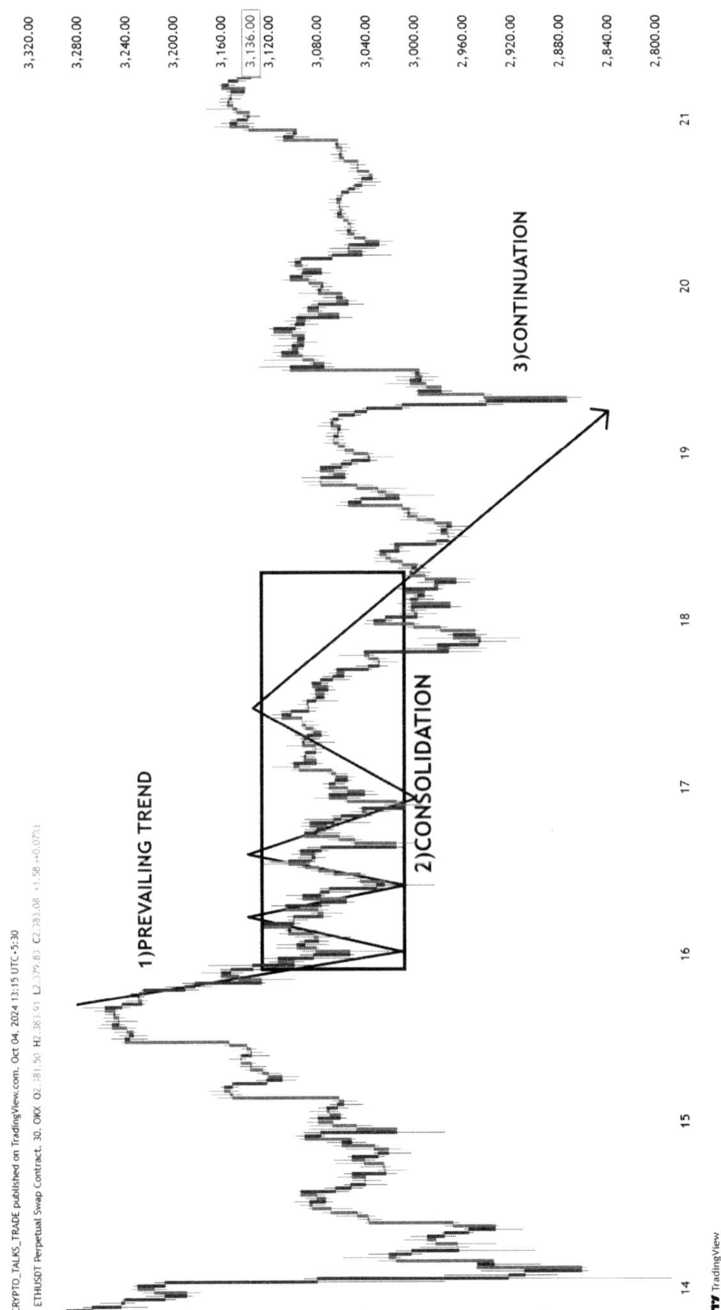
1)PREVAILING TREND
2)CONSOLIDATION
3)CONTINUATION

Pennants

A pennant pattern is a continuously forming chart pattern. It can be easily seen due to the high movement either upward or downward before moving in one direction with a trend line. This pattern looks like a small symmetrical triangle. Based on the direction of movement, it is usually classified as bullish or bearish.

1. **Bullish Pennants:** Bullish pennants are continuously forming bullish patterns found in strong uptrends. A pennant is created after a flagpole, which is an upward movement, followed by a consolidation period, and then a breakout leading to the continuation of the uptrend. Traders look for a break above the pennant to take advantage of the new upward momentum.

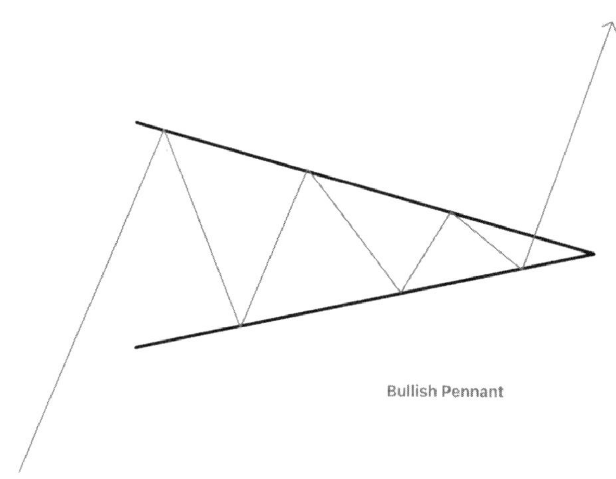

2. **Bearish Pennants:** Bearish pennants are essentially the opposite of bullish pennants moving in the opposite direction. These are continuously forming patterns found in strong

downtrends. They always start with a flag, indicating a significant drop in price, followed by a consolidation period where the downward movement pauses. This pause forms a triangular shape, known as a pennant. After the pennant, there is typically a breakout, and the downward movement continues. Traders look to enter short trades upon a break below the pennant to take advantage of the ongoing downward momentum.

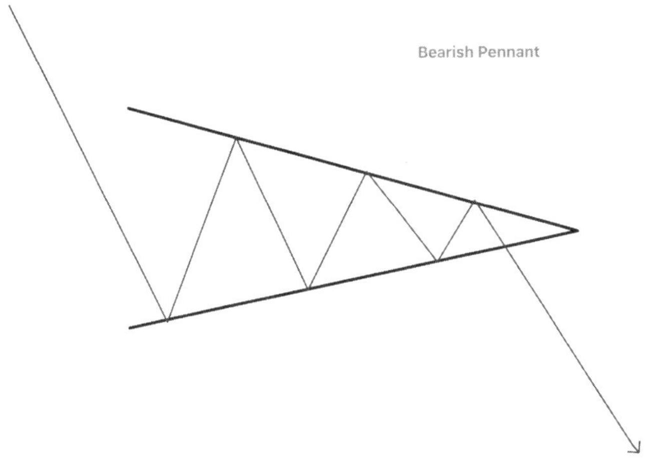

Note: When a flag and pennant combine, a flagpole is formed.

Triangles

In these charts, we can see a triangle formed with three corners. These patterns are further of three types, namely:

1. **Symmetrical Triangle:** In this triangle, there are very few opportunities to make trades in the market because it is uncertain whether the market will go up or down. To determine this, you start by observing the market moving upward from

the right side. Here, we need to observe whether the trend line is moving upward. If it is, it means the triangle is heading upward. Similarly, if the triangle moves downward, you need to look at the three points formed below. By observing the chart, you can easily understand where the trend line is finding support and where it isn't. Things can be challenging in this triangle.

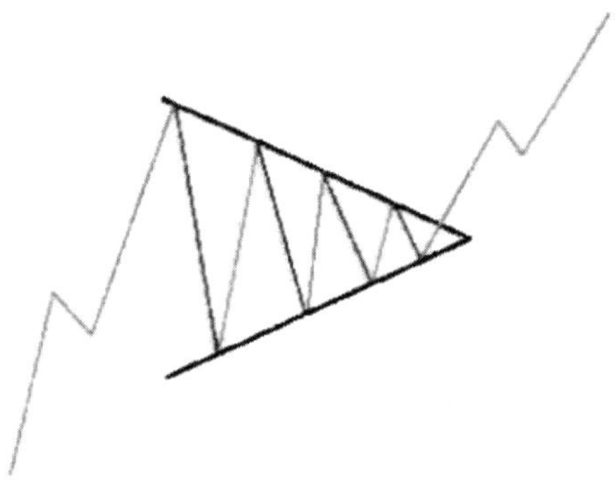

2. Ascending Triangle: In this pattern, the peak is always upwards. As the price moves within this triangle, it's getting squeezed between the two lines. The buyers are pushing the price higher, but they haven't yet broken past the resistance. When the price finally breaks through the top line, it usually signals that the market is ready to move upward. In simple terms, the Ascending Triangle shows that buyers are getting stronger, and there's a good chance the price will break out and go up. Traders often look for a strong upward move after the breakout.

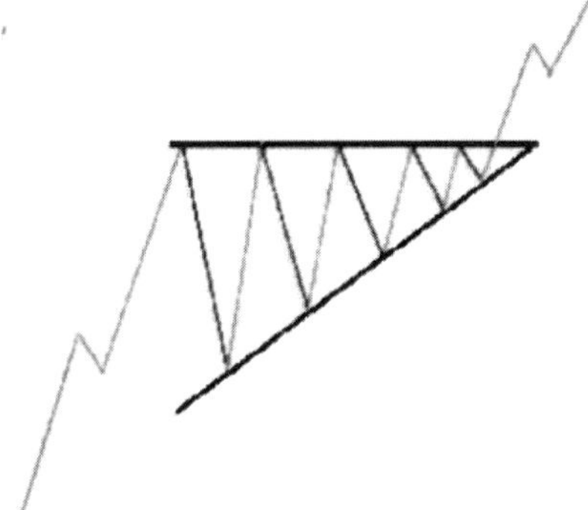

3. Descending Triangle: In this triangle, the peak is always downwards. Sellers are pushing the price lower, but the buyers are holding it at a certain level (the flat support line). When the price finally breaks below the support line, it often signals that the market is ready to move downward.

The market tends to move from top to bottom in this triangle. If we look inside the pennants, similar principles apply. There isn't much difference between the ascending and descending triangles. Pay close attention to these patterns because we will try to identify them in the charts.

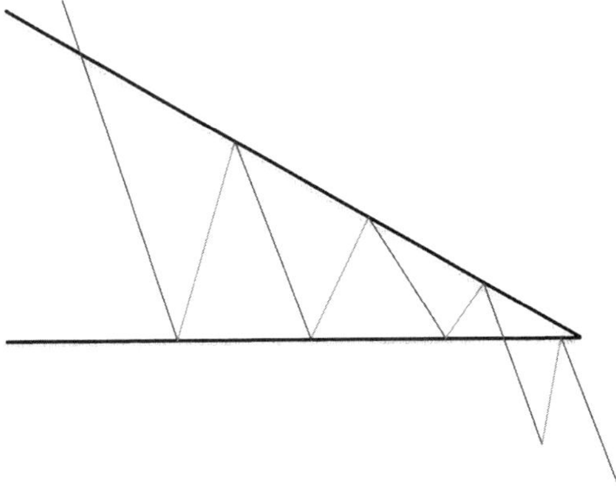

Head and Shoulders

There are two types of Head and Shoulder patterns—Bullish and Bearish, as shown below.

1. Bearish Head and Shoulders: This pattern typically forms at the top of an uptrend and indicates a potential reversal to a downtrend. In the market, there are still many people who believe that as soon as a Head and Shoulders pattern forms, the price will go up. But this is not always true. According to the pattern, if the price breaks below the neckline, it indicates that a downtrend is either starting or continuing, and the market is likely to remain in a bearish phase.

The Head and Shoulders pattern is confirmed when the price moves down again and breaks below the neckline. After this breakdown, the price may briefly rise again, testing the neckline before falling once more and breaking below it. This pattern indicates a downtrend, as the price continues to move downward after confirming the pattern. The Head and Shoulders pattern can sometimes exhibit a small "throwback" or "rally" before the downtrend continues again.

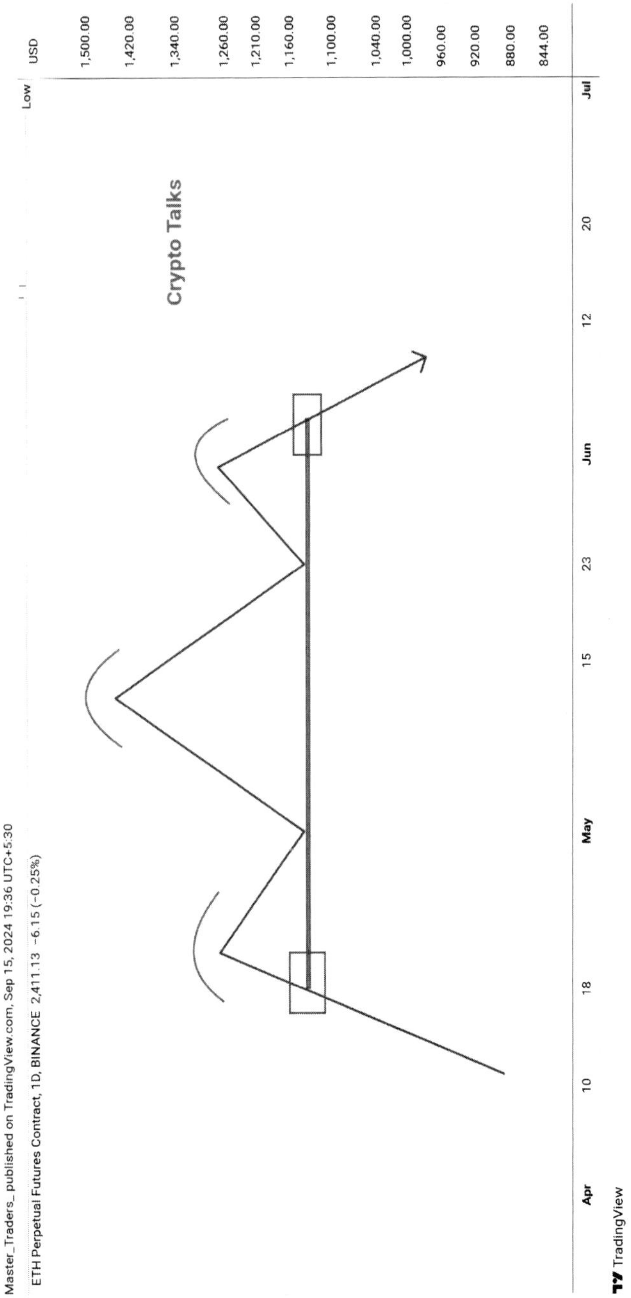

Master_Traders_ published on TradingView.com, Sep 15, 2024 19:36 UTC+5:30

ETH Perpetual Futures Contract, 1D, BINANCE 2,411.13 −6.15 (−0.25%)

Low USD

Crypto Talks

1,500.00
1,420.00
1,340.00
1,260.00
1,210.00
1,160.00
1,100.00
1,040.00
1,000.00
960.00
920.00
880.00
844.00

Apr 10 18 May 15 23 Jun 12 20 Jul

TradingView

2. Bullish Head and Shoulders - This pattern forms in the opposite direction of the Bearish Head and Shoulders. In a Bullish Head and Shoulders pattern, the price first declines to form the left shoulder, then rises to form the head and declines again to form the right shoulder. The neckline is confirmed when the price breaks above it. After this breakout, the price may dip slightly but then continues to rise, breaking above the neckline again. This indicates a bullish trend, as the price continues to move upward after confirming the pattern.

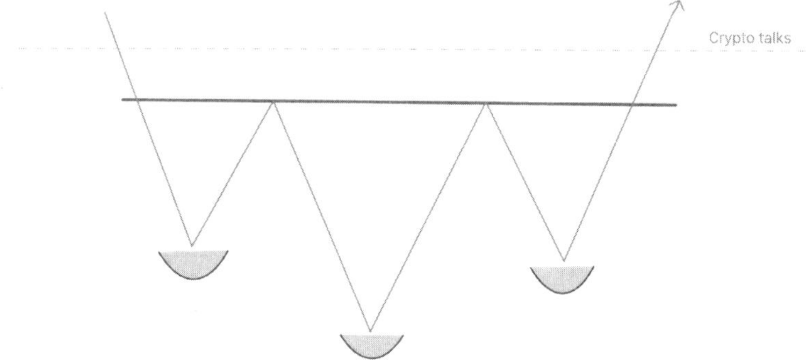

In the given patterns, if the Head and Shoulders are not confirmed, it is also necessary to form a Double Top.

How to Identify Trades in 'W' and 'M' Formations

These patterns are also known as Double Tops and Double Bottoms. They are frequently observed in trading. When an 'M' pattern forms, the market first moves upward to a peak (known as the "neckline"), then declines and forms another peak and eventually moves downward again. The take-profit level in this pattern is generally lower. If you examine this pattern, you will notice that double tops are formed.

Whenever double tops are formed, they signify a bearish signal. The meaning of this pattern is negative. Similarly, double bottoms, head and shoulders and wedges (which can be bullish or bearish depending on their formation) also follow this concept. In all these cases, particularly with double tops and double bottoms, the market generally follows the trend indicated by the pattern once it is formed. In this pattern, after a pullback, the market moves downwards and then rises above the neckline. The take-profit level in this pattern is higher. Wedges that are continuation patterns, head and shoulders that are inverted, double tops that form bearish signals, and double bottoms are all patterns indicating the direction of the market. Specifically, the market tends to rise with these bullish patterns.

Note: When discussing wedges, if it's a rising wedge, the market will generally go up. Similarly, if you see an inverted head and shoulders, the market will move up. For a double top, the market will go up, and for a double bottom, the market will also rise. Patterns like the head and shoulders, double tops, and double bottoms indicate upward movement. However, if the pattern is a top (whether a bearish top or a double top), the market will move downward.

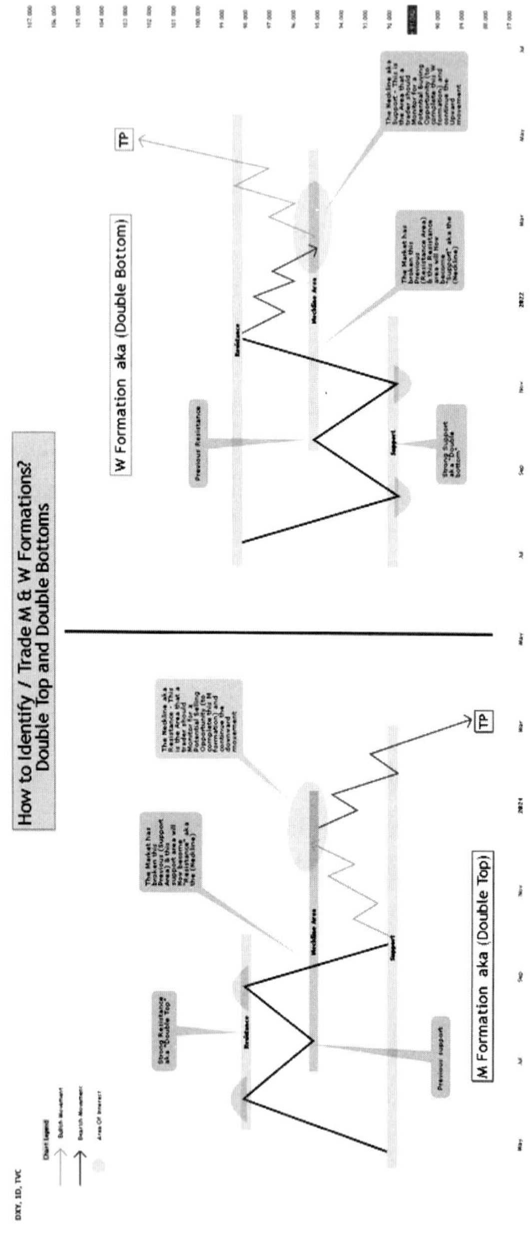

After the market reaches a peak, it will go up but it will continue to rise in areas where there is an error or where the

"M" pattern appears. This often results in the market starting to decline after a peak. Confirmation typically occurs in these specific areas. When two peaks form, it generally leads to the market declining further. This is referred to as a double top pattern. All the details are illustrated in the chart.

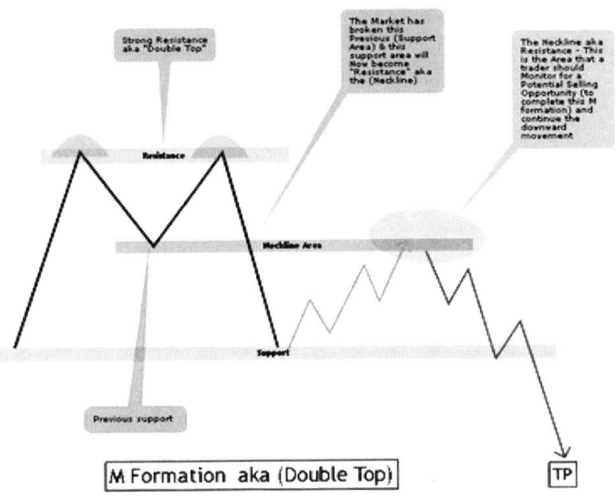

In this context, the "W" formation is the opposite of the "M" formation. It is referred to as a double-bottom pattern. It consists of two points or bottoms that are lower than the previous one. The blue section or area of the pattern is where the second bottom forms. The "W" starts forming from the point on the upper side and ends at the point, marking the completion of the pattern. These two points represent the confirmation areas. After forming the double bottom, the market starts to rise again. Confirmation occurs in these specific areas where the pattern completes. The pattern is known as the double bottom. All details are illustrated in the chart. If the lines shown in the chart do not match exactly, there is no need to worry.

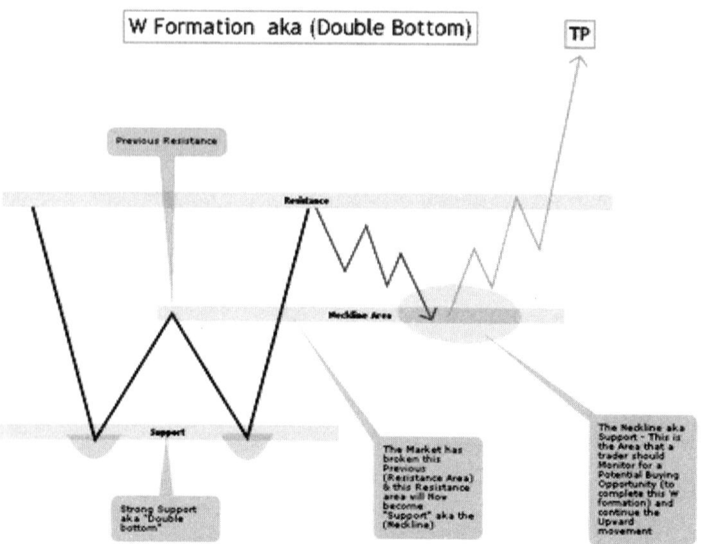

For this reason, a margin is maintained so that even if the market drops by 1-2 percentage points, it does not signal a significant issue. As a result, the market tends to move upward from this point.

Wedges

A wedge is a price pattern where the price forms a converging pattern on a chart. Typically, two trend lines are drawn to connect higher highs and higher lows or lower lows and lower highs over a period of 10 to 50 periods. These lines indicate whether the highs and lows are increasing or decreasing at different rates, creating the appearance of a wedge as the lines converge. Wedges can appear in either bullish or bearish price trends. In any case, there are three common characteristics of this pattern:

1. **Converging trendlines:** The lines narrow towards each other.

2. **Declining volume:** As the price moves through the wedge pattern, trading volume often decreases.

3. **Breakout from the wedge:** The price eventually breaks out from the wedge pattern, signaling a potential change in trend.

Wedges typically come in two forms:

1. Downward Converging Trend Lines or Falling Wedge: In the below figure, you can see a falling wedge. In this pattern, the trendlines are converging from top to bottom. According to the chart, these lines show that the price is moving up and down and confirmation is repeatedly occurring. The wedges appear to be going downward but ultimately the price is expected to rise, which is a certainty.

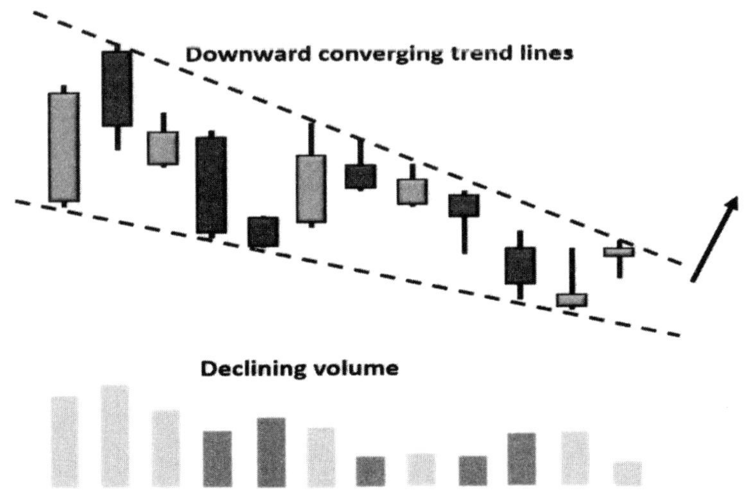

2. Rising Wedge: In this pattern, the trend lines converge from the bottom to the top, and the price moves up and down. Eventually, in this pattern, the price tends to move downward. This pattern is clearly illustrated in the provided chart. Therefore, pay close attention to the chart for a better understanding.

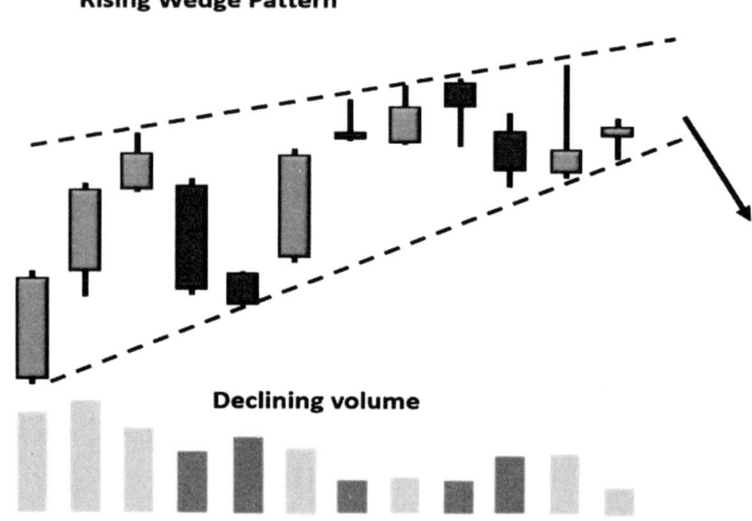

Note: As I have mentioned before, things that appear to be rising will generally indicate a positive market direction, while things that look straight will suggest a negative market direction.

Double Top and Double Bottom

In a Double Top pattern, there are two peaks at the top, forming an 'M' shape. The pattern typically includes a neckline at the base of the peaks.

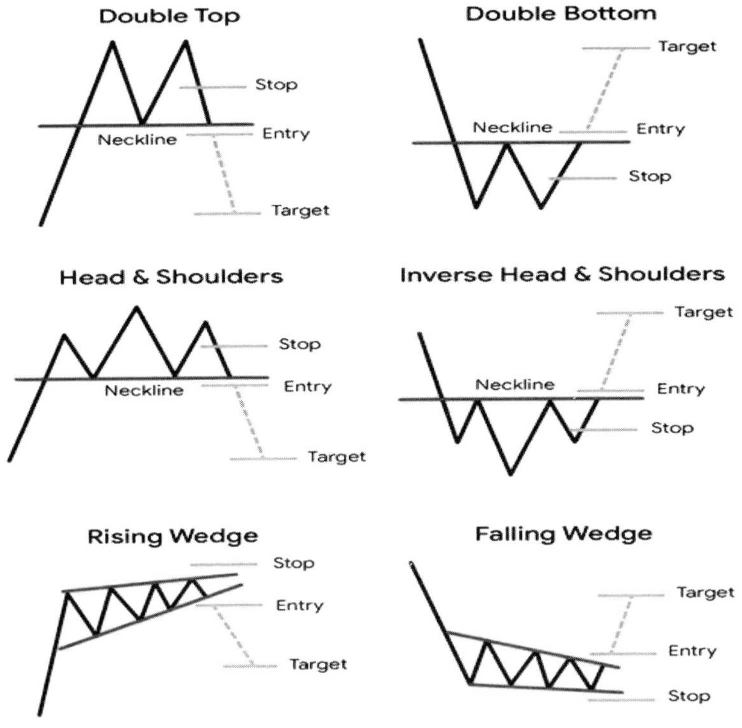

According to the chart, when the price moves downward and reaches the neckline, it might turn into a bearish reversal. If this happens, it forms a Double Top. If the price continues to decline, you should wait until the price is confirming the reversal. After that, you will act according to your strategy. The essence of the Double Top pattern is that the price is trending downward.

In a Double Bottom, there are two bottoms at the bottom, and a neckline is formed at the blue part, representing the 'W' shape. When the price moves downward and crosses the neckline, it continues to move downward. Here, your entry point is below the neckline. After this, you will act according to your strategy. The essence of the Double Bottom pattern is that the price is trending upward.

Note: I have already explained the Head and Shoulders and Rising and Falling Wedge patterns in detail. We usually take entry only after confirmation in any price movement. We did the same in the BTC chart; when this chart appeared, RSI and divergence provided confirmation, and only after that we had taken the entry.

Cup and Handle Pattern

In this pattern, whenever a cup and handle form, the price generally moves upwards. It's important to observe the cup and handle formations from the start to the end of the pattern. There should be no breaks or disruptions in this formation; otherwise it will not qualify as a proper cup and handle pattern, as shown below.

According to the chart, if the forming lines align with the similar trend lines, it will qualify as a cup and handle pattern; otherwise, it won't. All trend lines should be above the base, not below it.

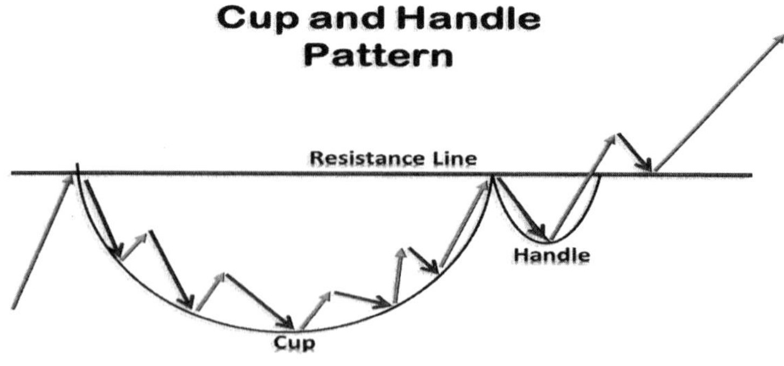

In this pattern, the cup can be an inverted cup or base, as shown in the chart. The handle forms on the side of this cup. The cup base trend line provides guidance because it is positioned above. The price movement from this base will generally be downward rather than upward. Both straight and inverted patterns are considered. The trend lines of the handle are informed by the lines of the cup, with the base at the top and extending backward. The price movement from the handle is expected to move downward not upward. Both straight and inverted patterns are relevant here.

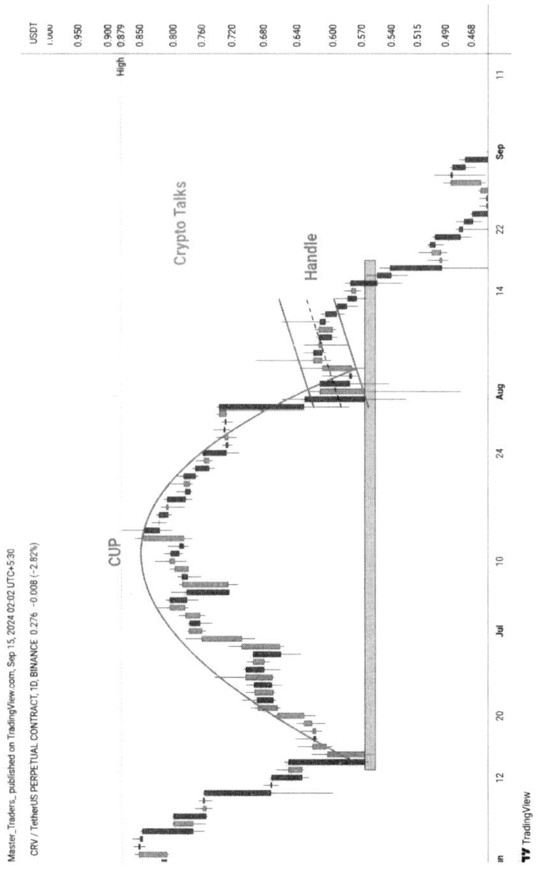

Triple Top Pattern

When a triple top is formed in a chart, all three points are aligned on the same line, as depicted in the given illustration. In the head and shoulders illustration below, points 1, 2, and 3 are distinct points that are formed at the same height. This pattern occurs in an uptrend. In a triple-top pattern, the market declines if a triple-top is formed. Conversely, if a triple bottom is formed, the market will rise.

Head and Shoulders: This pattern consists of three shoulders, with the middle shoulder being the highest, while the other two shoulders are of equal height. In this pattern, the market declines because it forms a direct head and shoulders. If it were to form a reverse pattern, the market would rise.

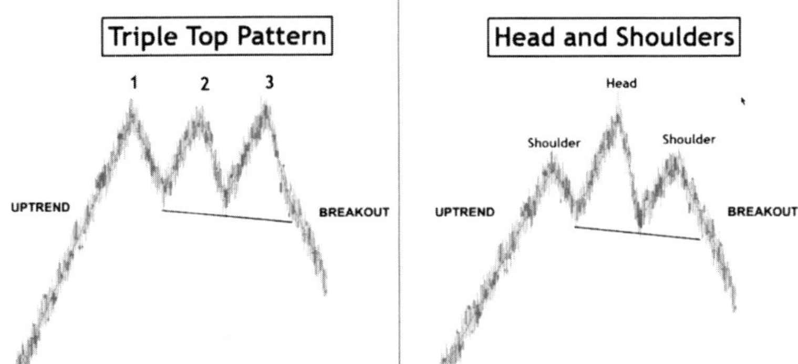

To fully understand everything you have learned so far, you need to diligently practice by marking these patterns on charts. If you do not make an effort to find these patterns on charts, you won't be able to learn. Along with this, I advise you to keep a notebook and pencil handy because every type of pattern should be noted in your notebook for future reference. This will ensure you can use them correctly.

You have studied flashcards covering bullish and bearish patterns. You also covered rising and falling wedges. After that, you learned about pennants, including bullish and bearish pennants. In head and shoulders, you studied both direct and reverse head and shoulders patterns. Additionally, you covered double tops, double bottoms, triple tops and triple bottoms. You also identified 'M' and 'W' patterns in double tops and bottoms. We need to practice identifying these patterns by marking them on charts to see how they look and how we can spot them.

Suppose we are analyzing the FET chart. Within this chart, we can easily find all these patterns. However, we must apply everything we have learned so far correctly to identify these patterns. We need to apply all concepts meticulously on the chart. By doing this, we can effectively practice and understand the usage of these patterns in real-time trading scenarios. It's crucial to be detailed and thorough in marking and identifying these patterns on the chart.

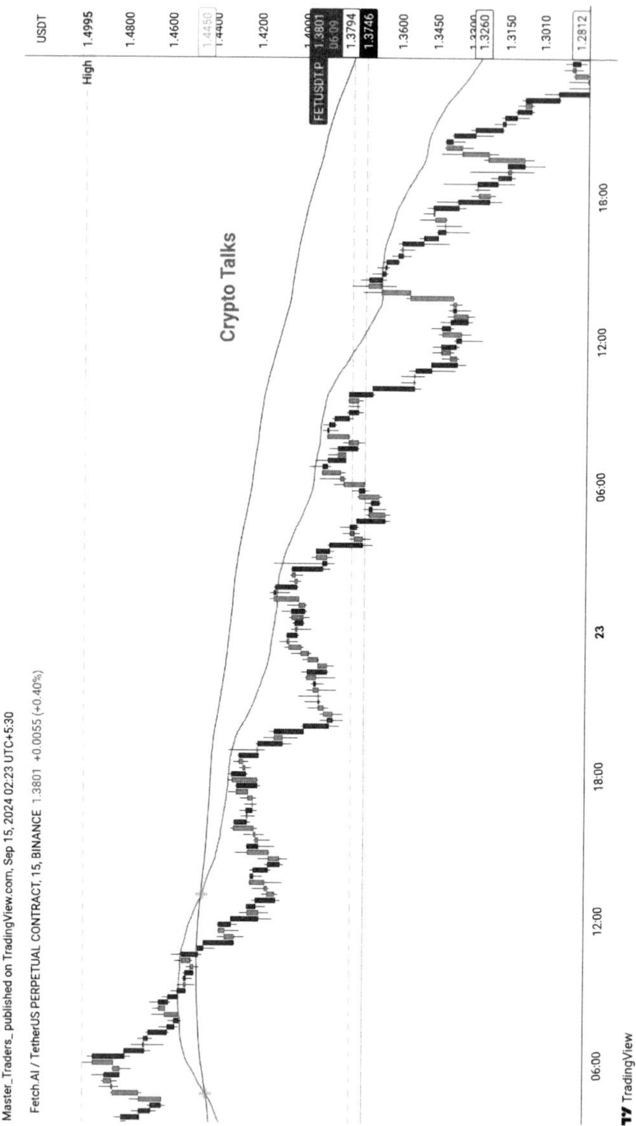

I focus more on smaller charts to ensure accurate plotting. If you want to do this consistently, it is very easy and will be interesting for you to observe. I am marking what appears in a simple form on this chart. Please pay close attention to it.

Inverse Flag

On the chart, we can see a simple inverse flag pattern, as shown in the diagram below. In this chart, we observe a downward trend indicating its completion.

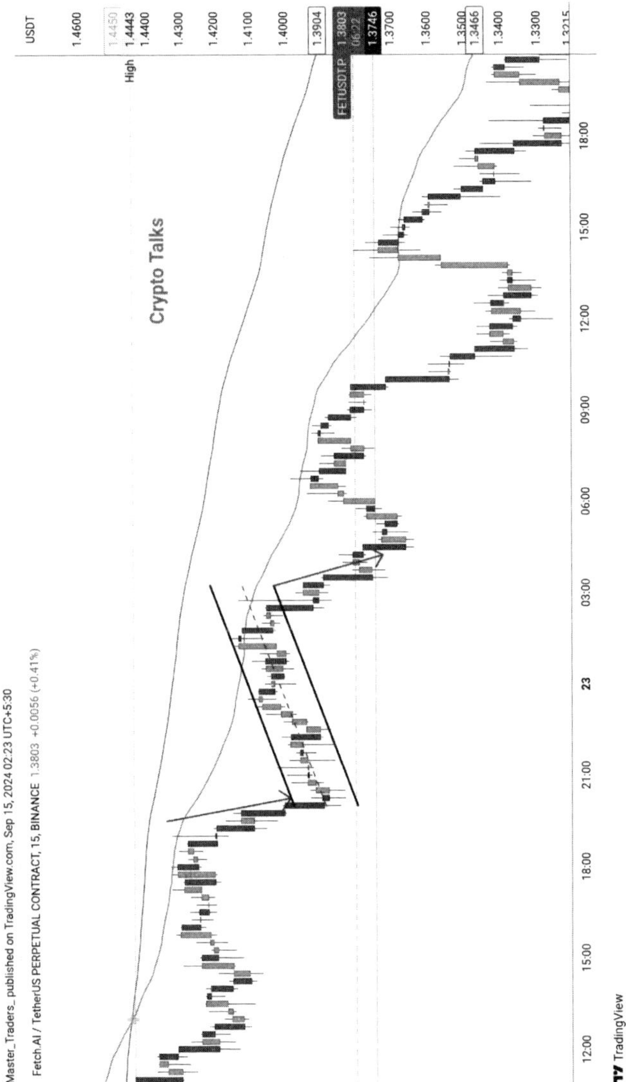

You can make your setup according to the chart. To close the trade, you will follow the arrows shown in the chart. While closing, always keep your starting point and closing point in mind. There isn't much risk because the last rise usually equals the last fall. For example, if you start your trade at $1.4078 and close it at $1.3835, you gain about $0.32, roughly $0.30. If you take the fluctuation between $1.4078 and $1.3835, it gives you about a 15% profit. Additionally, if you trade from the lower end of the flag, you still get around a 10% profit. There is no significant risk involved.

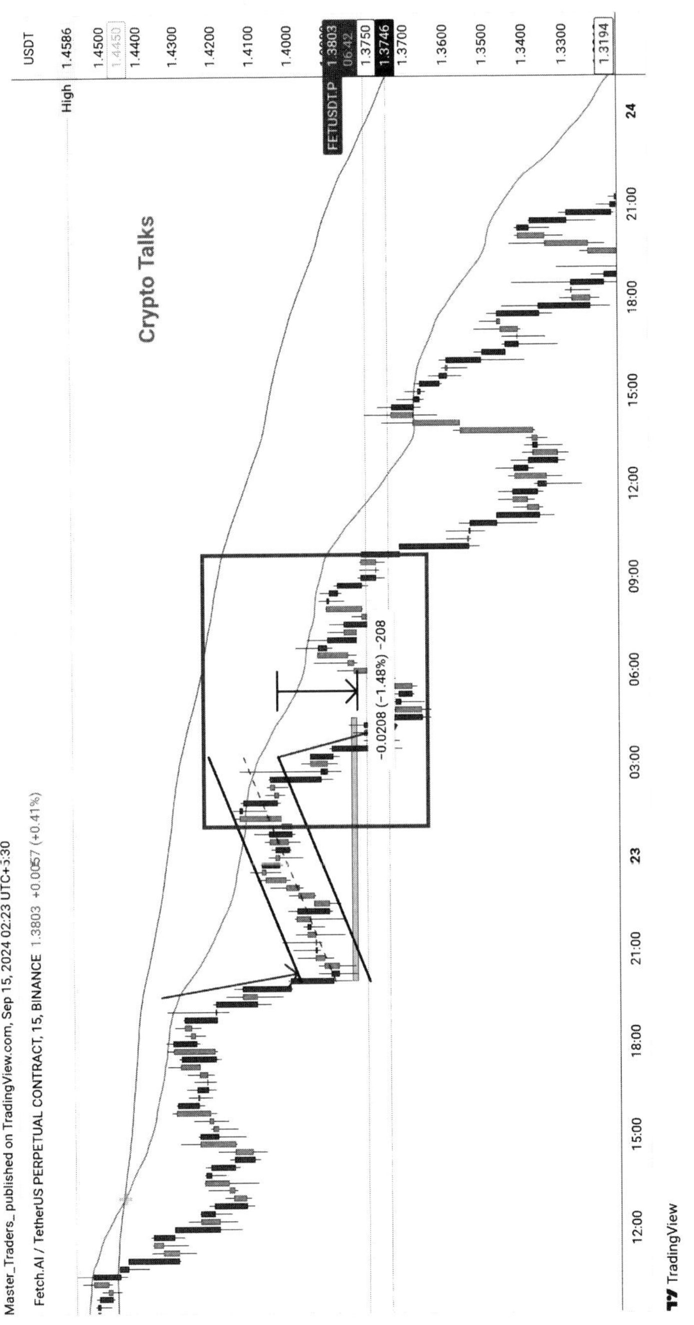
Master_Traders_ published on TradingView.com, Sep 15, 2024 02:23 UTC+5:30
Fetch.AI / TetherUS PERPETUAL CONTRACT, 15, BINANCE 1.3803 +0.0057 (+0.41%)
Crypto Talks
−0.0208 (−1.48%) −208
FETUSDT.P
USDT
High
12:00
15:00
18:00
21:00
23
03:00
06:00
09:00
12:00
15:00
18:00
21:00
24
TradingView

The more small charts you open, the more profit you will gain and the patterns on the charts will become easier to identify.

Double Bottom

This chart shows a specific pattern known as the Double Bottom Pattern. As explained, where there is a 'W' shape, if we draw a straight line, it acts as a neckline or support line. This support line allows the pattern to rise upward after the 'W' shape forms. The formation of the Double Bottom Pattern is indicated after the 'W' is complete. According to the chart, after the formation, you bought at $2348 and the pattern extended to $2387 after a 41-point movement. This resulted in approximately a 3% profit. If you follow a 41-point movement for your trades, everything will be clearer and you won't face any difficulties in formation.

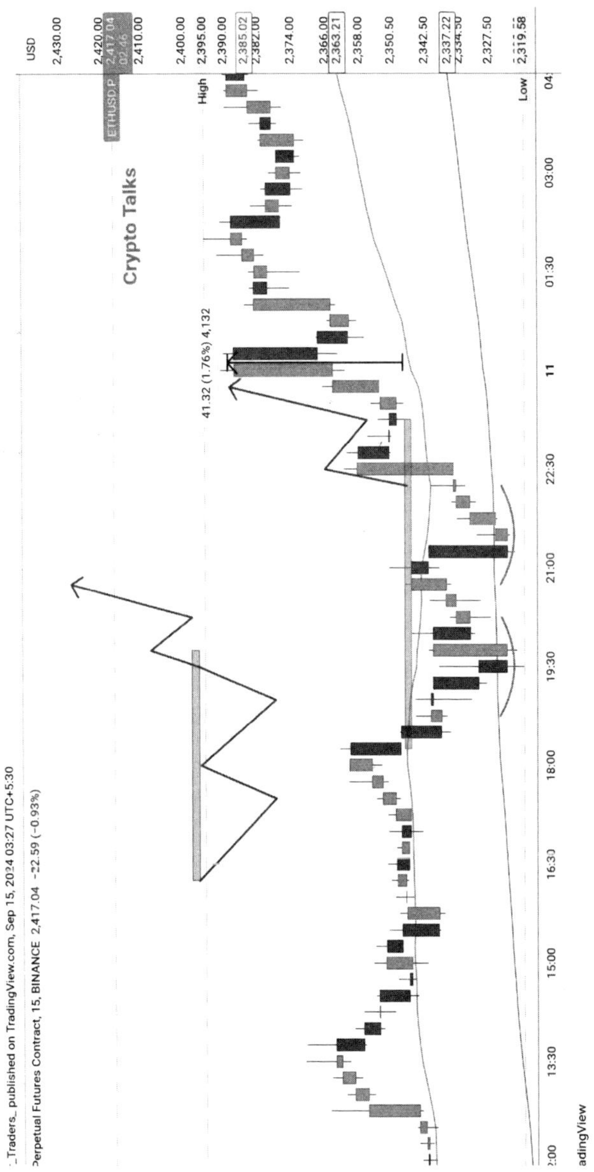

Now, we will open the chart for a 1-hour timeframe and analyze it. In this timeframe, you will clearly observe the pattern. If you look inside a small pattern, you will notice a

Reverse Flag Pattern that, after forming, takes a downward break. After the break, the trend lines typically rise upward for a while, following the confirmation. Subsequently, the trend will move downward again.

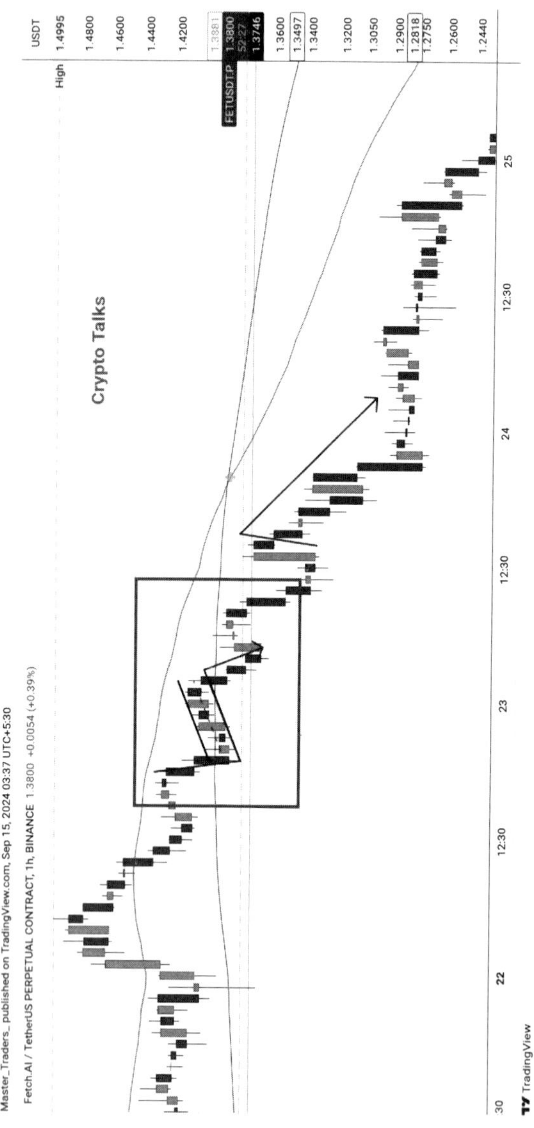

After this, once again, in the same chart, we notice a Straight Flag Pattern. The flagpole is formed downward. Here, after waiting for confirmation, the trend lines typically move upward. If you take a position starting from 1.34 dollars, the trend may reach 1.37 dollars upon confirmation. In this scenario, you can achieve a gain of about 2-3%. All these observations depend on the type of pattern you are identifying. Each pattern must be verified based on the specific timeframe, so it is crucial to carefully check your processes and patterns.

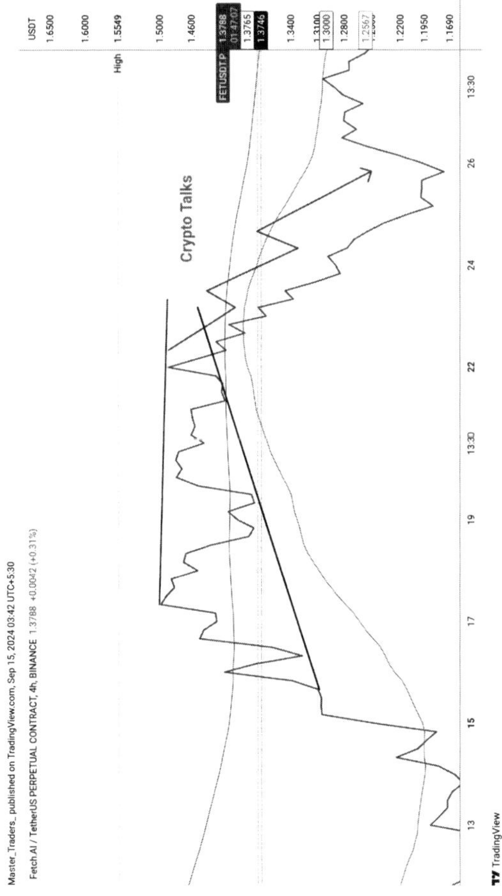

Here, you might feel that you're not understanding things clearly, but you'll get the hang of things as you practice. Now, it is important for you to select the trend lines accurately, as these are always significant for your analysis. The chart will then provide a clearer picture, though it's possible that these lines may seem a bit scattered. If you match all the points carefully, everything will become clear because I'm explaining things as quickly as possible. Otherwise, you might find that the process can be very slow.

You can repeat this process by using the examples and applying trend lines as demonstrated. If you correctly follow the patterns and strategies, you will definitely be able to see their effectiveness. Here, I am noticing again a pattern called the Falling Wedge. In this pattern, the market moves from top to bottom and after consolidation, continues to move downward. All these elements will become clear with the chart provided on the previous page. Please examine and understand this chart carefully.

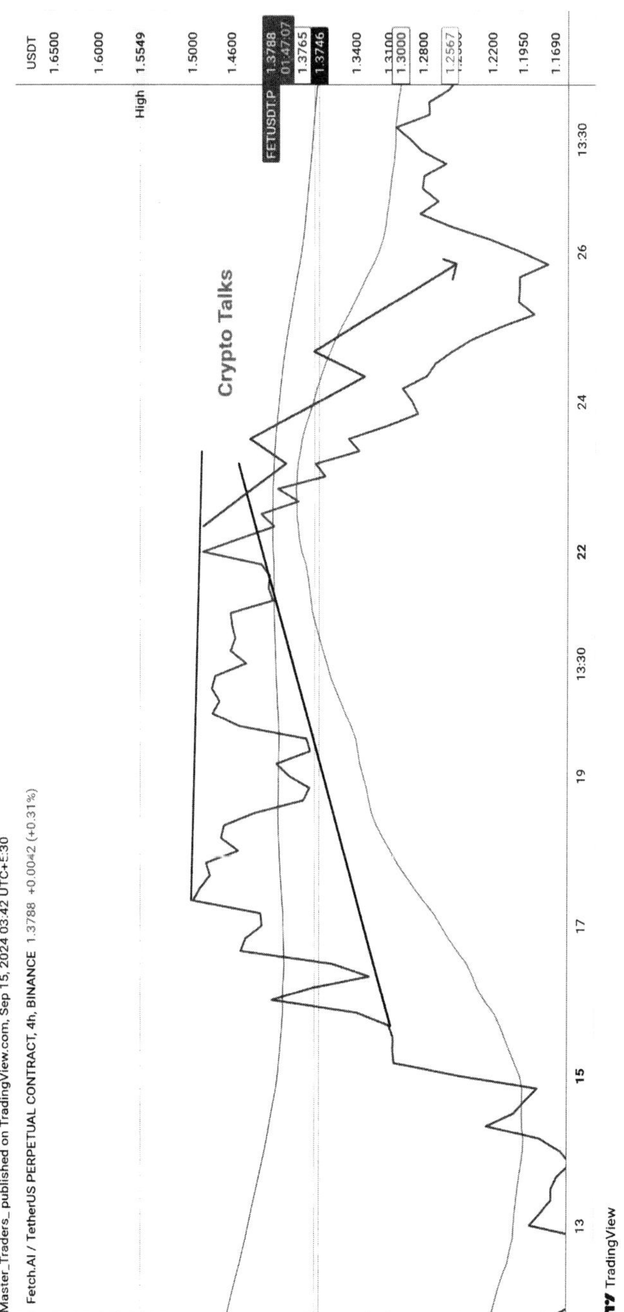
Master_Traders_ published on TradingView.com, Sep 15, 2024 03:42 UTC+5:30
Fetch.AI / TetherUS PERPETUAL CONTRACT, 4h, BINANCE 1.3788 +0.0042 (+0.31%)
Crypto Talks
High
FETUSDT.P
USDT
1.6500
1.6000
1.5549
1.5000
1.4600
1.3788
01:47:07
1.3765
1.3746
1.3400
1.3100
1.3000
1.2800
1.2567
1.2200
1.1950
1.1690
13
15
17
19
13:30
22
24
26
13:30
TradingView

Therefore, you should not face any difficulty in identifying patterns in any chart if you focus carefully on the chart and consider the time frame you are analyzing—whether it's a 1-hour, 4-hour, daily or weekly chart. Each time frame will provide different insights into patterns. If you have a clear understanding of these patterns, I suggest you apply them diligently. The best way to resolve any confusion is to work with line-by-line analysis and then convert those lines into patterns. It doesn't matter whether you focus more on trend lines or candlestick patterns, or whether you emphasize opening and closing prices. What matters is that you are able to identify any pattern clearly. By following this approach, you will definitely be able to recognize the patterns.

How To Take Entries and Exits Based on Certain Chart Patterns

Let's take a look at the Ethereum chart and understand how we can take entries and exits according to the patterns. I usually focus on this chart because it often shows clear patterns. Most of my analysis is centered on Bitcoin and Ethereum since their charts are usually easier to read and their price movements are more predictable. Money flow usually starts with Bitcoin, then moves to Ethereum, and finally to other altcoins. Bitcoin is the first to move, followed by Ethereum. That's why I pay more attention to these two and base most of my trades on them. Trading on Ethereum is usually straightforward and often leads to successful trades.

Flag Pattern:

As seen from the chart, I have identified several patterns, which I frequently use. One of these is the Bearish Flag.

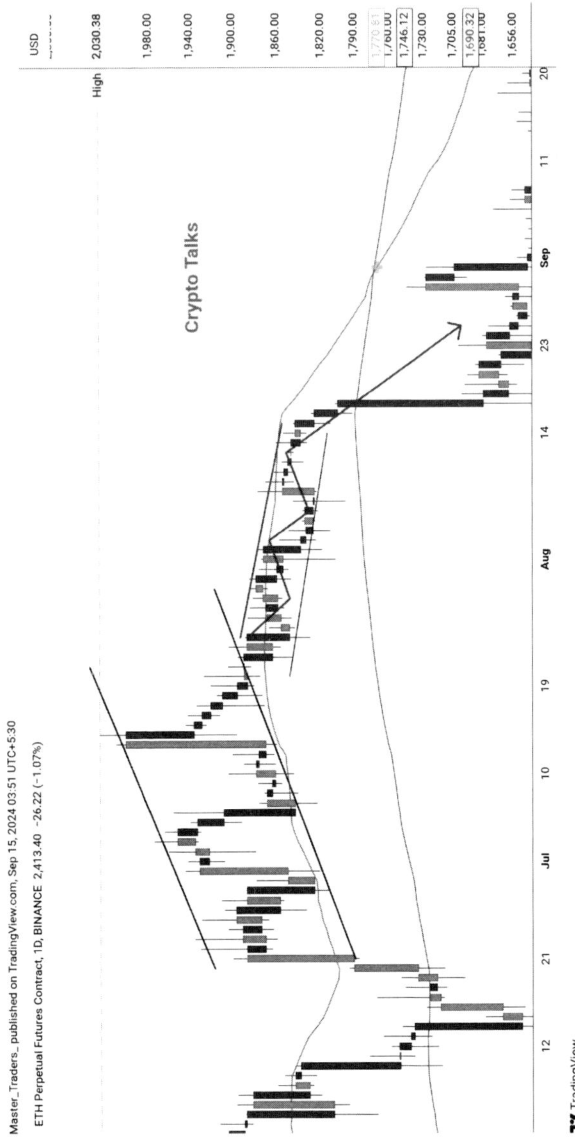

From the chart, it appears that a Bearish Flag pattern is forming. Here's how to interpret it. First, observe if the price is not clearly moving upwards and hasn't broken downwards. If these conditions are met, it may be a signal to enter a trade. Since the trend lines on the chart are moving significantly downward, you need to set an exit strategy. To do this, measure the length of the Flagpole. Use the Flagpole length to determine the target for exiting the trade, as the pattern indicates a continuation of the downtrend.

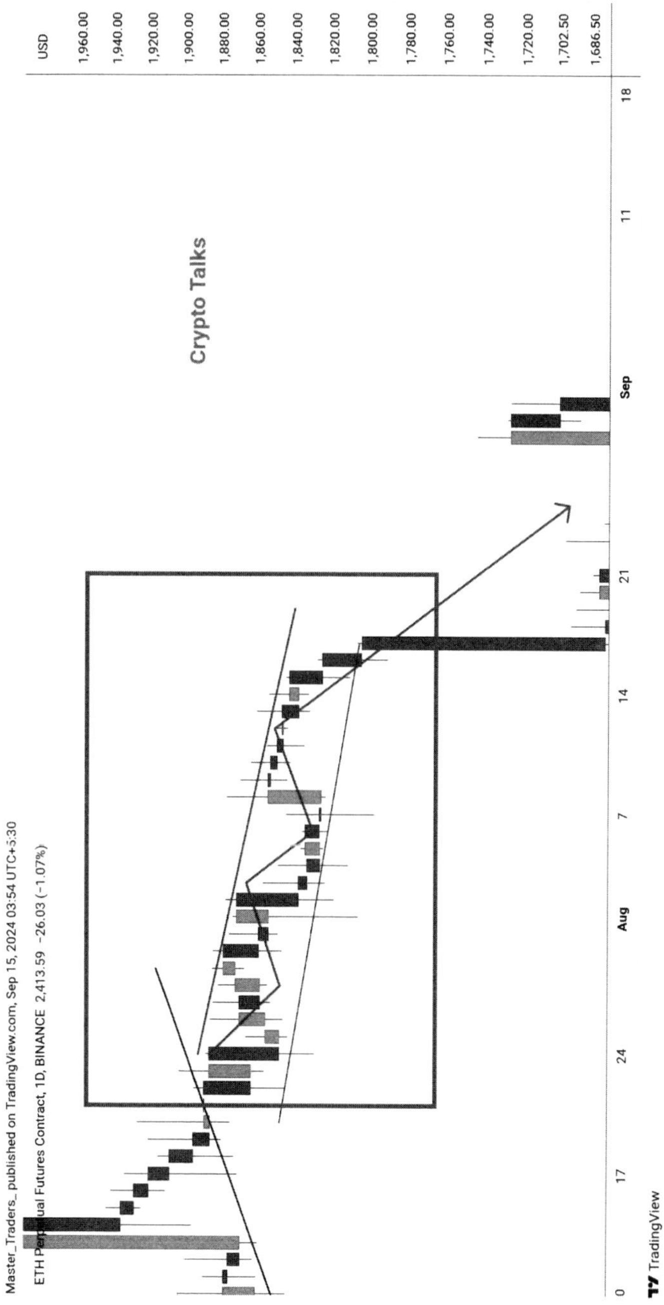
Master_Traders_ published on TradingView.com, Sep 15, 2024 03:54 UTC+5:30
ETH Perpetual Futures Contract, 1D, BINANCE 2,413.59 −26.03 (−1.07%)
Crypto Talks
USD
1,960.00
1,940.00
1,920.00
1,900.00
1,880.00
1,860.00
1,840.00
1,820.00
1,800.00
1,780.00
1,760.00
1,740.00
1,720.00
1,702.50
1,686.50
0
17
24
Aug
7
14
21
Sep
11
18
TradingView

If the Flagpole is approximately 12% on the chart, you will exit the trade when the price moves 12% below the entry point. At the exit point, the price might encounter support but you should stick to the exit strategy rather than adjusting for potential further movements. These principles apply to every pattern you observe. Whether you are dealing with a Cup and Handle pattern or any other pattern, follow the same approach.

For example, in the previous pages, we observed a Cup and Handle pattern. In the given chart, a Cup and Handle pattern starts at $4174 and completes at $3701, which is approximately an 11% drop. Based on this, you should exit the trade after confirming this pattern. If, for any reason, the price moves above the exit point, it's possible that it may end up about 6% above your exit level. This is the strategy for exiting trades.

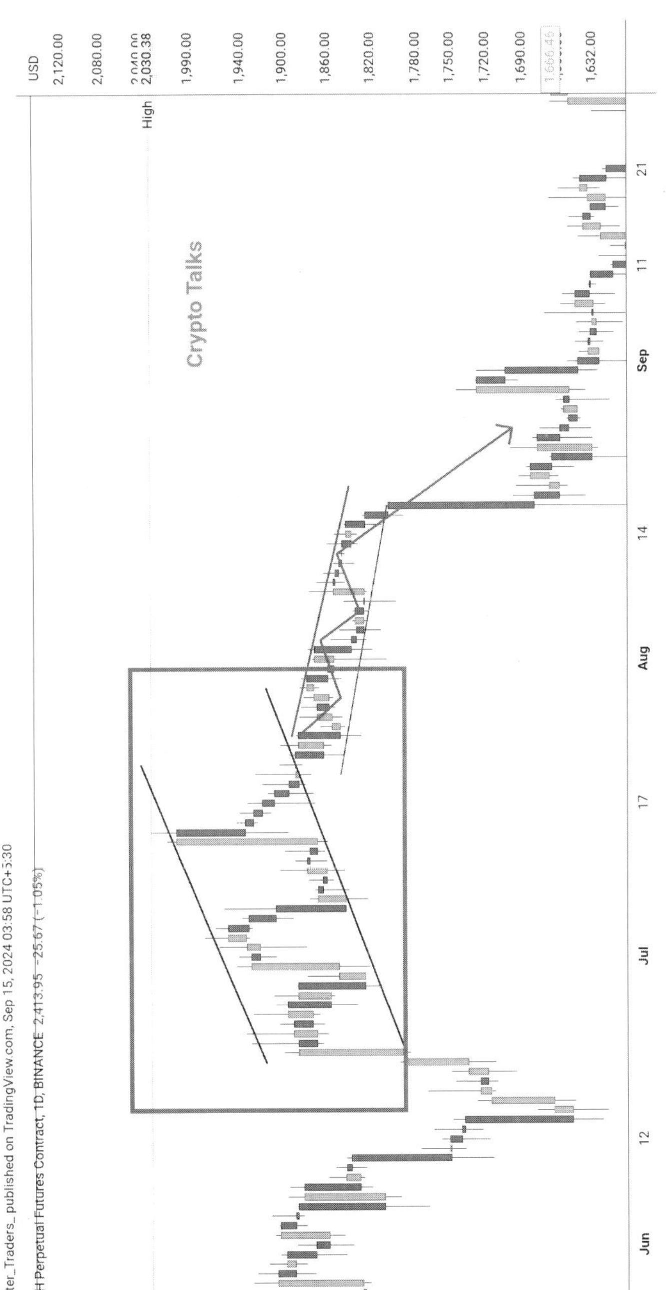
Master_Traders_ published on TradingView.com, Sep 15, 2024 03:58 UTC+3:30
ETH Perpetual Futures Contract, 1D, BINANCE 2,413.95 −25.67 (−1.05%)
Crypto Talks
High
USD
2,120.00
2,080.00
2,030.38
1,990.00
1,940.00
1,900.00
1,860.00
1,820.00
1,780.00
1,750.00
1,720.00
1,690.00
1,632.00
Jun
12
Jul
17
Aug
14
Sep
11
21
TradingView

Note: For this, a good sense of holding and patience is required. Those who do not maintain enough patience to hold tigh often achieve only a 10% margin in their trades.

Let's assume you had a 10% gain on a trade, according to a 5X leverage, you should have achieved a 50% profit. However, many people do not reach a 50% profit because, as soon as the market shows some volatility, they become anxious, fearing the market will either go up or they will hit a stop-loss. Such individuals exit the trade or plan to exit, resulting in a gain of only 10%. I also advise such individuals to target a 10% gain if they lack experience and patience but still aim for a reasonable profit with their trades. For example, if you have a 2% profit on a 5-8X leverage, it turns into a 10% profit. Exiting the trade at this point indicates good trading with patience. If we talk about a specific percentage gain, it often declines significantly. Hence, it's essential to be prepared and measure the error range between the entry point and the exit point.

Master_Traders_ published on TradingView.com, Sep 15, 2024 04:00 UTC+5:30
ETH Perpetual Futures Contract, 1D, BINANCE 2,413.61 −26.01 (−1.07%)
Crypto Talks
−149.41 (−8.25%) −14,941
USD
1,900.00
1,880.00
1,860.00
1,840.00
1,820.00
1,800.00
1,780.00
1,760.00
1,740.00
1,733.17
1,720.00
1,700.00
1,680.00
1,660.00
1,642.50
1,624.50
10
17
24
Aug
14
21
Sep
11
18
TradingView

According to the chart, you measured the specified segment and it is approximately 8%. As soon as the price moves slightly below the entry point, a breakout occurs. Now it becomes clear that you need to exit the trade from this point.

If you want to take the exit point after a breakout occurs, it is a safer method for you. However, if you take it from the beginning, it becomes a more proactive strategy.

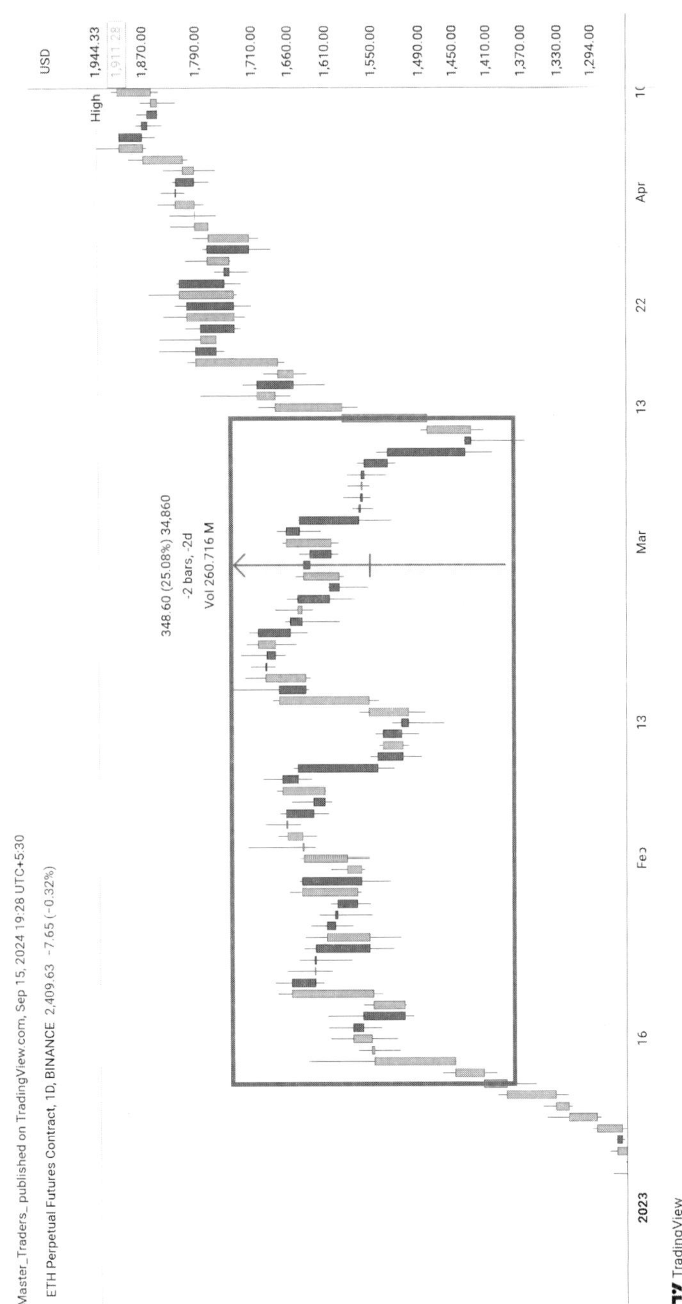

Master_Traders_ published on TradingView.com, Sep 15, 2024 19:28 UTC+5:30
ETH Perpetual Futures Contract, 1D, BINANCE 2,409.63 −7.65 (−0.32%)
348.60 (25.08%) 34,860
-2 bars, -2d
Vol 260.716 M
USD
High 1,944.33
1,911.28
1,870.00
1,790.00
1,710.00
1,660.00
1,610.00
1,550.00
1,490.00
1,450.00
1,410.00
1,370.00
1,330.00
1,294.00
2023
16
Feb
13
Mar
13
22
Apr
TradingView

Now, let's look at the second position where zig-zag trend lines are forming. These lines progress into parallel lines in this range. Here, we achieve a value of approximately 25%. If we need to take this value further, it will be according to the chart. Our profit depends on how long we hold the position. The longer we hold, the more profit we will achieve. In this case, rejection also occurs around the resistance level of 4779 dollars, which results in a retest. This means that the trend lines achieved their peak, giving us approximately 26% profit. All of this depends on your patience and how long you are willing to hold the position. Everything generally follows this pattern. Even with good profits, we may need to exit quickly due to the temptation of more gains.

Head and Shoulders Pattern:

Now, I will explain the elements of the Head and Shoulders pattern that we frequently observe on charts. According to the diagram on the next page, we have illustrated a Head and Shoulders pattern where the market starts from the bottom and moves upward or where the trend lines start from below and move upward.

The market rises from the bottom to form the first shoulder. The market continues to rise, creating a peak, then starts to decline, forming the head. The market rises again but does not reach as high as the head, forming the second shoulder. After forming the second shoulder, the market typically declines again. This downward movement often occurs after receiving a rejection from the upper side. The rejection point is crucial as it helps in determining the buy position. Ideally, you should consider buying near the rejection point or around it. If you choose to buy at the second rejection point, it will depend on your strategy. Pay close attention to the Head and Shoulders pattern and follow its guidelines for better trading decisions.

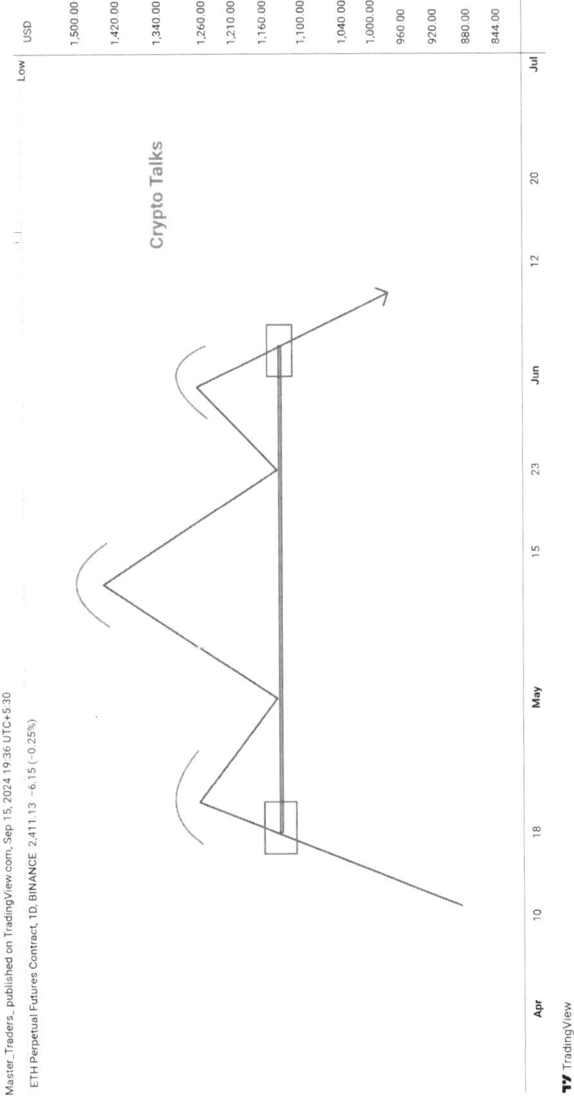

The height of the head from the neckline is approximately 26%. Therefore, this pattern will likely experience a breakdown of around 26% downward. While it is expected to drop this much, the actual movement will also depend on your patience. If you are patient, you will be able to achieve a good profit from this pattern.

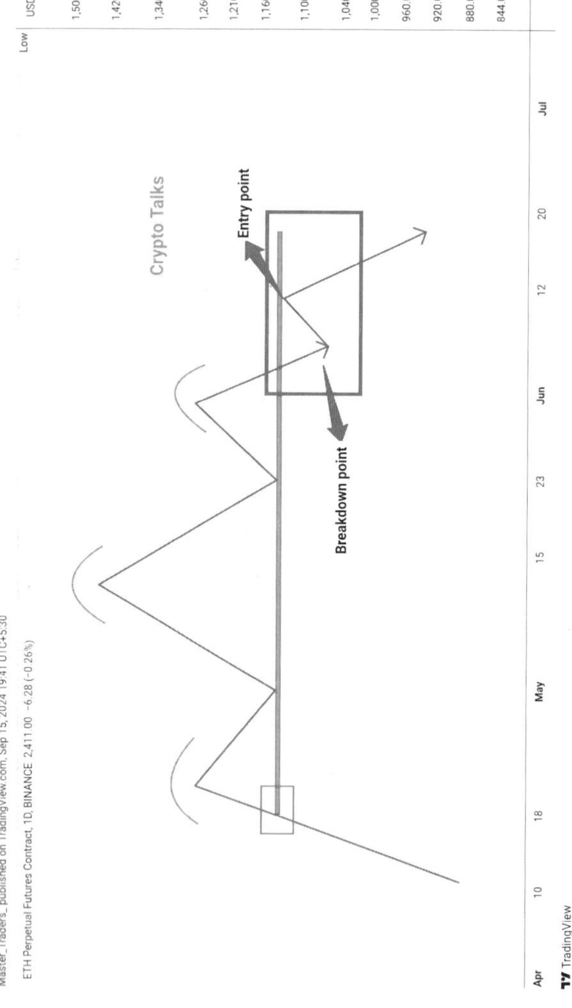

Assuming you have confirmed that the market will go down, you should take your exit point according to the chart. If you also exit from your target point, it will be approximately 23%. You should not be overly concerned; aim to secure a 10% profit.

For example, with 5X leverage, this translates to a 2% drop, resulting in a 10% profit. If you want to re-enter the market and notice that the market is dropping again, you can take another exit. However, it is important to secure your profit once the drop reaches 26%. There is no need to hold out beyond the 26% drop, as a further movement beyond this point will take the market outside of our zone and things may become unclear.

Technical analysis might sometimes be overshadowed by fundamental factors, causing price patterns to deviate from expectations. For example, a chart may show a head and shoulders pattern suggesting a downward trend but if fundamental factors or market sentiment shift, the market might move contrary to the technical prediction. Even if technical analysis suggests a certain trend, fundamental factors or market sentiment might cause unexpected price movements. For instance, A market could break downward according to a head and shoulders pattern but then rise due to positive news or market developments. Technical analysis alone might not always predict sudden changes in market direction caused by fundamental factors, such as significant news or events affecting the market. Always focus on securing your target profit, such as 10%. If you're trading with a target of 3% profit, but the market moves downward unexpectedly, adjust your strategy accordingly. If you are doing short trading and start at $6806 and exit at $6593, you will still make a profit of about 3%. Now, let's assume that the market is going straight down instead of going up. In that case, you need to re-enter at the entry point and exit with a 5-10% profit. Refer to the chart below.

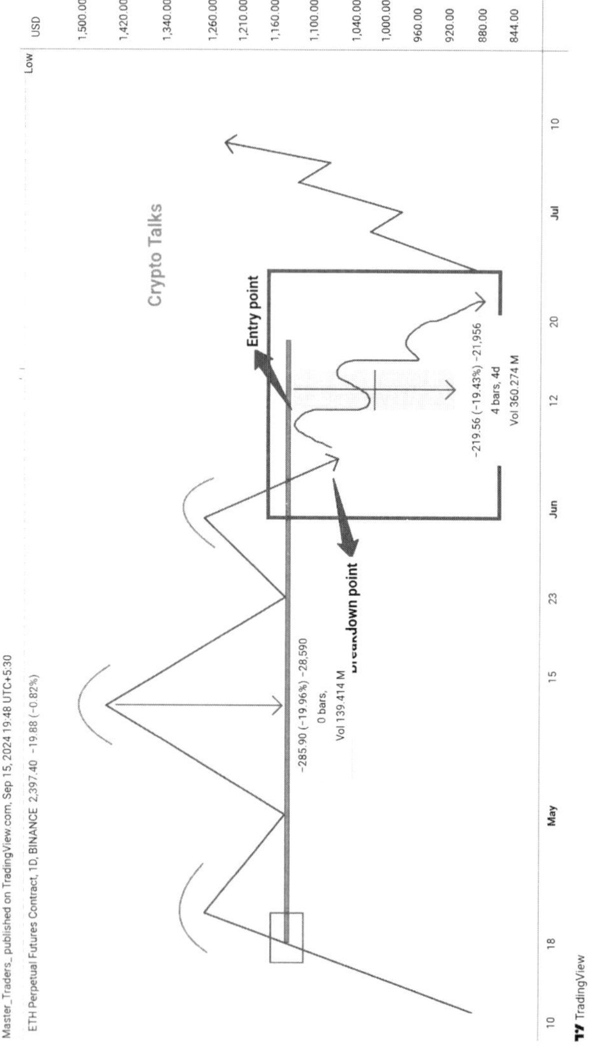

But if the market drops even further, you need to quickly adjust your exit strategy after reaching your target, because this might indicate that market manipulation is occurring. When both fundamental and technical analyses are not aligned with the market behavior, it suggests deliberate manipulation to push prices down.

If you see that the market is falling below your set points and the analysis is not consistent, it indicates that manipulation might be happening. In such cases, adapt your strategy accordingly and be cautious. Make sure to continually learn from both fundamental and technical analyses. The strategies I provide are meant to be applied when necessary, and they should be improvised based on the situation.

Inverse Head and Shoulders:

In the accompanying illustration, you will see an example of an Inverse Head and Shoulders pattern.

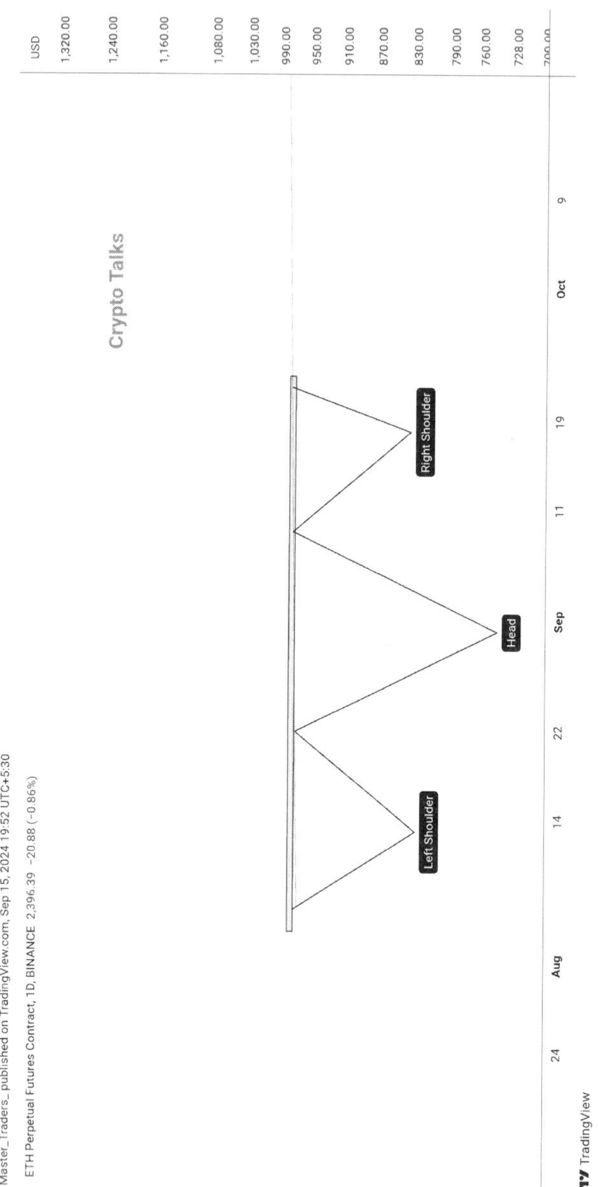

Here, you need to maintain the same level of vigilance as before. The height from the neckline in the Inverse Head and

Shoulders pattern is approximately 17%. Now, you should create a measurement based on this 17%, to determine whether it indicates a manipulation above this level. Refer to the accompanying illustration for clarification.

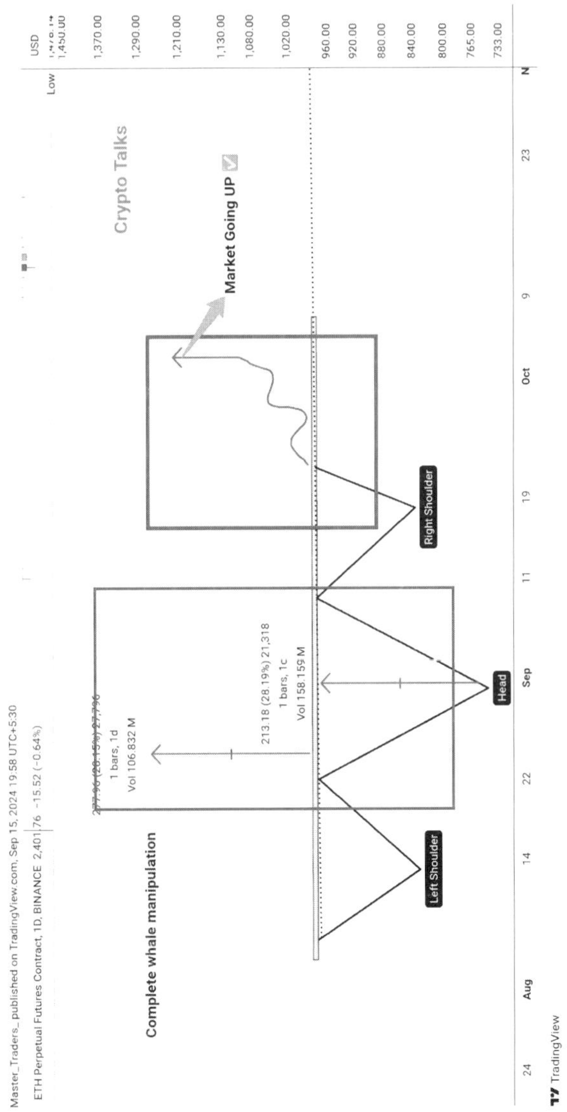

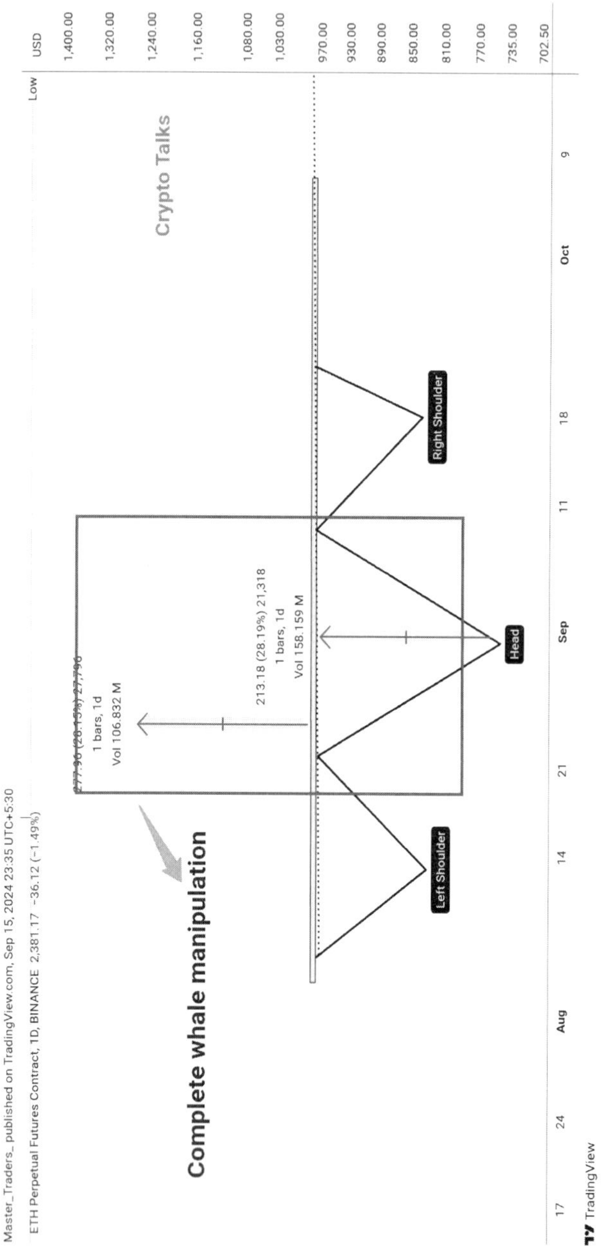

Master_Traders_ published on TradingView.com, Sep 15, 2024 23:35 UTC+5:30
ETH Perpetual Futures Contract, 1D, BINANCE 2,381.17 −36.12 (−1.49%)

Complete whale manipulation

Crypto Talks

1 bars, 1d
Vol 106.832 M

213.18 (28.19%) 21,318
1 bars, 1d
Vol 158.159 M

Left Shoulder
Head
Right Shoulder

Low
USD
1,400.00
1,320.00
1,240.00
1,160.00
1,080.00
1,030.00
970.00
930.00
890.00
850.00
810.00
770.00
735.00
702.50

17
24
Aug
14
21
Sep
11
18
Oct
9

TradingView

According to the chart, when the market moves above the neckline, it is essential to get confirmation, and it will go up again. You need to decide whether to set your exit based on this information. If you set your exit before or after confirmation, you might incur some loss, so you should exit at this point. If for some reason the market moves down, you should exit based on the market's behavior to avoid substantial losses. It's important not to rely solely on the market. To avoid such losses, a stop loss is applied. Always set a stop loss at 2% on a 5X leverage to ensure that your loss does not exceed 10%.

Assume you have taken a long position with a 5X leverage. You should set your stop loss at 2% to avoid exceeding a 10% loss. After this, you will need to check for support and resistance levels, as well as other key points. If you set your exit near $7000 and exit around $6878, you will incur minimal loss. For example, if you set your exit at a confirmation point on the neckline, you might exit with a 2-3% loss. Ensure that the stop loss is placed in such a way that it doesn't go below the neckline. Always set your exit point from the breakout point.

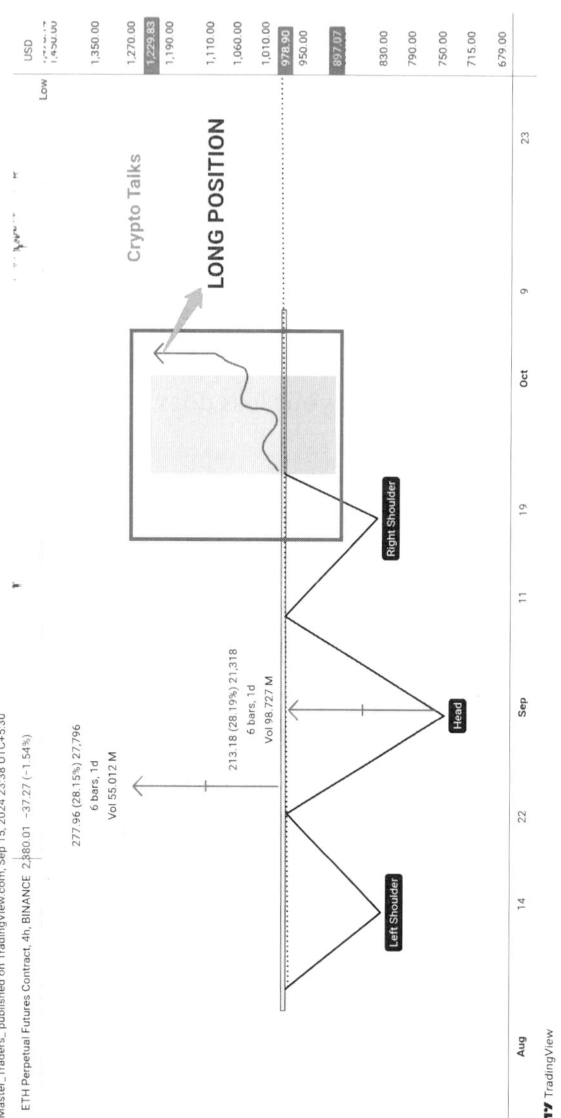

Notes: Always set the stop loss according to market conditions. Both the flag wedge and head and shoulders patterns follow the same principle.

Cup and Handle

Now, we'll discuss the cup and handle patterns. In the chart, we see that the handle is forming near the support line marked by the lower arrow. This indicates that the pattern is taking support here and the market is moving upward from this point.

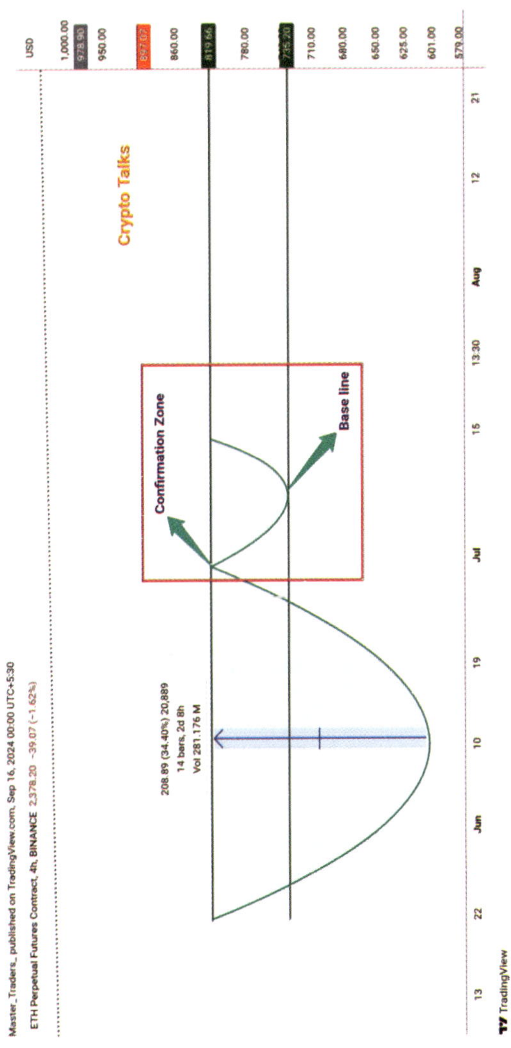

This line is also known as the baseline. It is crucial for the handle to form on this baseline and taking support at this line is very important. If the cup and handle pattern aligns with the baseline, it will not be considered a proper cup and handle pattern. The confirmation zone of the cup is usually a gap of about 13%, so you need to set the stop loss according to this 13% to ensure that the taking of the profit is in line with the pattern's principle.

Common Mistakes and Pitfalls

When trading with candlestick and chart patterns, it's easy to make mistakes that can lead to bad decisions and potential losses. By understanding these common mistakes—misinterpreting patterns, over-relying on candlestick patterns and ignoring the market context—and learning how to avoid them, you can improve your trading strategy and make better decisions in the market. Remember successful trading isn't just about recognizing patterns; it's about understanding the whole market picture and making informed choices based on all the available information.

1. **Misinterpreting PatternsL:** A common mistake traders make is misunderstanding or misreading candlestick and chart patterns. This can happen when a trader thinks they've identified a pattern, but they either get it wrong or don't fully understand what the pattern is signaling. For example, a trader might see a pattern that looks like a bullish engulfing pattern (which usually suggests prices might go up) and assume the market will rise, without realizing that the overall market conditions don't actually support this move.

To avoid misinterpreting patterns, it's important to study and understand each pattern thoroughly before making a trade. Practice identifying patterns on historical charts to get a better feel for how they work. It's also helpful to confirm the pattern with other technical indicators or signals to ensure you're reading the market correctly. Don't rush into trades based solely on a single pattern—double-check your analysis to make sure it aligns with the broader market conditions.

2. Over-Reliance on Candlestick Patterns: Another mistake is depending too much on candlestick patterns alone. While these patterns can be useful, they should not be the only tool you rely on. Candlestick patterns are just one part of a bigger picture. If you focus only on these patterns without considering other factors, you might miss important signs that could impact your trade. For example, a pattern might suggest a price will go up, but if you ignore other indicators that show weak market momentum, you might enter a trade that doesn't go your way.

To avoid over relying on candlestick patterns, always use them in conjunction with other technical indicators, such as moving averages, RSI, or MACD. These tools can provide additional context and help confirm whether the signals from the candlestick patterns are strong or weak. By combining multiple indicators, you'll have a more well-rounded view of the market, which can lead to better trading decisions.

3. Ignoring Market Context: A big mistake traders make is not paying attention to the overall market context. Candlestick patterns are more meaningful when viewed within the broader market situation. For instance, a pattern might suggest a certain price movement but if it's happening during a low-volume period or against a strong trend, it might not be reliable. Ignoring the larger market conditions can lead to poor trading decisions because you're not seeing the full picture.

To avoid ignoring market context, always analyze the broader market environment before making a trade. Look at the overall trend, trading volume, and any external factors (such as news events) that could impact the market. Make sure the candlestick pattern you're seeing fits within this larger context. By doing so, you'll be able to make more informed and accurate trading decisions.

Chapter 8

Trading Strategies

In cryptocurrency trading, there are many strategies designed to suit different trading styles, time frames, and market conditions. While some of these strategies are similar to those used in traditional markets like stocks or forex, the unique features of the crypto market—such as its high volatility, the fact that it trades 24/7, and how quickly news and social media can impact prices—have led to the creation of strategies that are specifically suited for trading cryptocurrencies.

Scalping Strategies

In this section, we'll go over different strategies. To do this well, we'll use tools like Moving Averages (MAs), Exponential Moving Averages (EMAs), Divergence Indicators, and the Relative Strength Index (RSI). Since we covered indicators in the previous chapters, you should already be familiar with them and how they are used. Some of the key indicators to focus on are Divergence Indicators and the RSI. These are commonly used in trading and are very important for understanding market conditions.

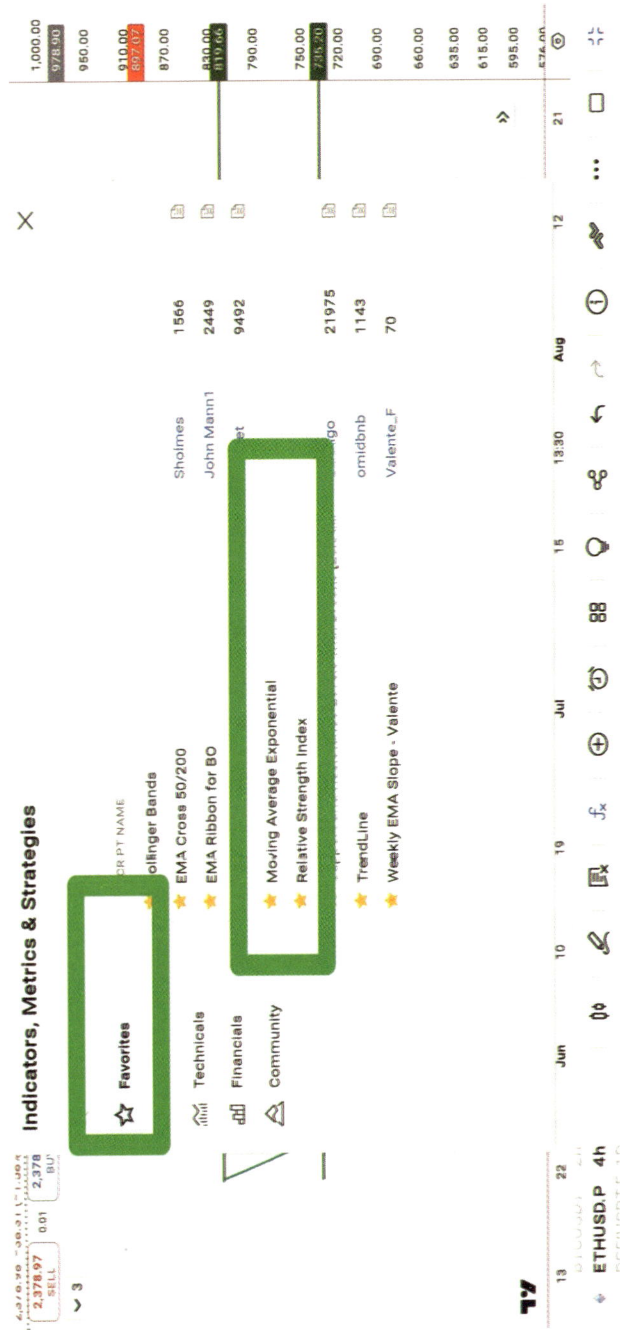
Indicators, Metrics & Strategies
Favorites
Technicals
Financials
Community
EMA Cross 50/200
Sholmes
1566
EMA Ribbon for BO
John Mann1
2449
Moving Average Exponential
9492
Relative Strength Index
21975
TrendLine
omidbnb
1143
Weekly EMA Slope - Valente
Valente_F
70
2,378.97
SELL
0.01
1,000.00
978.90
950.00
910.00
897.07
870.00
830.00
819.66
790.00
750.00
735.20
720.00
690.00
660.00
635.00
615.00
595.00
13
22
Jun
10
19
Jul
15
13:30
Aug
12
21
ETHUSD.P 4h

If you're familiar with divergence indicators and the Relative Strength Index (RSI), you'll know that they work in similar ways. Both of these tools help you understand market trends and how strong price movements are. They can show you the market's buying power or help you spot any misleading signals.

When looking at trends, both indicators can be used with different assets and typically work with ratios like 70:30. For example, if the lines on the chart are moving downwards, it could mean the market is oversold, suggesting that prices might go up soon. On the other hand, if the lines are moving upwards, it might mean the market is overbought, suggesting that prices could drop.

In simple terms, RSI and divergence indicators help you spot these conditions on charts. If the lines are trending down in the oversold area, the market might be ready for a rise. If the lines are in the overbought area and moving up, the market might be about to fall.

Master_Traders_ published on TradingView.com, Sep 16, 2024 00:17 UTC+5:30
Bitcoin / TetherUS, 4h, BINANCE 59,793.85 −199.18 (−0.33%)
Crypto Talks
Overbought Zone
USDT
62,000.00
61,000.00
High 60,625.00
59,993.03
BTCUSDT 59,793.85
58,000.00
57,200.00
56,400.00
55,400.00
54,600.00
53,800.00
70.00
RSI-based MA 65.14
RSI 58.28
50.00
40.00
30.00
3
5
7
9
11
13
16
18
20
23
TradingView

If you look at the two indicators on the chart above, you'll notice that there isn't much difference between them. Both indicators move in the same way. The chart shows that the divergence indicator is giving signals while the RSI is showing the market's strength and how money is moving in and out. When the market is done with buying or when it reaches an overbought level, selling usually starts. In this case, the RSI has gone up to 75.2 and might even reach 77. When the RSI goes beyond a certain level, the market often drops, and this area is known as the overbought zone.

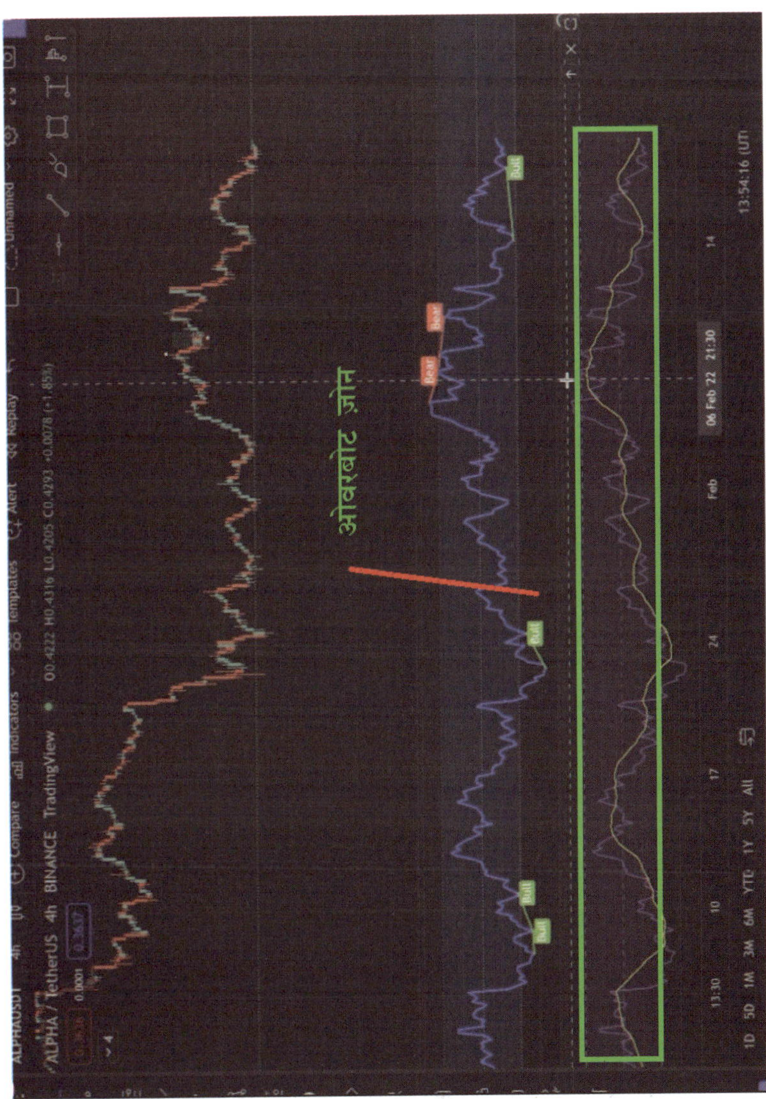

So, whenever this indicator goes up and shows a bearish signal, people often say it comes too late, and they wonder how they can buy a position at the right time. I'd say these signals are more suited for swing trading. Now we're going to learn about futures trading and how to use these indicators effectively.

First, I'll start with the basics, open a chart with a shorter time frame and apply the RSI. In this setup, the 50 Moving Average (MA) acts as both support and resistance, which you can clearly see on the chart.

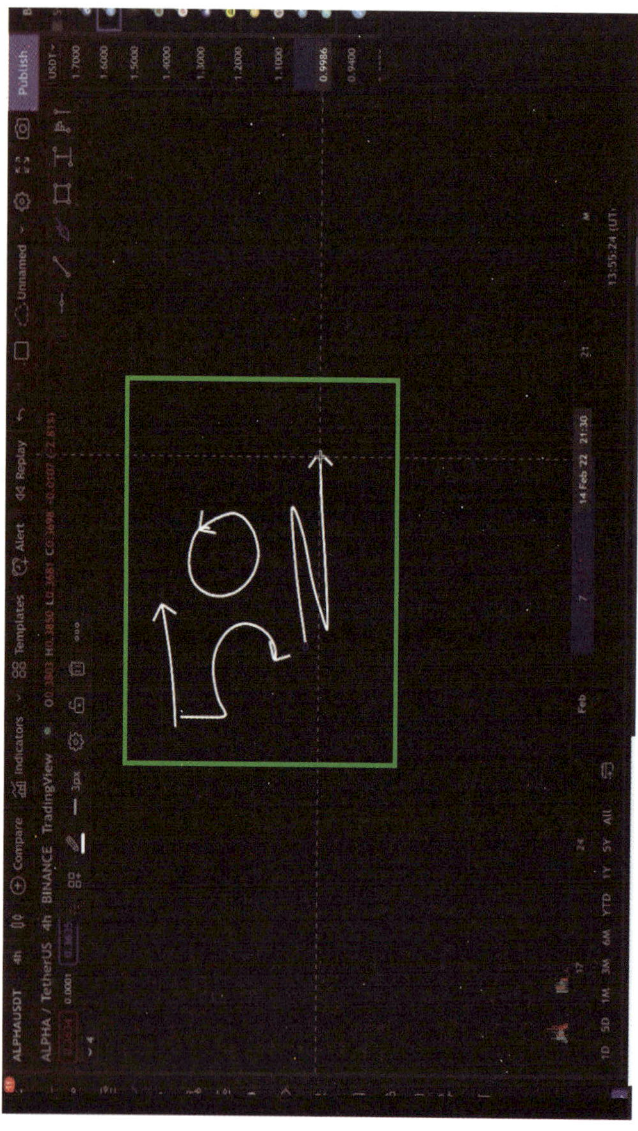

Here's the most basic rule - if you're scalping on a chart, always use a lower time frame. In scalping, we focus on very short time frames like 1 minute, 5 minutes and 15 minutes. We analyze the 1-minute, 5-minute and 15-minute candles on the chart to decide when to enter and exit trades based on the market trend.

For example, if you're looking at 5-minute candles over a 15-minute period and see that 3 candles are positive, you might make a 2-3% profit on one of those candles, which is great for scalping. Sometimes, the market is so favorable that you can make even more like 10-15% profit. Even aiming for a 10% profit is very good. The key is how well you observe the chart, which is why it's important to keep a close eye on your trades.

In day trading, it's not a big deal if you get distracted for a moment. In swing trading, where trades last a few days or weeks you can work actively but also take breaks when needed. If the market drops, it often returns to its original position. In position trading, being occasionally active is usually enough.

But in scalping, you need to be very active. You only hold trades for a few minutes and holding them longer can lead to losses. You can trade every day and take multiple trades in a single day, depending on how well you focus on analyzing the chart.

Now, let's get back to our chart. As I mentioned earlier, we use the 50 Moving Average (MA) on our chart, so let's start by activating it, just like shown in the example.

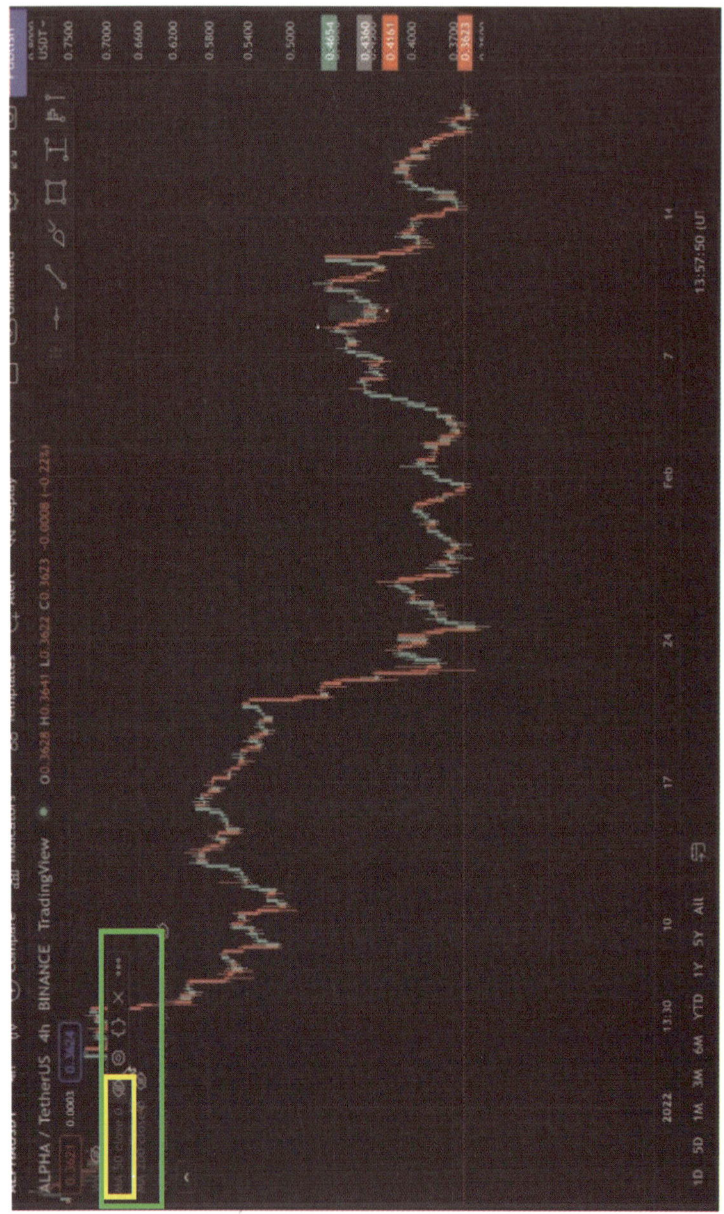

To activate the 50 MA, we click on the upper left corner of the chart and then right-click to apply it to the chart. After this, we open a 15-minute chart. If you look at this chart carefully, you will see that it is forming good support at the 50 MA. After a while, you will notice a short movement down to 0.368 and then it will move back up, expected to reach 0.3656, as shown in the illustration.

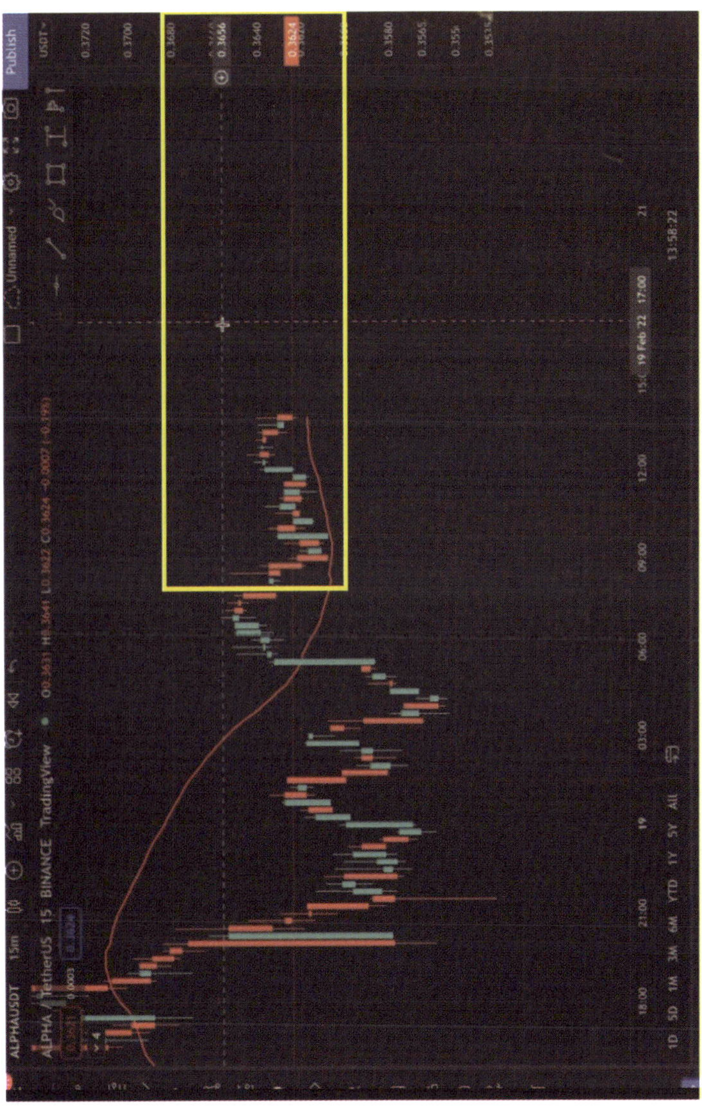

Here, you can open your price range and see that you make a profit of approximately 1%. This means that if your leverage is 5X, you get a direct profit of 5%. This happens in scalping. Even if your profit is less for some reason, it is not an issue. In scalping, you can choose your leverage according to your preference. You can take leverage up to 5X, 10X, or 15X. You can also set a stop loss to ensure that your loss does not exceed a certain limit. Suppose you want to set a stop loss at around 5%, you must set it at 5% below. By doing so, your loss will not exceed 5%.

Assume you take a 10% loss in a call, you can recover that loss in another future call. Therefore, I believe that taking such a loss is not a problem. Sometimes the market falls significantly and setting a stop loss is crucial to recover from such situations. Scalping is very basic trading and you can observe it everywhere; you just need to pay attention. Here, you can take long and short calls simultaneously, depending on the market.

Strategy-1

According to the chart provided, I've marked various levels on the chart. The use of levels helps us gauge the market's strength and trend. These Levels give us an idea of the strength and validity of the market's trend. Additionally, you can draw trend lines to analyze or refine the market. Different types of trend lines can be used as needed. Trend lines clearly depict the market's strength. You should draw various types of trend lines to observe the actual strength of the market. For example, if you have identified a 2.5% profit based on a certain level, and you use 5X leverage, the profit would be 12.5%. Even if the profit is not very significant on any single trade, this method is effective. The 50 MA (Moving Average) is a very reliable tool for this purpose.

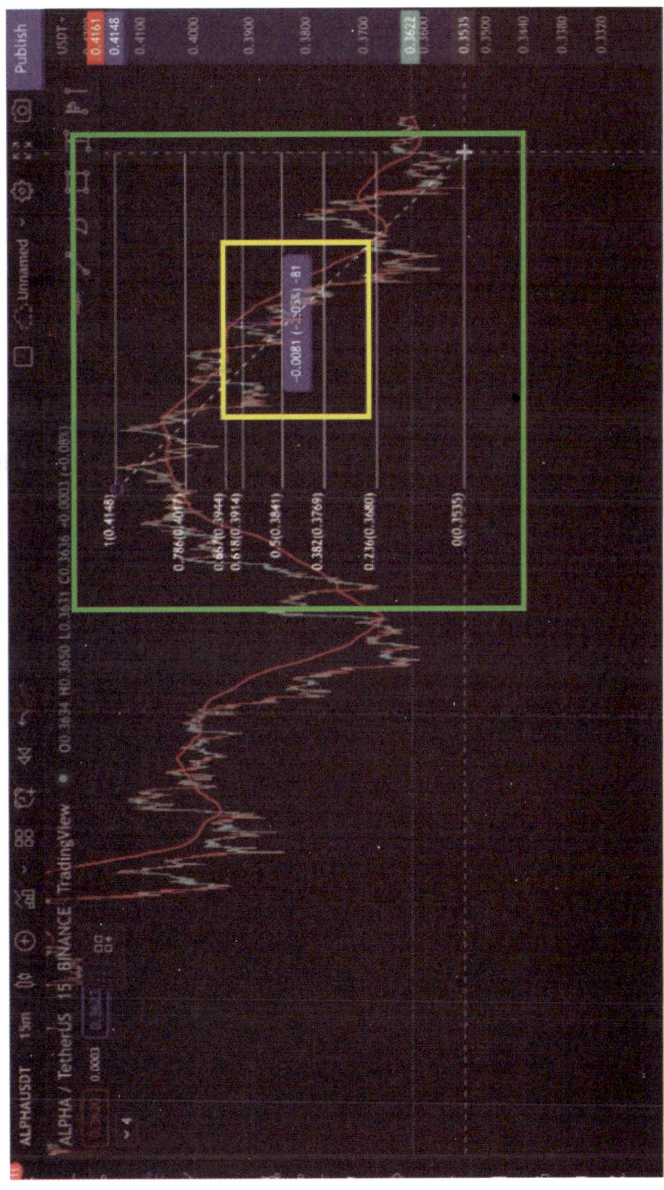

Strategy-2

In this strategy, we use both the 50 MA and 200 MA. We will work with a 15-minute time frame. For this, we select both the 50 MA and the 200 MA, applying them together on the chart, allowing us to analyze them together on the chart.

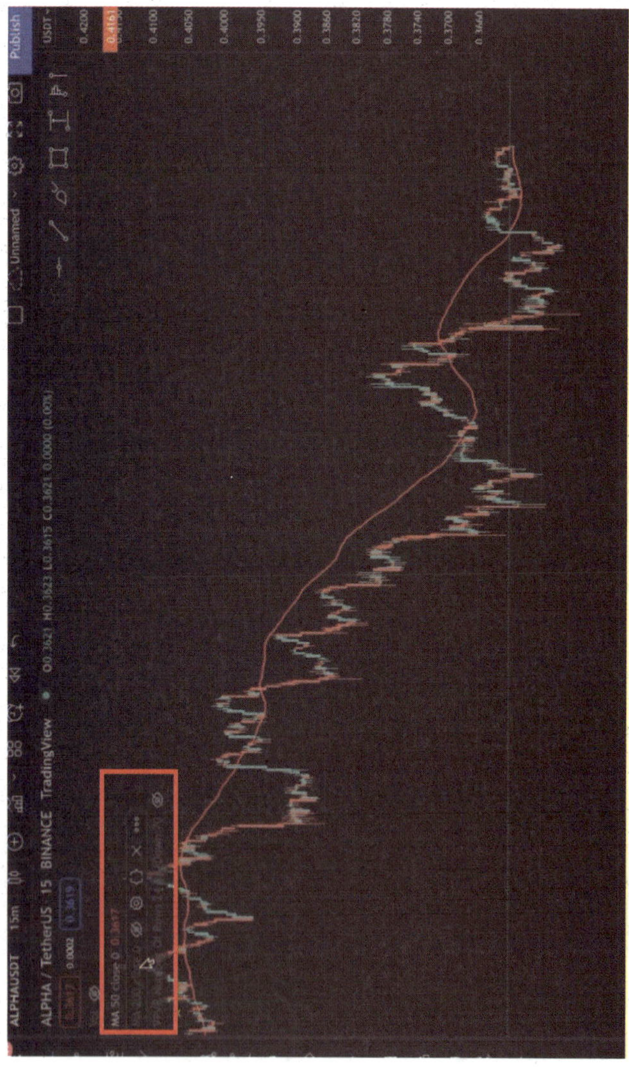

In the provided chart, the green line represents the 200 MA while the red line represents the 50 MA. You need to look for situations where the red line is above the green line and then observe when this configuration occurs. Whenever this happens, you should consider taking a trade. The chart clearly shows that the red line has moved below the green line and has reached a point where it has turned into support and is moving upward. You should take a trade at this point.

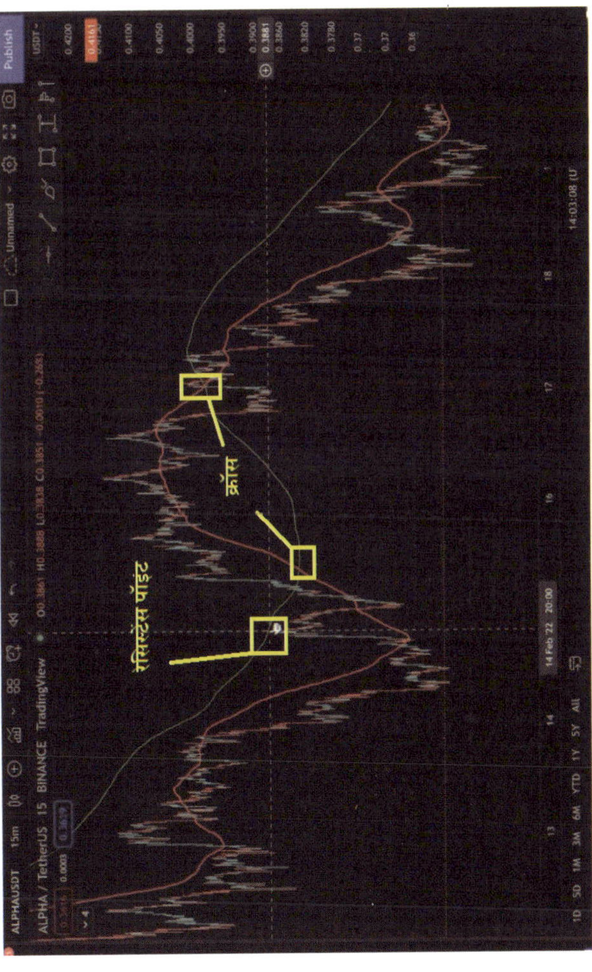

In the previous chart, the reversal point has been highlighted. When the red line crosses from below to above, it often takes a certain reversal point into consideration. While the 200 MA doesn't play a significant role in resistance and support, the 50 MA is more impactful. In the chart, you can observe where the red line reaches the reversal point and you should close your trade at this point. The significance of the RSI is also noted here, which is why we place more emphasis on the crossover points between the red and green lines. According to the chart, these two lines cross at different points. At the first crossover, you should consider the initial point for trade setup, and only after that should you take the trade.

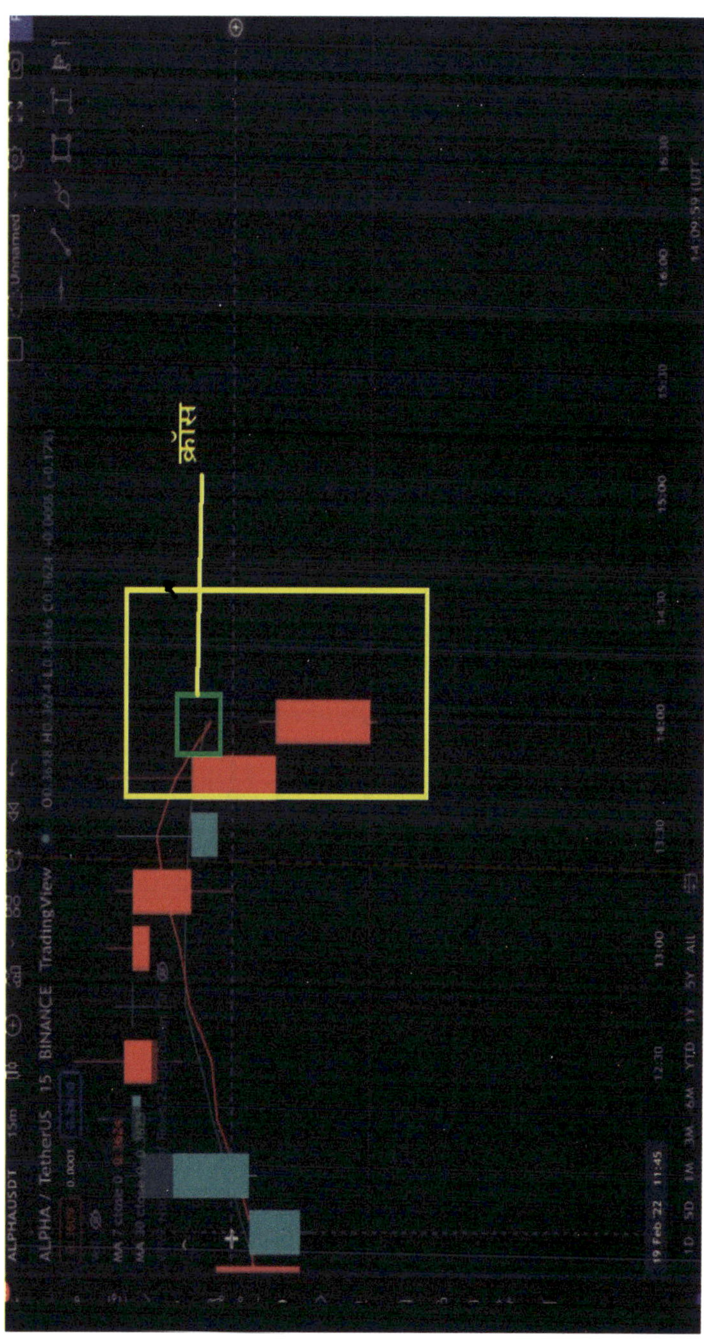
ALPHAUSDT
ALPHA / TetherUS 15 BINANCE TradingView
क्रॉस
12:30
13:00
13:30
14:00
14:30
15:00
15:30
16:00
16:30
19 Feb '22 11:45
1D 5D 1M 3M 6M YTD 1Y 5Y All

As shown in the relevant chart, we have taken the trade at a specific trading point and the reversal point was observed above it. Here's how we proceed: We exit the trade with a profit of 2% from the market. With 5X leverage, this 2% profit translates into a 10% return. Although the trend is showing an increasing pattern, which means that with 5X leverage, a 4% profit could yield up to 20%, we are choosing to exit at a 2% profit due to the uncertainty of the exact exit point. Therefore, despite the potential for higher gains, we will secure our profits at the 2% mark for a more certain outcome.

In this scenario, we will examine a few key points when the 50 MA is trending upwards and a trade has been confirmed: Confirm Trade Location: Identify where the confirmation of the trade is occurring. Check if the trade aligns with the upward trend of the 50 MA. Monitor Trade Duration: Observe the trade for a duration of around 25-30 minutes to ensure it continues to perform well. Evaluate Trade Strength: If the trade shows increasing strength, you can decide to hold the position longer according to your preference. Exit Strategy: If the market trend continues upward, it indicates that the market is less likely to drop significantly. Therefore, you should plan to take the trade and manage it according to your strategy.

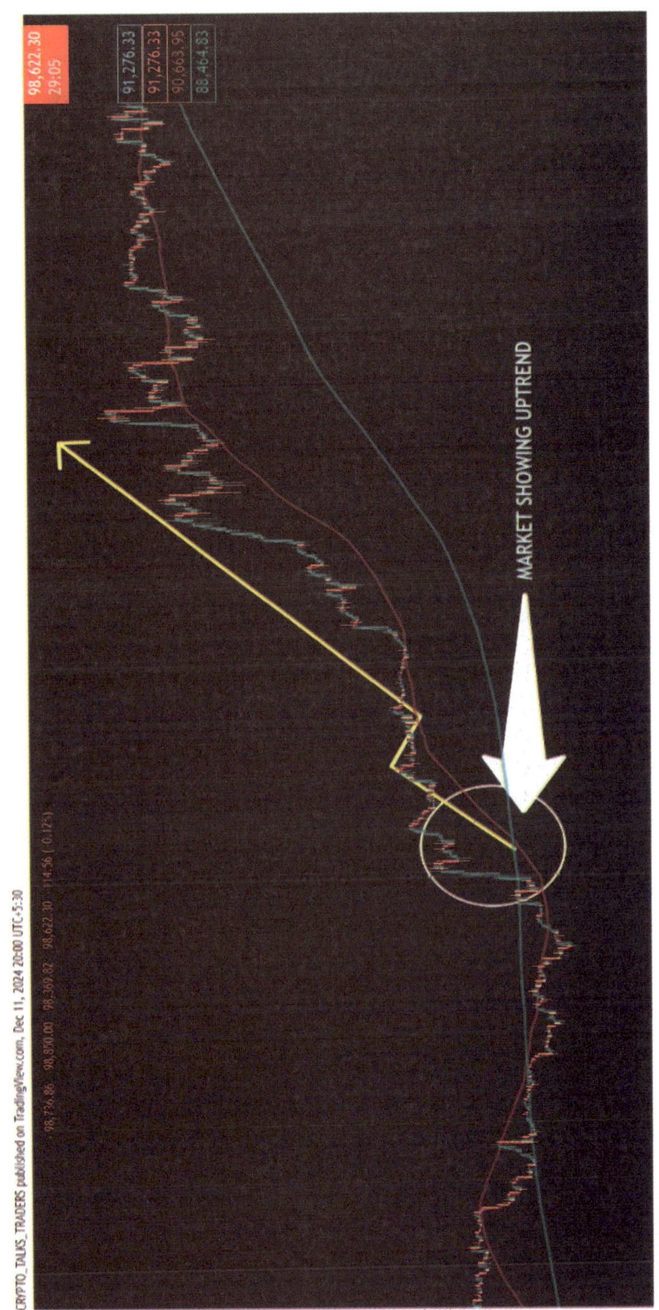
CRYPTO_TALKS_TRADERS published on TradingView.com, Dec 11, 2024 20:00 UTC+5:30
98,622.30
29:05
91,276.33
91,276.33
90,663.95
88,464.83
MARKET SHOWING UPTREND
TradingView

According to the chart, when the market is in such a condition, we take trades with small positions. When the market is in an uptrend, hold your trades for a short time and exit with a 2-3% profit. If the market shows continued upward movement, take profits again with 2-3% and exit from the market. This kind of trading helps you avoid losses. These are also referred to as scalping strategies. This way, your strategy becomes effective, using either 50 MA or 200 MA.

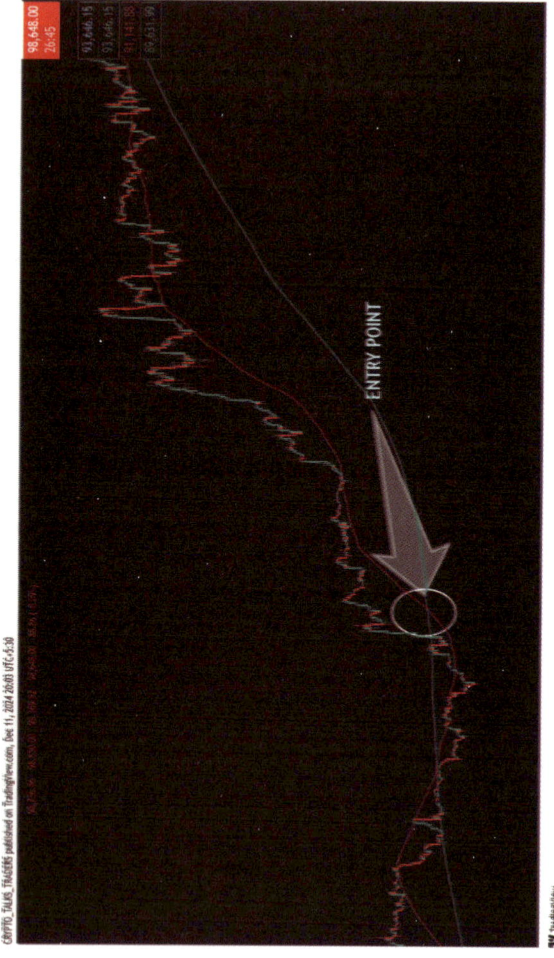

You can also use the EMA (Exponential Moving Average) in your strategies. According to the chart, when you see that the red line (representing the EMA) is below the green line and is continuously moving upwards, you should always prefer a long position rather than wasting time on a short position. The duration of a long position can start from 15-20 minutes and can extend up to half an hour or even an hour. Similarly, you can take a 2-3% profit and exit from the market. In this strategy, if the market moves downward from the resistance point, you should enter the market with a long position. For instance, if you aim for a 2% profit and you have the risk that the market might go back up, you should set a stop loss at 2% to protect yourself from losses. This strategy involves using both 50 MA and 200 MA for identifying resistance points.

Strategy-3

In this strategy, we also use the EMA (Exponential Moving Average) bands but I also have a specific method for this, which I shall explain in detail. Before starting with this strategy, you must make a slight adjustment to the chart's settings. For this adjustment, you will apply the EMA bands on the chart, which will reveal additional options for analysis.

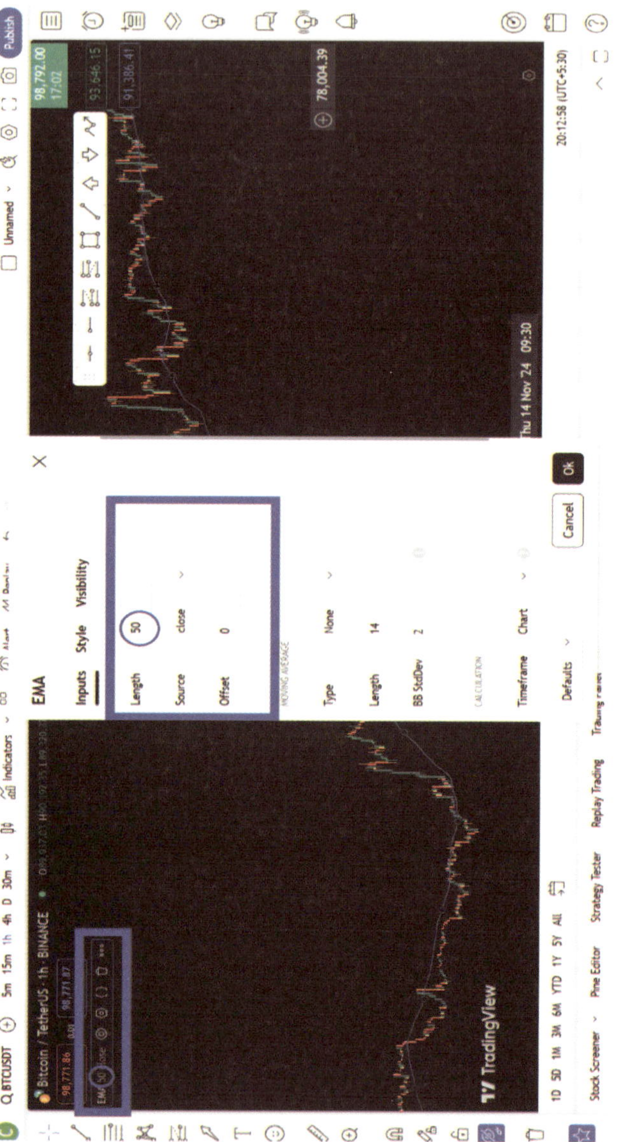

In the chart settings menu, instead of 50, you can change the time frame to 7 and then click on the button. By doing this, we will obtain a new format for the chart, as shown in the illustration.

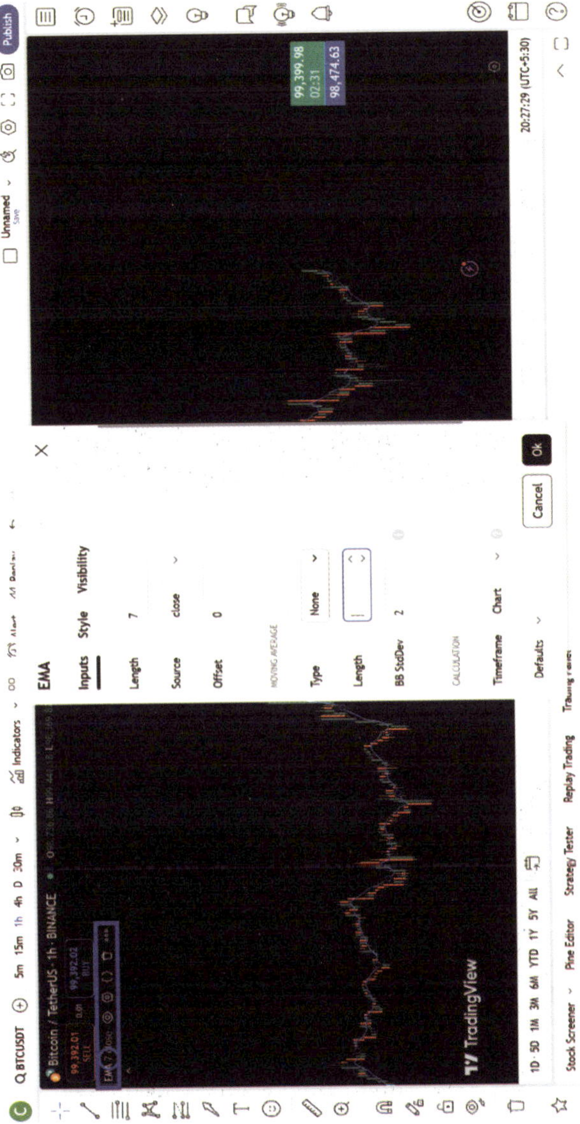

Moving forward in this direction, you can also make changes to the 200 MA. To do this, click on the 200 MA and the settings button will appear. Once you click on the settings button again, the options will appear as shown in the illustration.

Here, instead of 200, you can change the time frame to 30 and then click on the button, as depicted in the chart below.

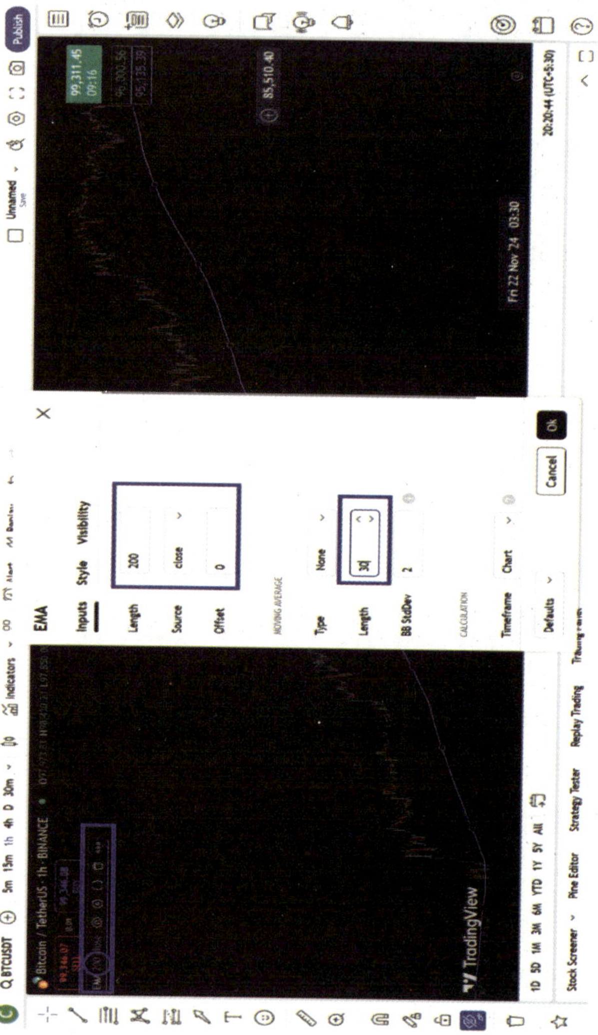

This way, the resulting chart will be very effective in the short time frame. The shorter the moving average, the clearer the chart appears. You can easily see the prices and identify support and resistance levels, making trading easier.

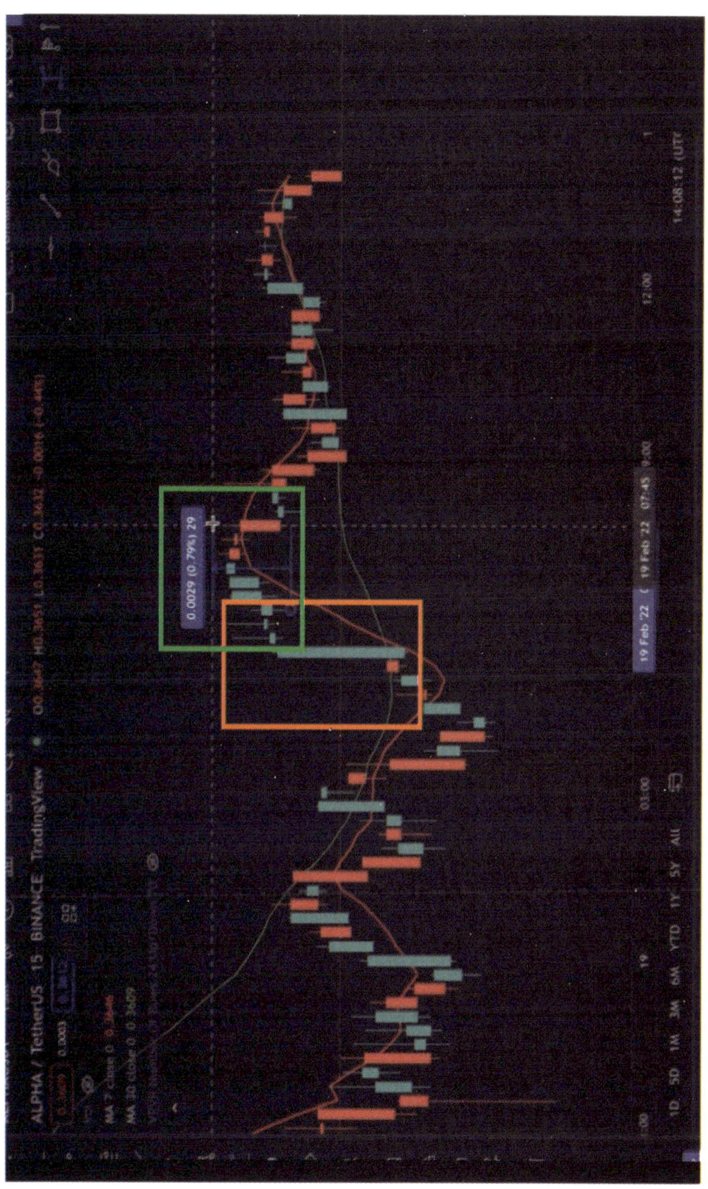

In the chart, there are some large green candles highlighted in boxes. When the price goes above these green candles, you can take a trade. Above this, the price finds support, allowing you to aim for approximately a 0.50% profit. Since your leverage is 5X, your total profit will be 2.5%. A simple point to remember is that your monitoring should be for 15-30 minutes or at most for a single candle. Any profit you gain should be taken as soon as possible. In scalping, traders sometimes use high leverage, which is also feasible here without any issues.

If for some reason your leverage increases to 10X, your profit will increase to approximately 5%. It becomes clear that the higher the leverage you take, the higher your profit will be. However, when taking higher leverage, make sure your potential profit is not equal to your stop loss. If you keep this in mind, there won't be any issues. This is specifically applicable in scalping. If you increase leverage for any other trade lasting 4 hours, you might face significant losses. Therefore, in scalping, you need to be cautious about these factors.

When the red line of the 7 MA is above the green line of the 30 MA, it indicates that the market is going up. Conversely, if the green line is above and the red line is below, the market is moving downward. In the next chart, you can see that at the marked section, both lines are crossing each other. This clearly shows that after the crossover, the red candles are moving downward, indicating that the market is going down from this point. In this situation, you should exit the market as quickly as possible and, if necessary, make a quick entry as well. Try scalping, but if for some reason the losses increase, you can always switch to normal trading because it's not essential to take future trades only in scalping. However, for consistent profits, scalping is very important.

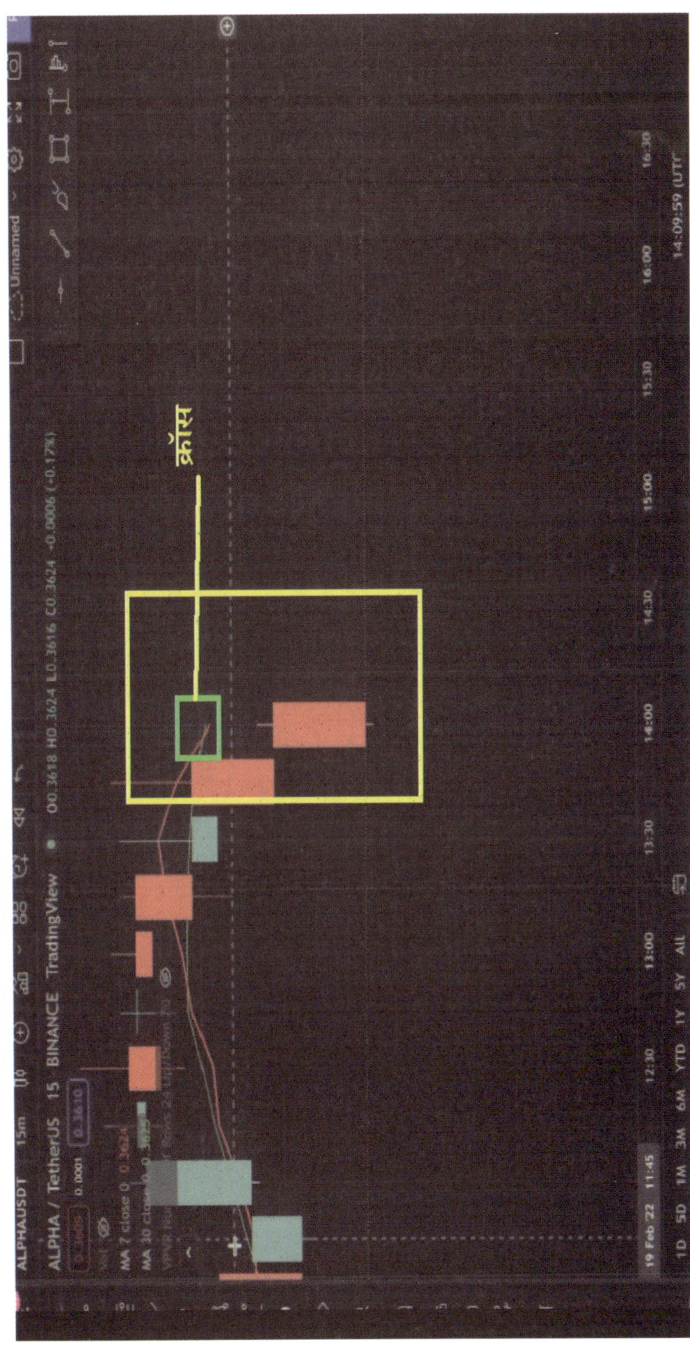
क्रॉस
ALPHAUSDT 15m
ALPHA / TetherUS 15 BINANCE TradingView
O0.3618 H0.3624 L0.3616 C0.3624 +0.0006 (+0.17%)
Unnamed
19 Feb '22 11:45
12:30
13:00
13:30
14:00
14:30
15:00
15:30
16:00
16:30
1D 5D 1M 3M 6M YTD 1Y 5Y All
14:09:59 (UTC

Strategy-4

My personal favorite; for this scalping strategy, we will need to clear all the data on this chart or work on another one. You can work on any chart, whether it's the default chart or any other. For a new chart, you can go to "My Scripts" in the trading platform, as shown in the illustration, and select the "Long/ Short By CryptoTalks" option. You can enable this whenever you want.

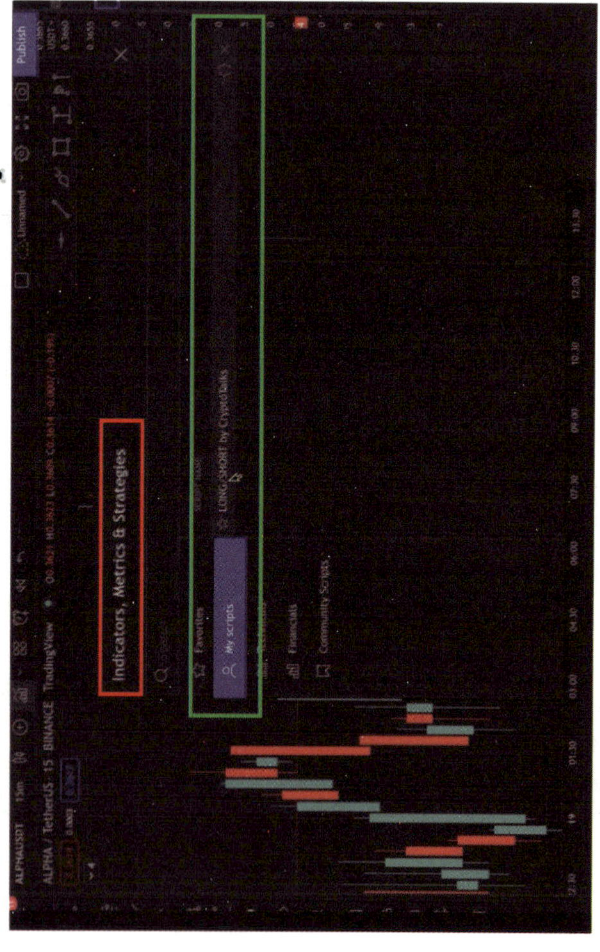

To do this; Now, Open TradingView; Go to Google and open TradingView. You can search for My profile. Once TradingView is open, search for my name in the search bar. Select the Correct Profile: You will see many options with similar names. Look for my profile, which will have my specific logo and a verified badge. This is the profile you need to select. Refer to the following illustration for clarity.

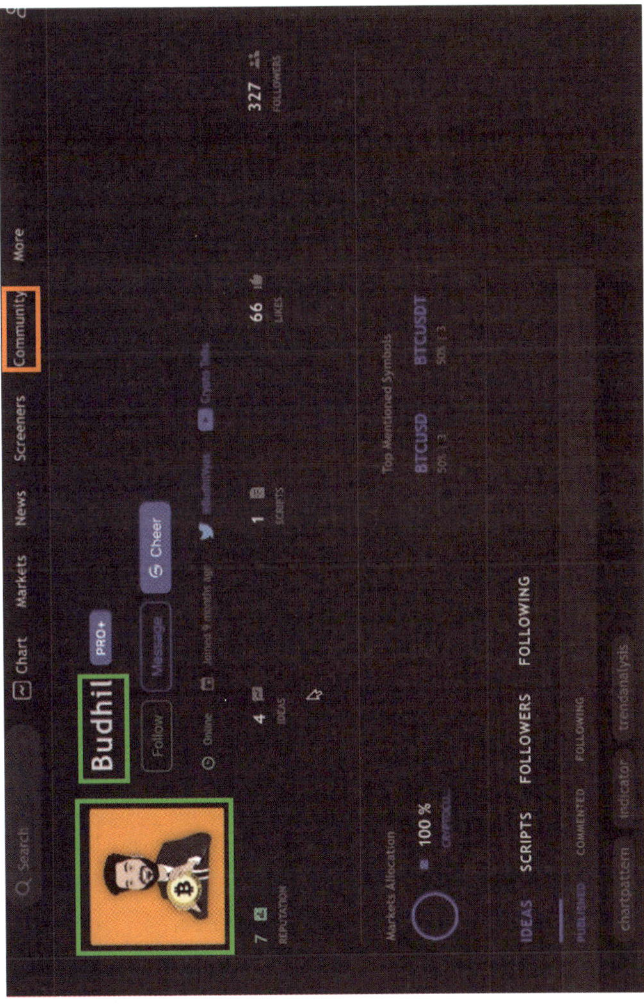

Here, you can also follow my profile. You can follow me, see my followers, or you can also send me messages. It is important to follow the script I share.

Now, in this chart, I've used two EMAs (Exponential Moving Averages) to identify upcoming trends for those who prefer trading strategies. By applying a shorter time frame, we can use this effectively. When one EMA crosses above the other, it signals a trade opportunity. As soon as we take a trade, we will get two different indicators for the strategy. One will indicate a long position and the other will indicate a short position. When the long signal appears, you should take a long trade, and when the short signal appears, you should take a short trade. This needs to be done with short time frame charts. Here, a green arrow indicates a long position and a red arrow indicates a short position. See the chart for reference.

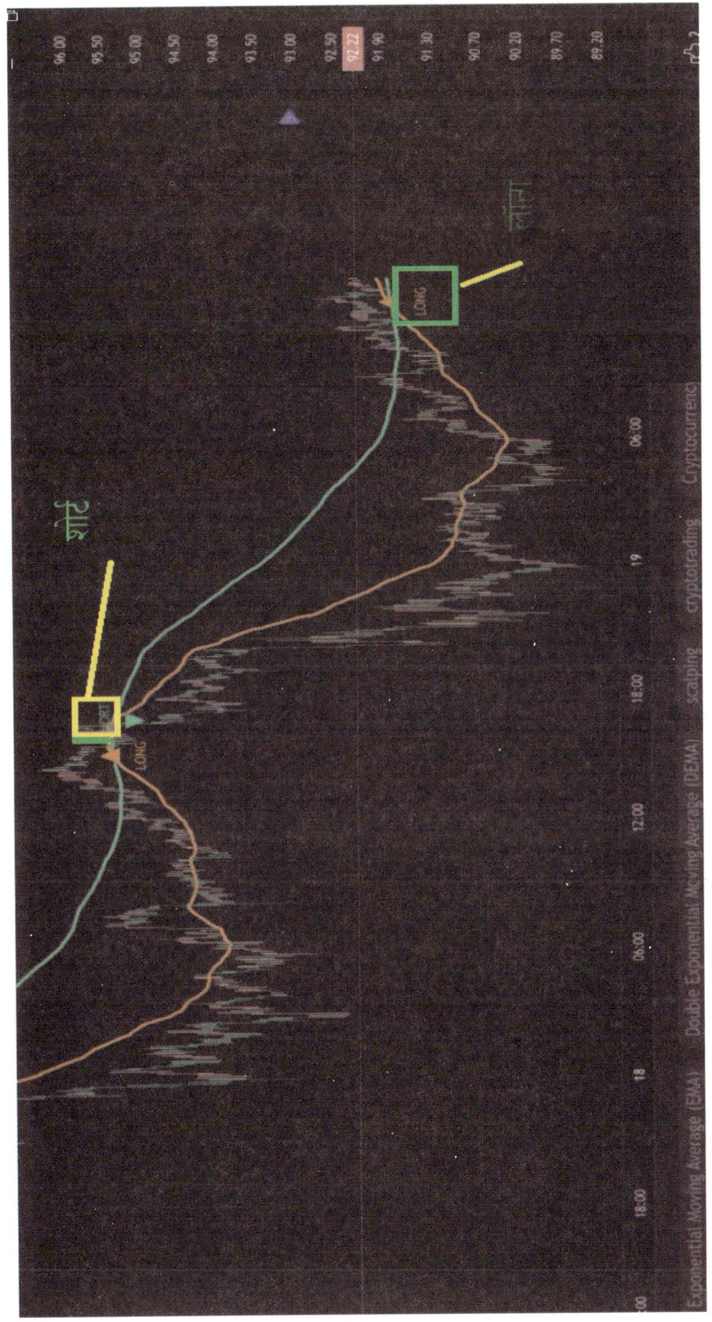
96.00
95.50
95.00
94.50
94.00
93.50
93.00
92.50
92.22
91.90
91.30
90.70
90.20
89.70
89.20
LONG
LONG
18:00
18
06:00
12:00
18:00
19
06:00
Exponential Moving Average (EMA)
Double Exponential Moving Average (DEMA)
scalping
cryptotrading
Cryptocurrenc

I have applied 'Long/Short By CryptoTalks' as you can see on the chart. When you place this indicator on the chart, you will notice that the market is trending downwards. According to the chart, a short signal is occurring. Therefore, if you take a trade here, it should align with the short position signal.

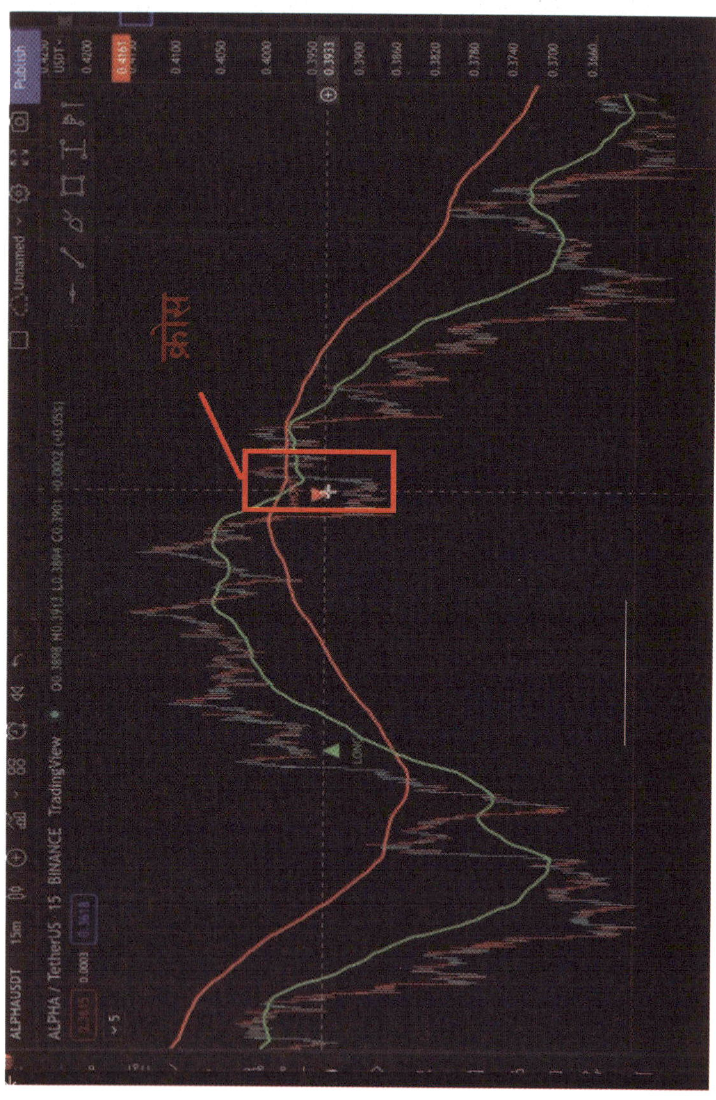

The chart shows that the market was in a short position and you held the position for a while. Even after that, the market has remained in the same downward trend. This indicates that the short trend is still valid, as the market is moving downward due to its current fluctuation. Overall, the market is trending downward.

On the same day, you observed a long position signal, which looked more promising within a 5-minute chart. Therefore, you opened a 5-minute chart. On this chart, you initially did not have confidence in the first green candle, so you decided to take your long position on the subsequent candle.

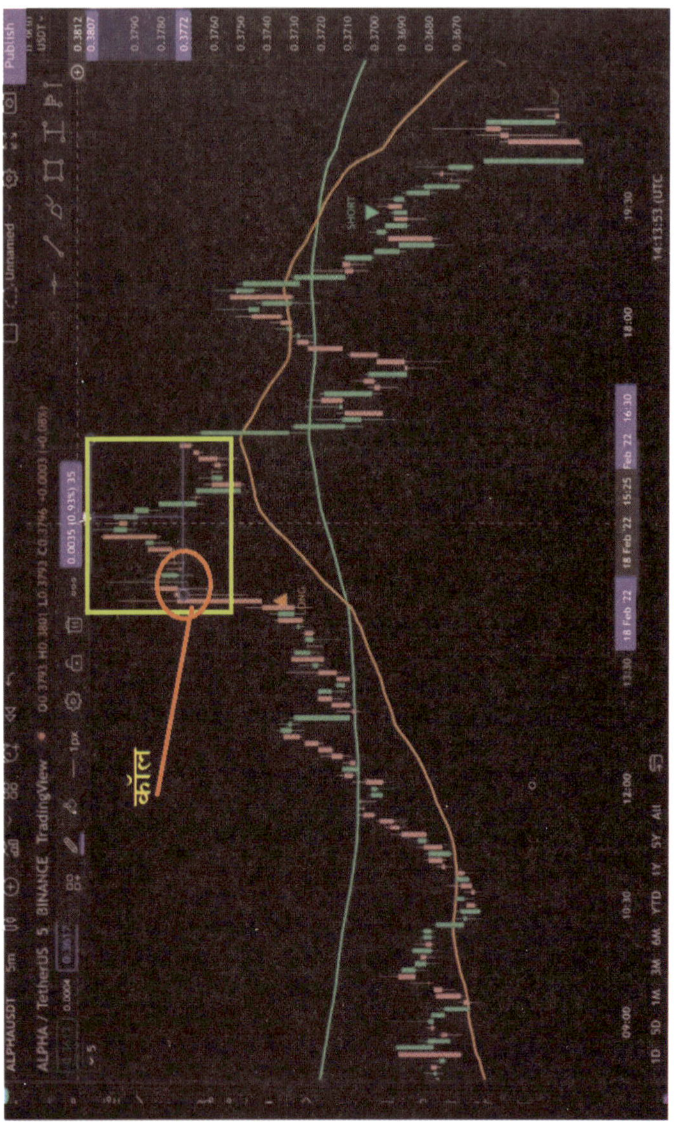

If you take a long position on the subsequent candle, you can achieve approximately 1% profit, depending on your leverage. Similarly, if you take a short position and manage it for a short period, you might notice that the candle forms significantly downward. This could result in about 3% profit. The reason for the substantial downward candle is that a strong downtrend has formed in the market, causing the price to decline sharply. For better results, it's advisable to analyze this on a 15-minute chart rather than a 30-minute chart.

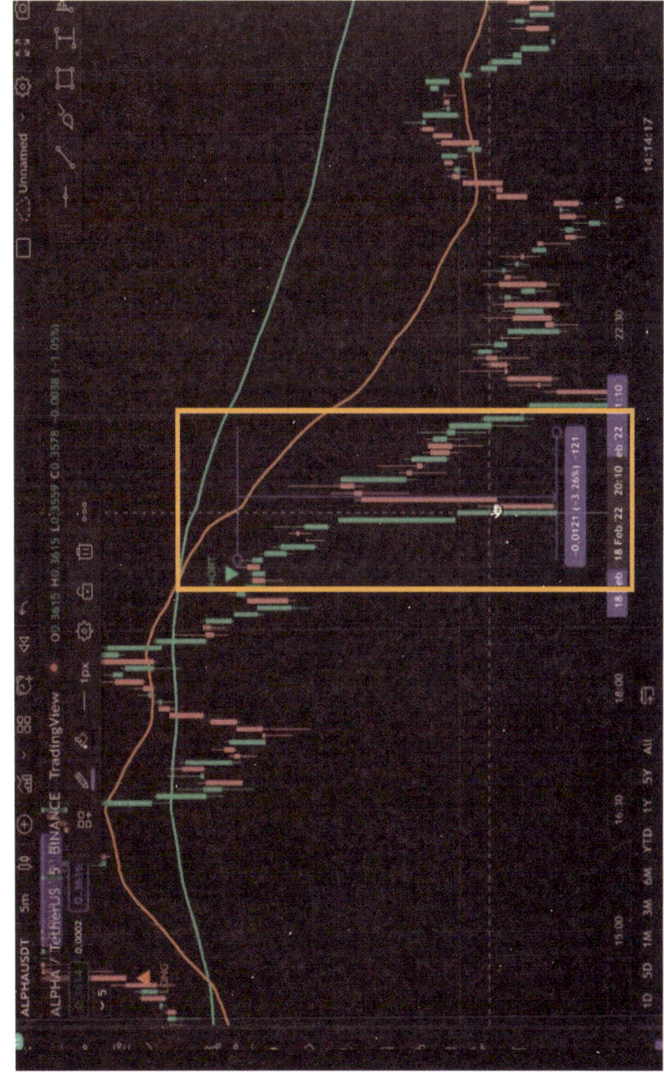

If you check a 5-minute chart again, you may observe that another short signal is present. For this strategy, we use two EMAs—21 EMA and 51 EMA. Essentially these are the 21-period and 51-period moving averages. By using these two EMAs, I've created a script that can help you analyze the market. According to the chart, if you took a short position and waited for 2-3 candles, you might achieve a profit of approximately 1%. If you hold this position for a longer time, it will depend on how much profit you can make, based on the prevailing market conditions.

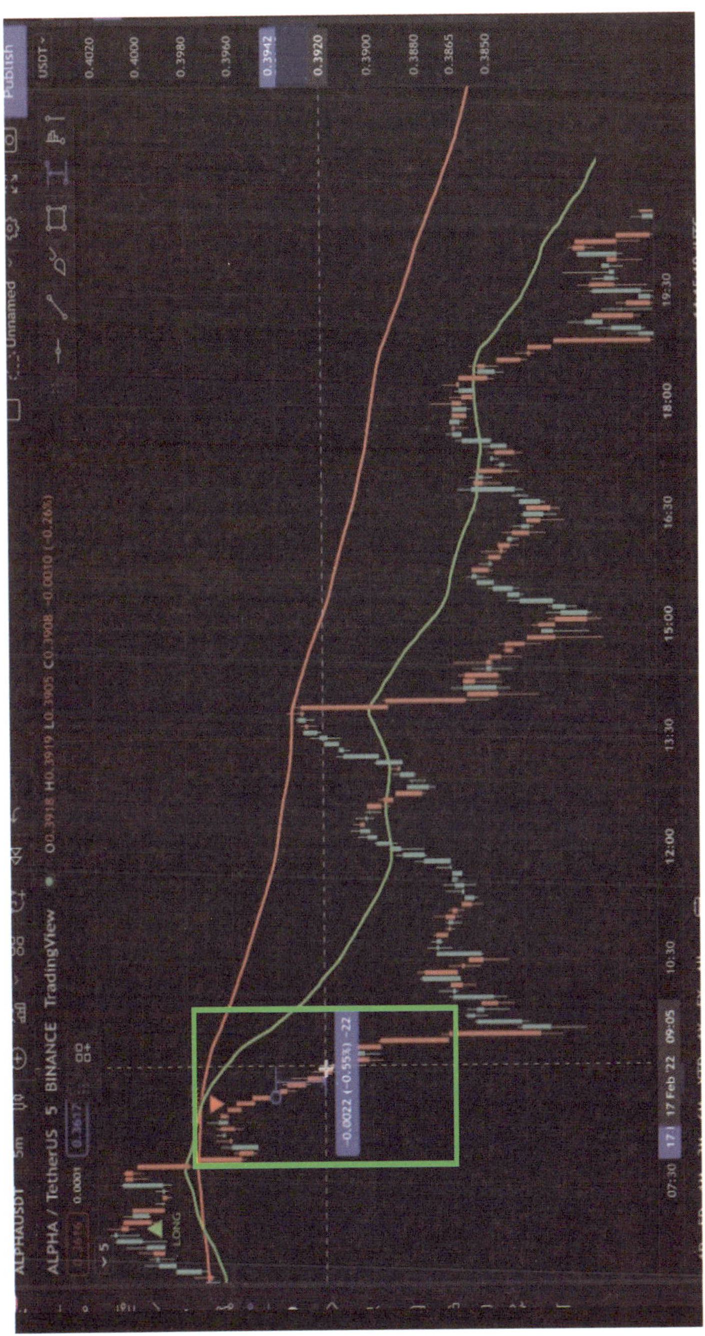

You should hold your trade until the next candle does not confirm the signal. Otherwise, there can be a situation where the trade gets invalidated. Sometimes, the market can behave unpredictably even after you have taken the position based on confirmation. If you find yourself in a loss, it's advisable to exit the position to avoid further losses. In similar situations, when you take a short position, keep it open until the next long signal appears. According to the chart, you can achieve approximately a 1% profit, which would be 5% with a 5X leverage.

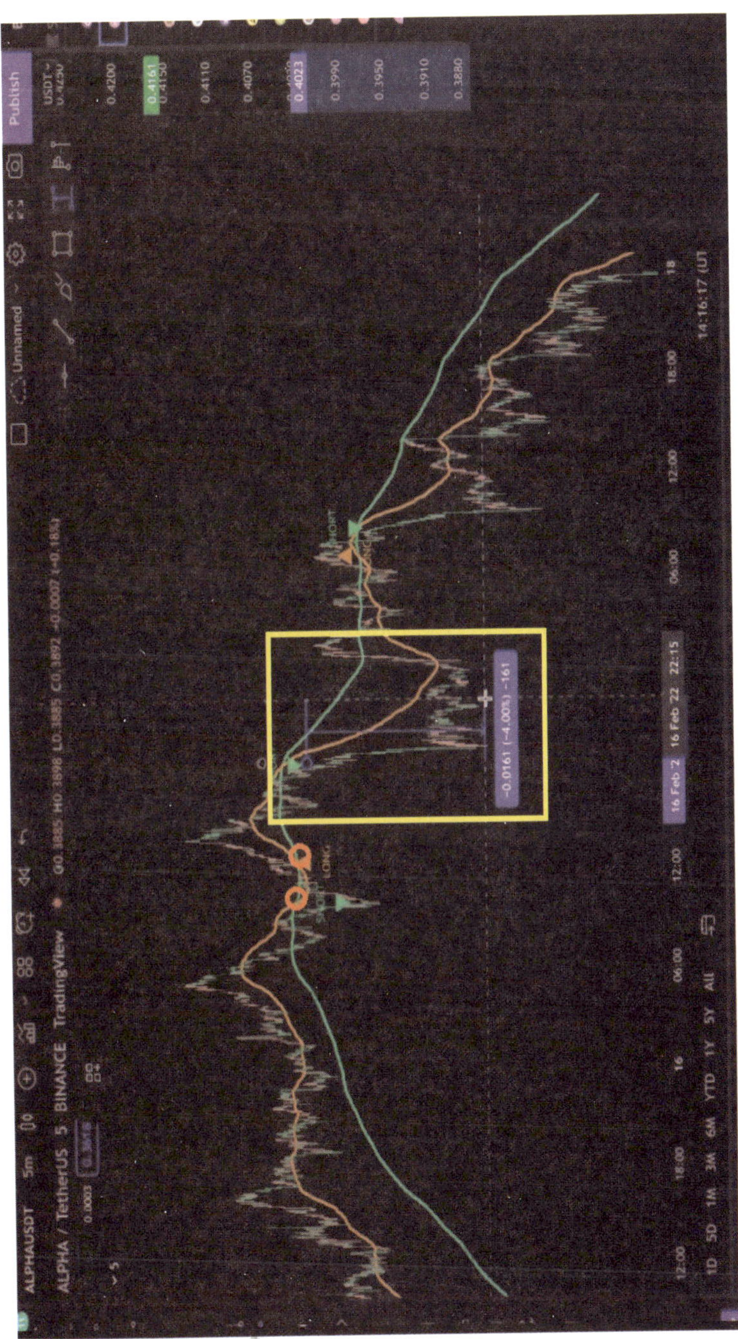
ALPHAUSDT 5m
ALPHA / TetherUS 5 BINANCE TradingView
Unnamed
Publish
USDT
0.4200
0.4161
0.4150
0.4110
0.4070
0.4023
0.3990
0.3950
0.3910
0.3880
LONG
SHORT
−0.0161 (−4.00%) −161
16 Feb '22 22:15
12:00
18:00
16
06:00
18
14:16:17 (UT
1D 5D 1M 3M 6M YTD 1Y 5Y All

Let's return to this chart and see that when we get a short call at the first crossover. Here, it only manages to form a single long candle, but due to significant buying in the market, it immediately reverses and rises again. In such a situation, our stop losses are hit and we incur a loss because not all strategies work all the time. This situation occurs when there is substantial buying in the market, causing it to shoot up and then come back down. This is when stop losses are triggered. This doesn't happen every day but occasionally. Afterward, there are many situations where we recover. You can notice the chart anywhere in a single day without any problem. It is important to note that where there are frequent reversals, the chances of loss increase. Therefore, we incur losses in areas with heavy buying. Generally, if you notice the chart in a shorter time frame, you will see many things. A 1-minute chart becomes very small, so you should consider at least a 5-minute or 15-minute chart.

Strategy-5

This is the ultimate strategy and involves using the EMA Ribbon. According to the chart, if you go to the "My Scripts" section in TradingView and select the EMA Ribbon type, you will see the EMA Ribbon displayed with yellow lines on the third level from the top. Applying this will help you make timely decisions to avoid any potential issues. Based on the attached chart, there are different types of ribbons, but you need to choose the one that I am guiding you about. If you use other types of ribbons without proper knowledge, you might face difficulties. Therefore, it is essential to gather information about the specific type of ribbon you plan to use. This will help you prevent your trade from going into a loss. The next page shows a chart related to the EMA Ribbon. Please pay close attention to the chart for better understanding.

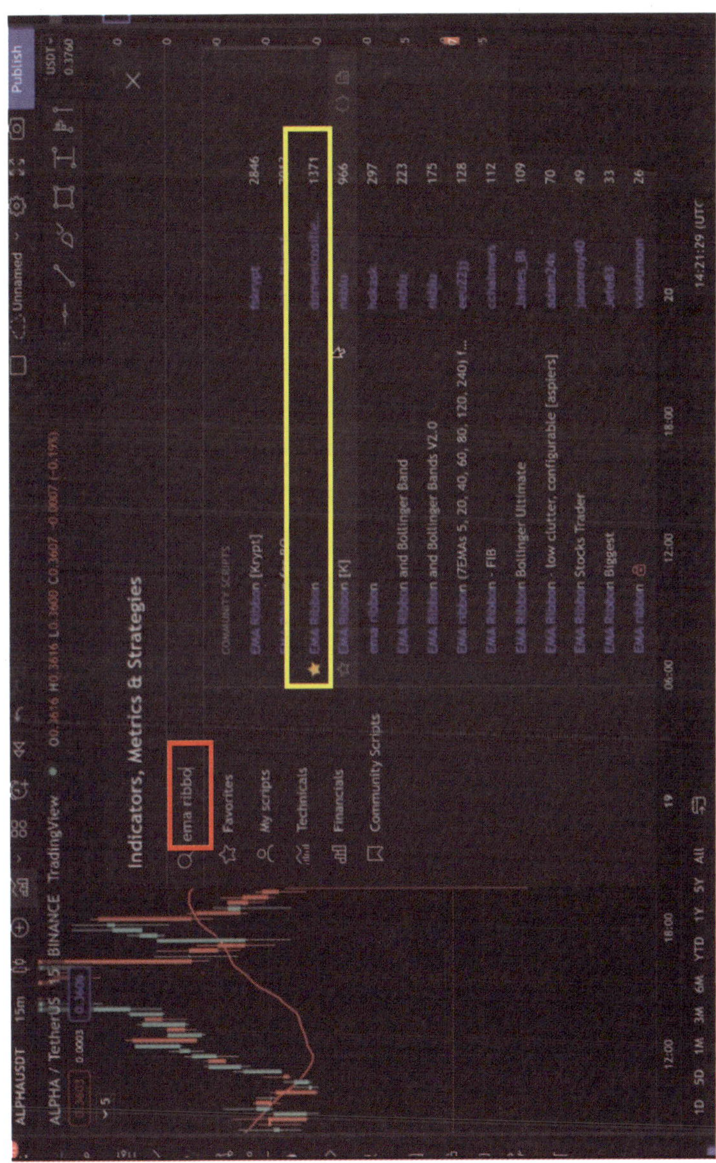

When we apply EMA ribbons on a chart - it looks like the following picture:

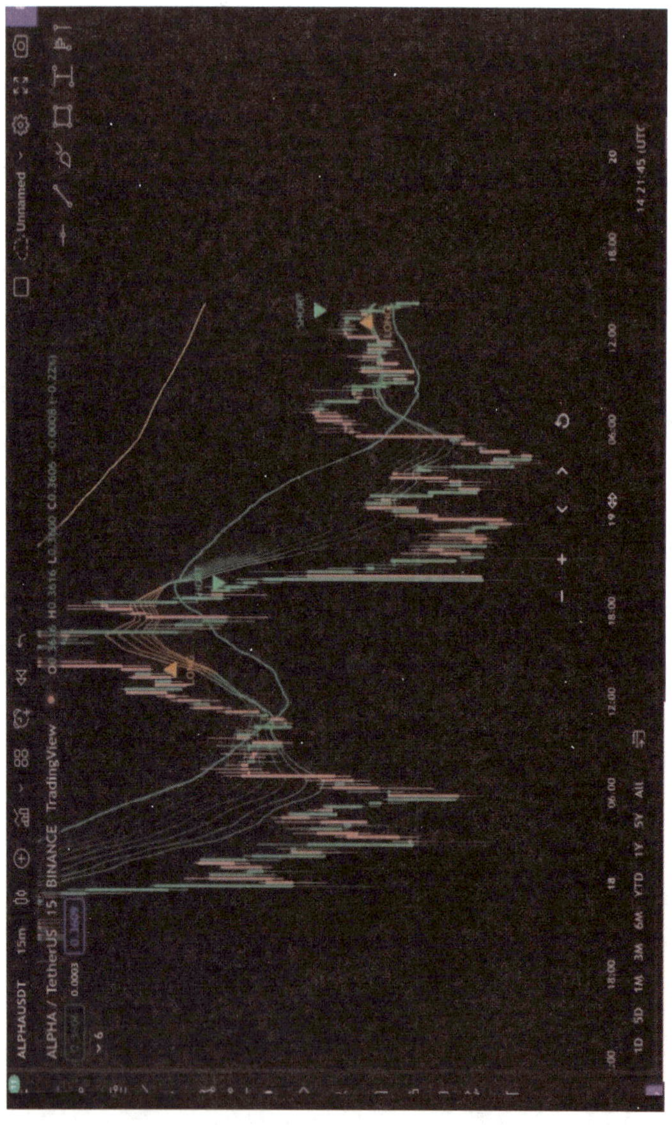

In this chart and the previously mentioned chart, there is not much difference. Here, the EMA Ribbon is present, so based on the ribbon, you can determine where the long trades are. Different EMAs are used in the ribbon, and apart from this, there is not much else that distinguishes it. Understanding this in a 15-minute chart can be quite challenging. Based on the chart, you can see that the short trades occur above the ribbon, as highlighted in the chart.

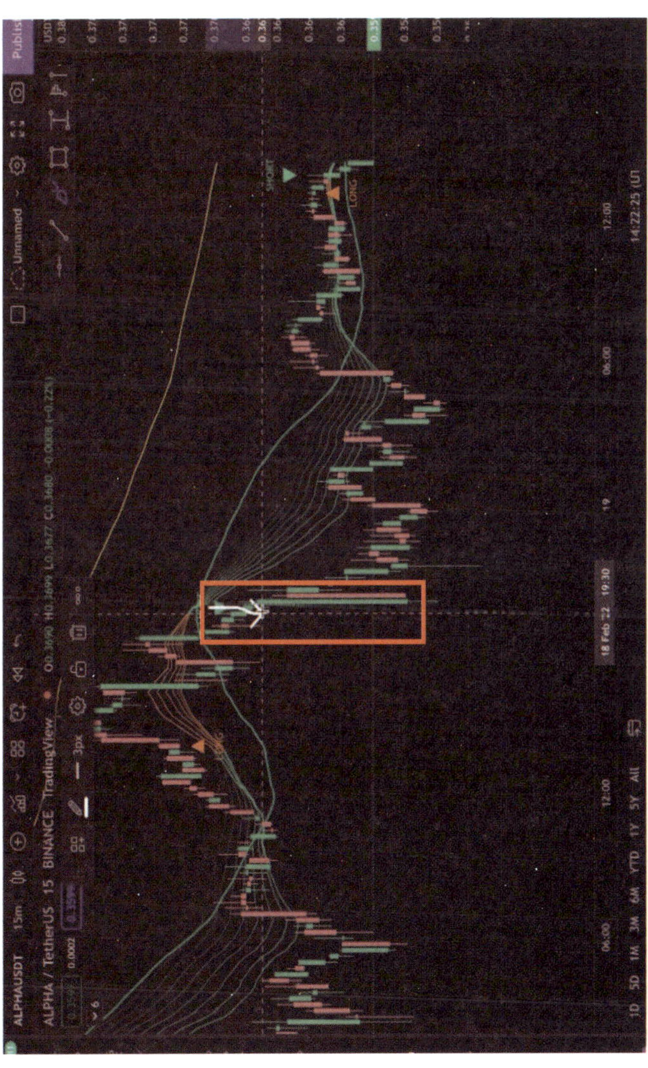

Now, I remove the EMA Ribbon from the chart and use a simple strategy where trades are based on similar positions and similar signals. Let's look at the 5-minute chart. Regarding the ribbon, short trades were slightly different as shown in the given chart. However, you will see that the trades occurred a bit earlier, about 1-2 candles before.

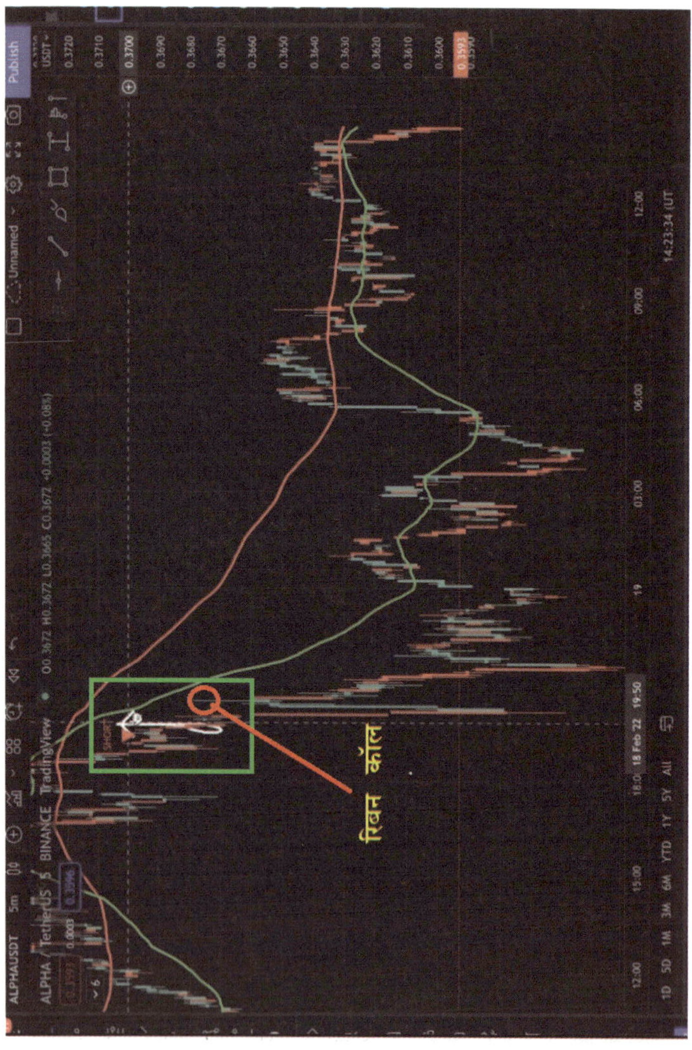

This is why I created my own indicator to increase accuracy in trading and to ensure that it aligns with market conditions. This indicator can be quite useful for you, especially in short-term trading.

Here's a summary of the strategies:

1. **First Strategy:** Use 50MA for support and resistance on a lower time frame.

2. **Second Strategy:** Combine 50MA and 200MA. Take a long position when 50MA is above and a short position when 200MA is below. Conversely, take a short position when 50MA is below and 200MA is above.

3. **Third Strategy:** Use 7MA and 30MA (or 30EMA) on a 15-minute chart. Take a long position when 7MA is above 30MA/30EMA and a short position when 7MA is below.

4. **Fourth Strategy:** Personal strategy involving EMA 21 or EMA 51, or MA 21 and MA 51.

5. **Fifth Strategy:** Use EMA Ribbon for analysis, with detailed application provided.

Chapter 9

How to Use Tradingview

In the previous chapter, you were introduced to the basics as well as advanced concepts that you can apply in your trading practice. It is possible that some of you found it a bit dull since it mostly involves theory. However, this chapter is a practical lesson for the ones who are starting from scratch. We will start from zero and progress to the final advanced level, learning everything necessary so that you can confidently make your own trades and make decisions for yourself.

The first and foremost requirement to get started is to be mentally prepared, following that, having a stable internet connection is crucial. The next key requirement is to have either a mobile phone or a laptop. On your mobile, you can download the TradingView application. If you are using a laptop, you can visit www.tradingview.com and register yourself to create an account. Similarly, on your phone, after installing the application, open it and use your email ID to register and activate your account. So go ahead, open it as you read along.

Next, we need to learn about the features of your account. To begin with exploring TradingView, let's begin with the example of Bitcoin. When we talk about Bitcoin, it holds around 45-47% of the trading volume. This means that out of all the trading done in the cryptocurrency world, 45-47% of the amount is invested in Bitcoin. From the beginning, Bitcoin has been seen as the king of cryptocurrency. Therefore, whenever there is any change in Bitcoin, whether it is a downfall or a market pump, it influences altcoins in some way. Money flow also plays a role in this.

Within the cryptocurrency world, 17-20% of the amount involved in trading volume is in altcoins. This is why we don't rely solely on the dominance chart. Based on the changes in Bitcoin, you can make predictions about how altcoin rallies might occur or how we might see roll-ups. Specifically, I want to inform those who are engaging in futures trading. If you have 1000 rupees in your portfolio or have deposited 1000 rupees in your account for trading, you should only use 100 rupees for futures trading. Even these 100 rupees should not be invested all at once.

For example, you should not invest all your money at once. Instead, invest 40% initially, then another 30%, and finally the remaining 30%. This is because the market can fluctuate and it is not guaranteed that the price at which you bought the coin will remain the same. By doing this, you get an opportunity to reinvest if the market dips. Whether you invest 50-50% or 40-30-30%, you should always invest in future trading as advised, because it is risky. You should only invest 10% of your portfolio in the market.

Now, let's move forward with TradingView. We'll cover various aspects of TradingView and all the essential elements. The first and most important thing is to understand which charts you need to open. As soon as you click on the BTCUSD icon in the corner, you'll need to open the respective chart.

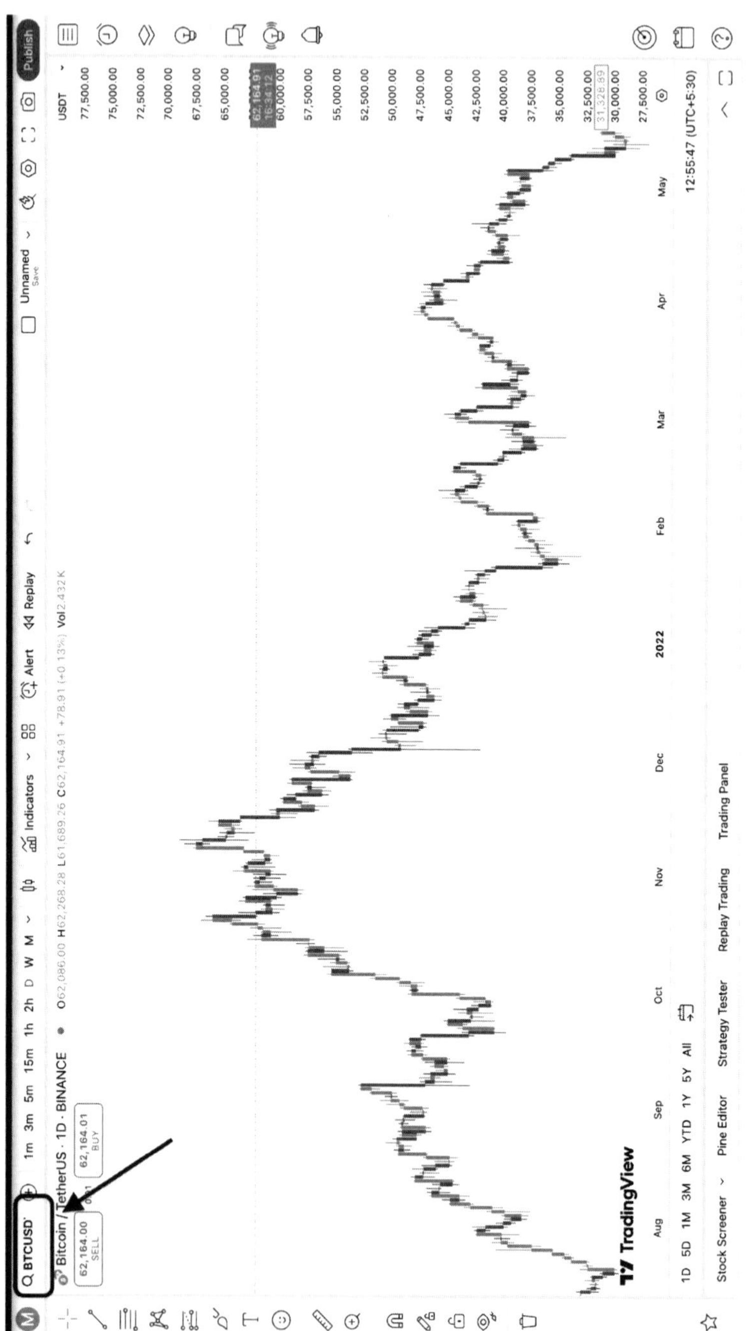
BTCUSD
1m 3m 5m 15m 1h 2h D W M
Indicators
Alert
Replay
Unnamed
Save
Publish
Bitcoin / TetherUS · 1D · BINANCE
62,164.00 SELL
62,164.01 BUY
USDT
77,500.00
75,000.00
72,500.00
70,000.00
67,500.00
65,000.00
60,000.00
57,500.00
55,000.00
52,500.00
50,000.00
47,500.00
45,000.00
42,500.00
40,000.00
37,500.00
35,000.00
32,500.00
30,000.00
27,500.00
Aug
Sep
Oct
Nov
Dec
2022
Feb
Mar
Apr
May
TradingView
1D 5D 1M 3M 6M YTD 1Y 5Y All
12:55:47 (UTC+5:30)
Stock Screener
Pine Editor
Strategy Tester
Replay Trading
Trading Panel

By doing this, the specific index opens where BTCUSD is written. Here, you need to select the coin on which you want to perform your analysis.

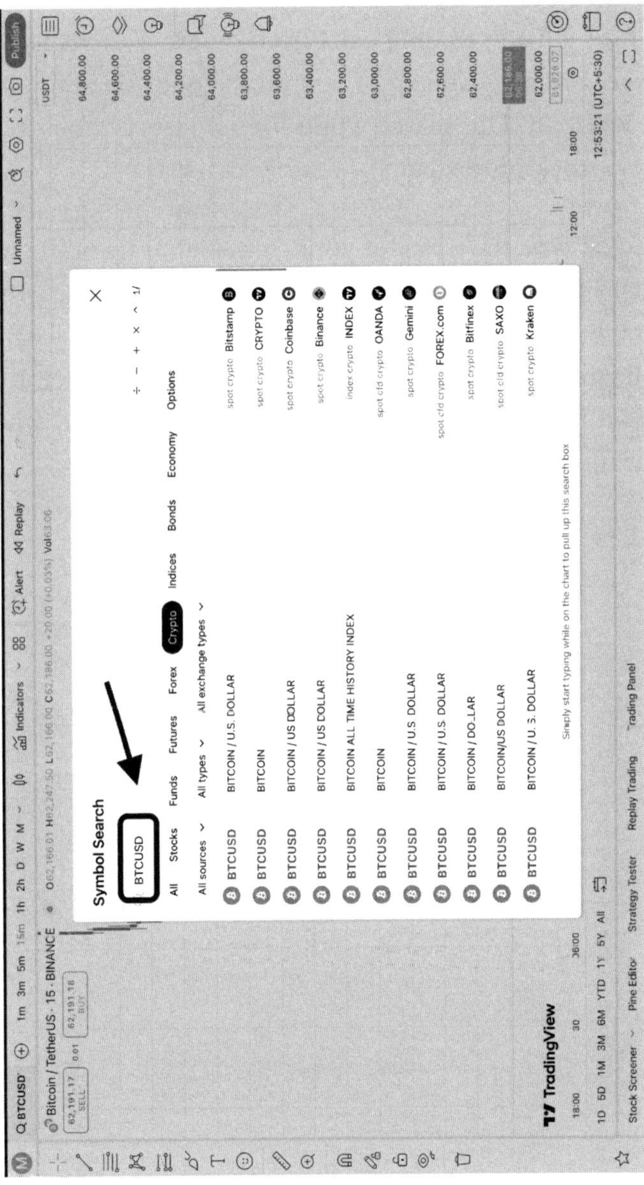

Here, At the top of the screen, there's a search bar. This is where you can look up cryptocurrencies or other assets. Just type the symbol or name of the cryptocurrency you want to check, like "BTCUSD" for Bitcoin or "ETHUSD" for Ethereum. You'll see a list of trading pairs from different exchanges (like Binance, Bitfinex, Kraken). Click on the one you want and its chart will load. This search works for not just cryptocurrencies but also stocks, forex pairs and other markets.

when you type the name of your coin, it appears in the search results. For example, if you type "BTC," you'll see related results. But if you need BTCUSD on Binance, you'll also see the Binance label alongside other coin names. Since I often trade on Binance, I prefer to focus on Binance data, whether it's for futures trading or spot trading.

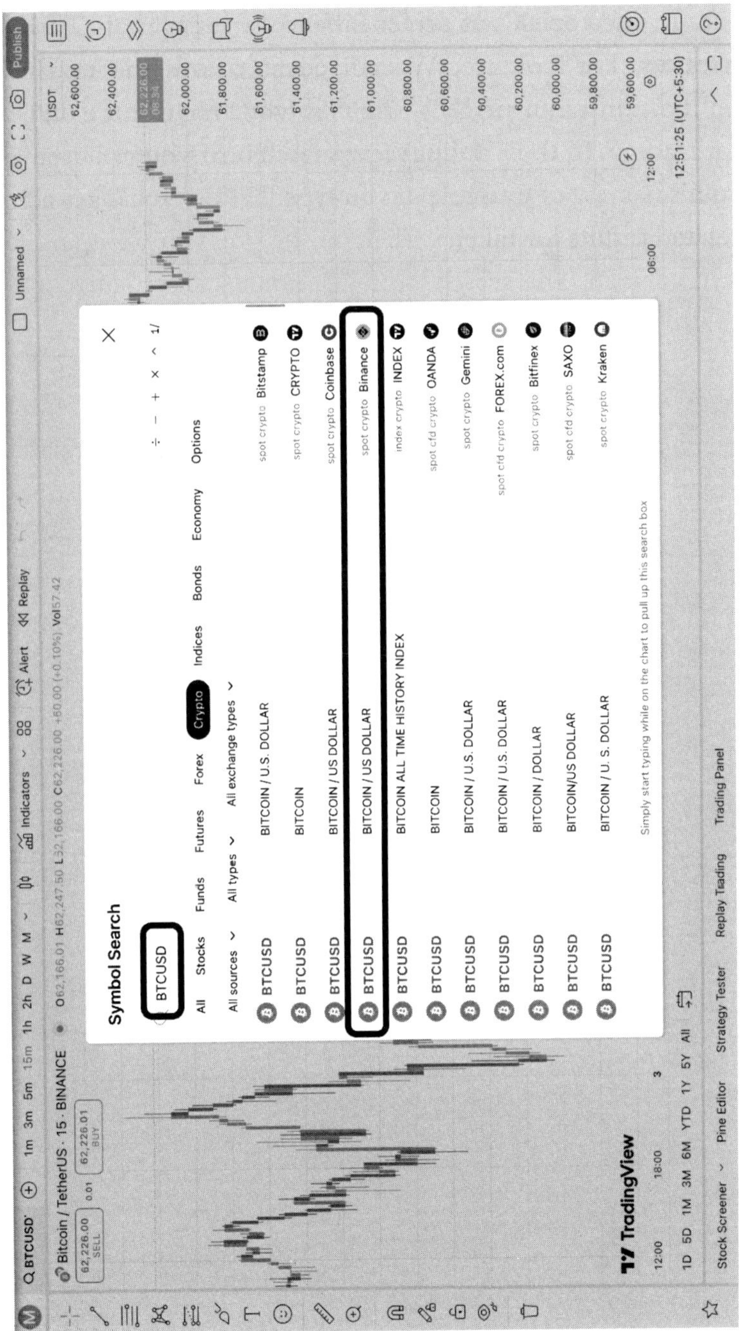
BTCUSD
Bitcoin / TetherUS · 15 · BINANCE
Indicators
Alert
Replay
Unnamed
Publish
Symbol Search
BTCUSD
All
Stocks
Funds
Futures
Forex
Crypto
Indices
Bonds
Economy
Options
All sources
All types
All exchange types
BTCUSD BITCOIN / U.S. DOLLAR spot crypto Bitstamp
BTCUSD BITCOIN spot crypto CRYPTO
BTCUSD BITCOIN / US DOLLAR spot crypto Coinbase
BTCUSD BITCOIN / US DOLLAR spot crypto Binance
BTCUSD BITCOIN ALL TIME HISTORY INDEX index crypto INDEX
BTCUSD BITCOIN spot cfd crypto OANDA
BTCUSD BITCOIN / U.S. DOLLAR spot crypto Gemini
BTCUSD BITCOIN / U.S. DOLLAR spot cfd crypto FOREX.com
BTCUSD BITCOIN / DOLLAR spot crypto Bitfinex
BTCUSD BITCOIN/US DOLLAR spot cfd crypto SAXO
BTCUSD BITCOIN / U. S. DOLLAR spot crypto Kraken
Simply start typing while on the chart to pull up this search box
TradingView
Stock Screener
Pine Editor
Strategy Tester
Replay Trading
Trading Panel
12:51:25 (UTC+5:30)

I trade on WazirX but prefer Binance because it offers better features. For instance, WazirX doesn't have the necessary options for trading in INR, which is why I focus more on USD for trading. In the TradingView search box, you can type any coin's name. For example, if you type "ETH," you'll see all the related results for ETH.

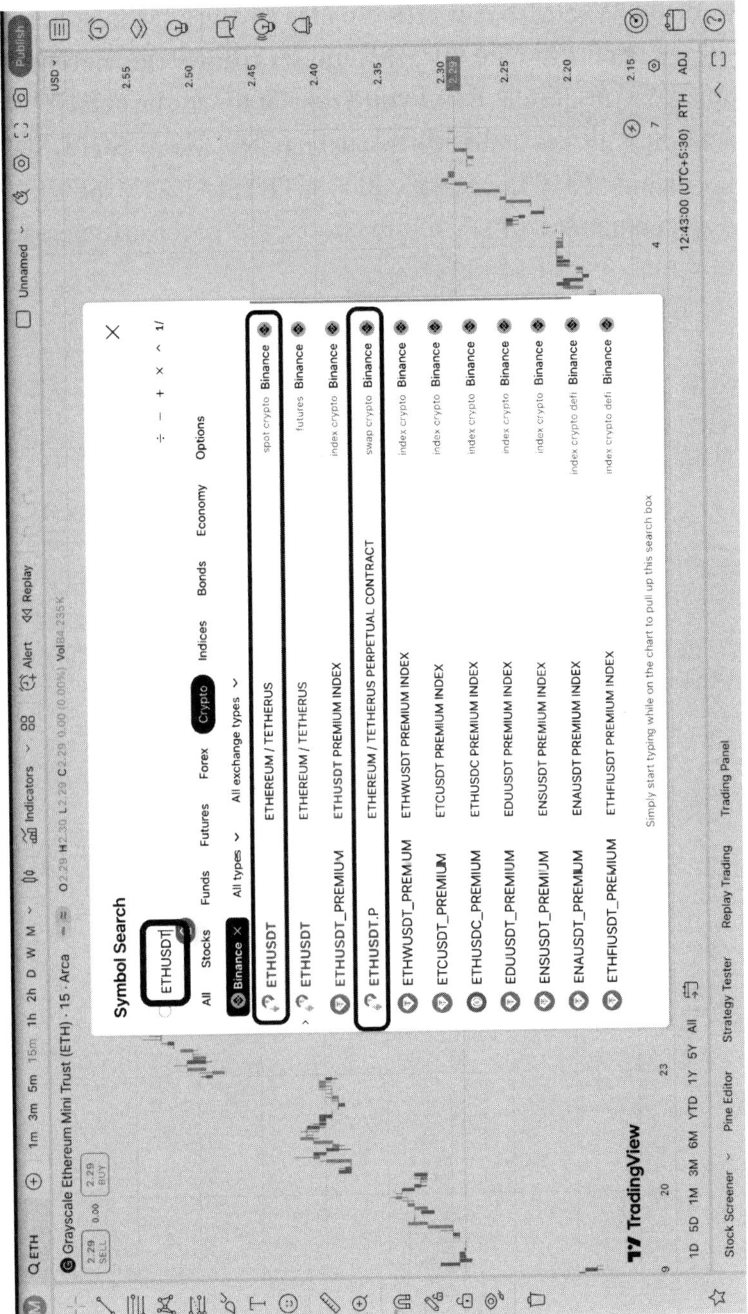
Symbol Search
ETHUSDT
All
Stocks
Funds
Futures
Forex
Crypto
Indices
Bonds
Economy
Options
Binance
All types
All exchange types
ETHUSDT ETHEREUM / TETHERUS spot crypto Binance
ETHUSDT ETHEREUM / TETHERUS futures Binance
ETHUSDT_PREMIUM ETHUSDT PREMIUM INDEX index crypto Binance
ETHUSDT.P ETHEREUM / TETHERUS PERPETUAL CONTRACT swap crypto Binance
ETHWUSDT_PREMIUM ETHWUSDT PREMIUM INDEX index crypto Binance
ETCUSDT_PREMIUM ETCUSDT PREMIUM INDEX index crypto Binance
ETHUSDC_PREMIUM ETHUSDC PREMIUM INDEX index crypto Binance
EDUUSDT_PREMIUM EDUUSDT PREMIUM INDEX index crypto Binance
ENSUSDT_PREMIUM ENSUSDT PREMIUM INDEX index crypto Binance
ENAUSDT_PREMIUM ENAUSDT PREMIUM INDEX index crypto defi Binance
ETHFIUSDT_PREMIUM ETHFIUSDT PREMIUM INDEX index crypto defi Binance
Simply start typing while on the chart to pull up this search box
Grayscale Ethereum Mini Trust (ETH) · 15 · Arca
Indicators
Alert
Replay
Unnamed
Publish
TradingView
Stock Screener
Pine Editor
Strategy Tester
Replay Trading
Trading Panel
12:43:00 (UTC+5:30)
RTH
ADJ

In TradingView, if you type "ETH" in the search box, you will see results like ETHUSDT and ETHPERP, indicating the Binance icons. Similarly, if you type "SOL" in the search box, you'll see all related results, such as SOLUSD, SOLUSDT, SOLBUSD, SOLBTC, SOLEUR, SOLTRY, and SOLUSDPERP, all with Binance icons. You can choose any of these to perform your analysis or trading.

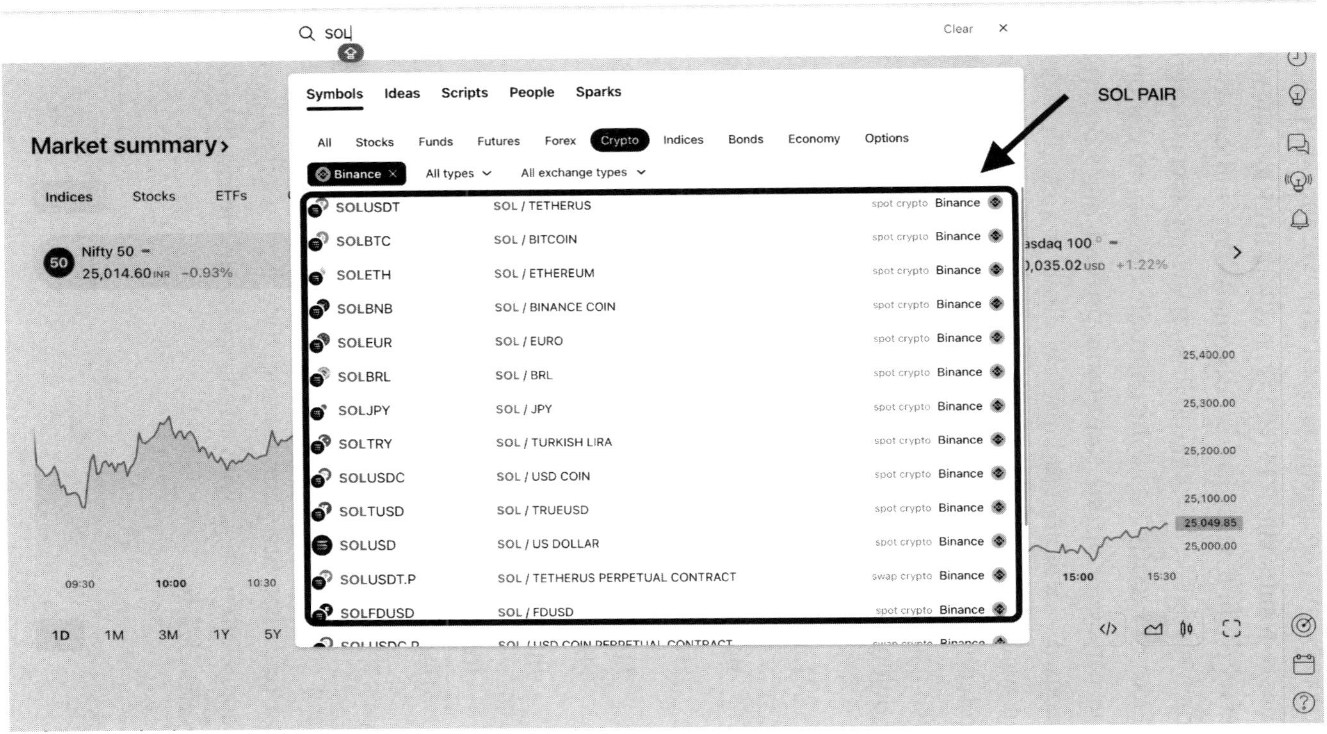
SOL
Clear
SOL PAIR
Market summary ›
Indices
Stocks
ETFs
Nifty 50
25,014.60 INR −0.93%
asdaq 100
),035.02 USD +1.22%
Symbols
Ideas
Scripts
People
Sparks
All
Stocks
Funds
Futures
Forex
Crypto
Indices
Bonds
Economy
Options
Binance
All types
All exchange types
SOLUSDT SOL / TETHERUS spot crypto Binance
SOLBTC SOL / BITCOIN spot crypto Binance
SOLETH SOL / ETHEREUM spot crypto Binance
SOLBNB SOL / BINANCE COIN spot crypto Binance
SOLEUR SOL / EURO spot crypto Binance
SOLBRL SOL / BRL spot crypto Binance
SOLJPY SOL / JPY spot crypto Binance
SOLTRY SOL / TURKISH LIRA spot crypto Binance
SOLUSDC SOL / USD COIN spot crypto Binance
SOLTUSD SOL / TRUEUSD spot crypto Binance
SOLUSD SOL / US DOLLAR spot crypto Binance
SOLUSDT.P SOL / TETHERUS PERPETUAL CONTRACT swap crypto Binance
SOLFDUSD SOL / FDUSD spot crypto Binance
25,400.00
25,300.00
25,200.00
25,100.00
25,049.85
25,000.00
09:30
10:00
10:30
15:00
15:30
1D
1M
3M
1Y
5Y

After you pick an asset, the chart area will appear in the center. This is where you can see how the prices are moving. By default, you'll see a candlestick chart, but you can switch to other types like bar charts, line charts, or special charts like Renko or Heikin-Ashi. The chart area is easy to customize so you can set it up for short-term price changes or long-term trends. By default, TradingView displays a candlestick chart, but you can easily switch to other chart types based on your preferences or the type of analysis you wish to do. To change the chart type, simply click the chart icon on the top toolbar, and you'll get a dropdown menu with multiple options like:

- **Line Chart:** Useful for quickly identifying price trends.
- **Bar Chart:** A classic chart type, though less common for crypto trading.
- **Heikin-Ashi:** A smoother version of the candlestick chart that helps identify trends by filtering out minor fluctuations.
- **Renko, Kagi, Point & Figure:** Advanced chart types that focus more on price movement and ignore time intervals, are helpful for spotting longer-term trends.

Each chart type has its own strengths, so experiment to find the one that fits your trading style best. Generally, crypto traders often stick with candlesticks or Heikin-Ashi to spot trends clearly.

Time Frame:

Just above the chart, there's a dropdown menu where you can change the timeframe of the chart. On the left side of the BTCUSD chart, click on the "D" icon to access time frames ranging from 1 minute to 1 month. This lets you see price data over different time periods—from 1-minute views for day traders to monthly or yearly views for long-term investors. Crypto traders often switch between 5-minute, 15-minute, 1-hour, and daily charts, depending on their strategy. You can easily switch between these timeframes to find trends or spot short-term opportunities.

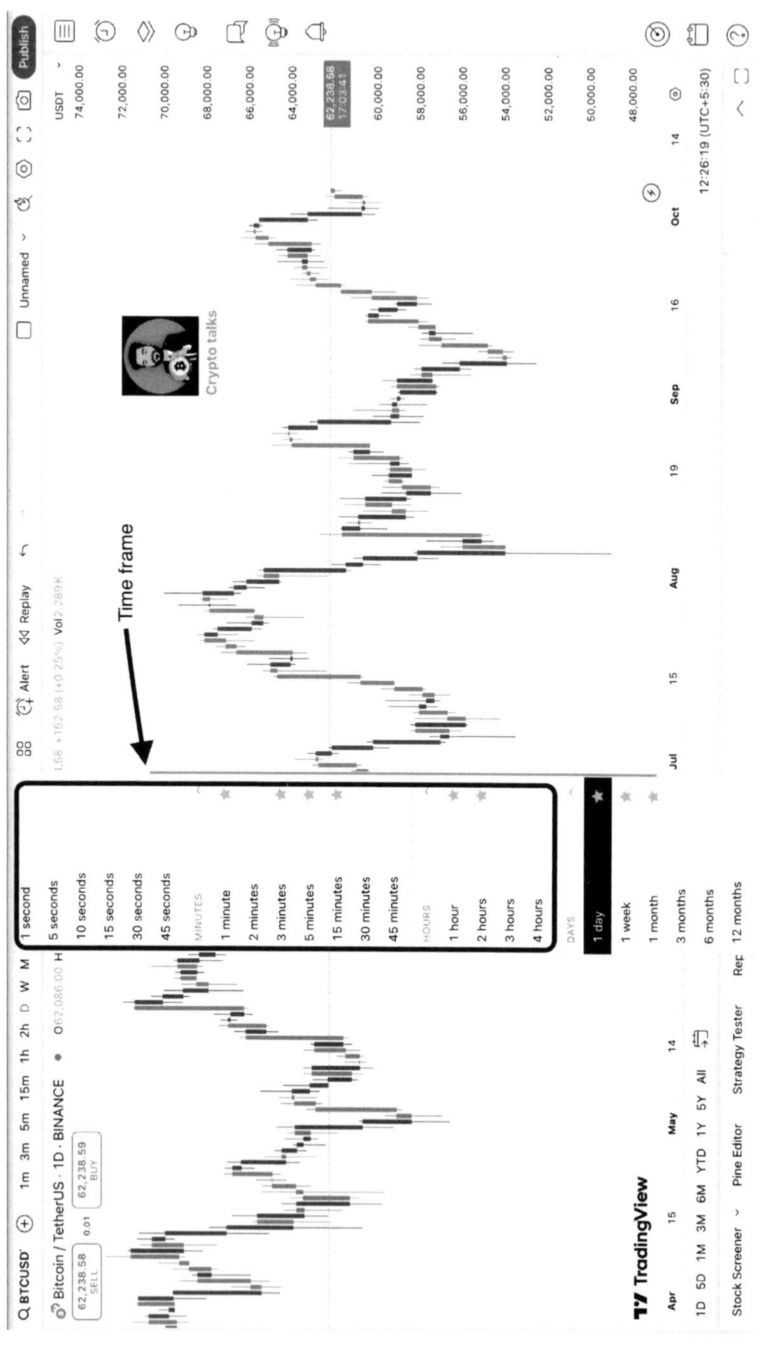
BTCUSD
1m 3m 5m 15m 1h 2h D W M
Bitcoin / TetherUS · 1D · BINANCE
62,238.58 SELL
62,238.59 BUY
Alert
Replay
Unnamed
Publish
Time frame
1 second
5 seconds
10 seconds
15 seconds
30 seconds
45 seconds
MINUTES
1 minute
2 minutes
3 minutes
5 minutes
15 minutes
30 minutes
45 minutes
HOURS
1 hour
2 hours
3 hours
4 hours
DAYS
1 day
1 week
1 month
3 months
6 months
12 months
Crypto talks
TradingView
1D 5D 1M 3M 6M YTD 1Y 5Y All
Stock Screener
Pine Editor
Strategy Tester
12:26:19 (UTC+5:30)

Toolbars

TradingView has several toolbars, each with its own functions:

- **Left Toolbar:** This has drawing tools like trendlines, Fibonacci retracement, and tools for adding text and shapes to make your analysis clearer.
- **Top Toolbar:** This lets you change chart types, adjust timeframes, and add technical indicators. You can also save your chart layouts, take screenshots, or share your chart with others.
- **Bottom Toolbar:** This is where you can access watchlists, alerts and your paper trading portfolio. It also has links to ideas and scripts from other traders so you can explore new strategies.

Watchlist

On the right side of the screen, you'll see your watchlist. This helps you keep track of multiple cryptocurrencies and other assets at once. You can add any asset you're interested in by clicking the "+" icon, and it will show up here, making it easy to monitor price changes without switching charts. The watchlist updates in real-time, so you can keep an eye on several markets at once.

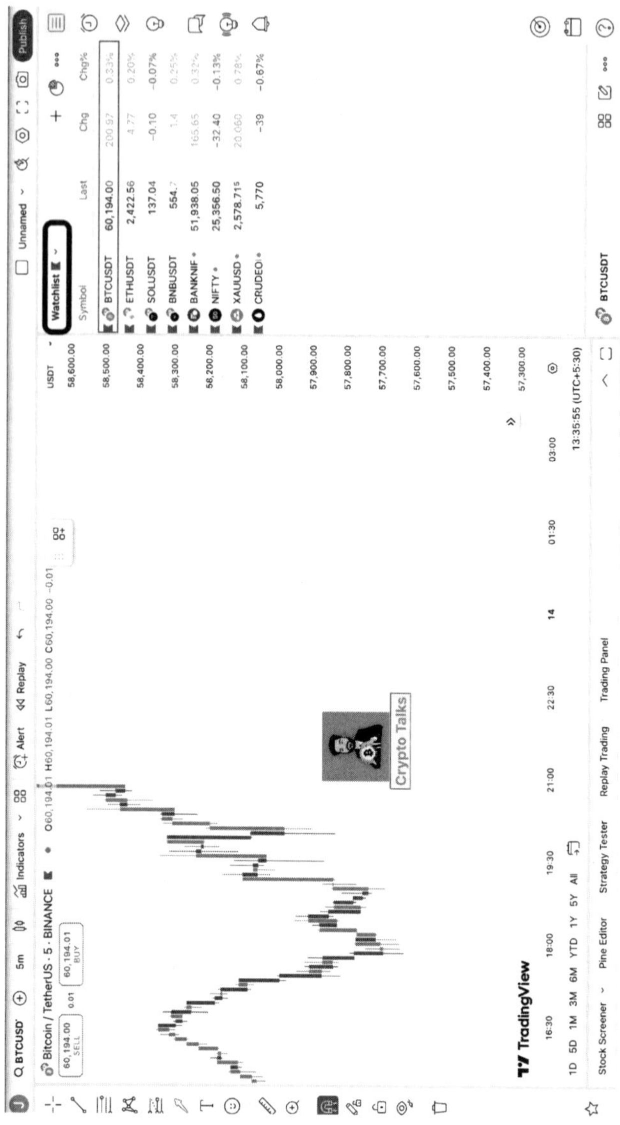

Ideas and Community

One of TradingView's best features is the community-driven ideas section, located in the right-hand panel. Here, you can find trade ideas, technical analysis, and chart patterns shared by other traders. This is great if you're new to crypto trading, as you can learn from more experienced traders. You can also interact with the community by liking, commenting, and sharing your own ideas.

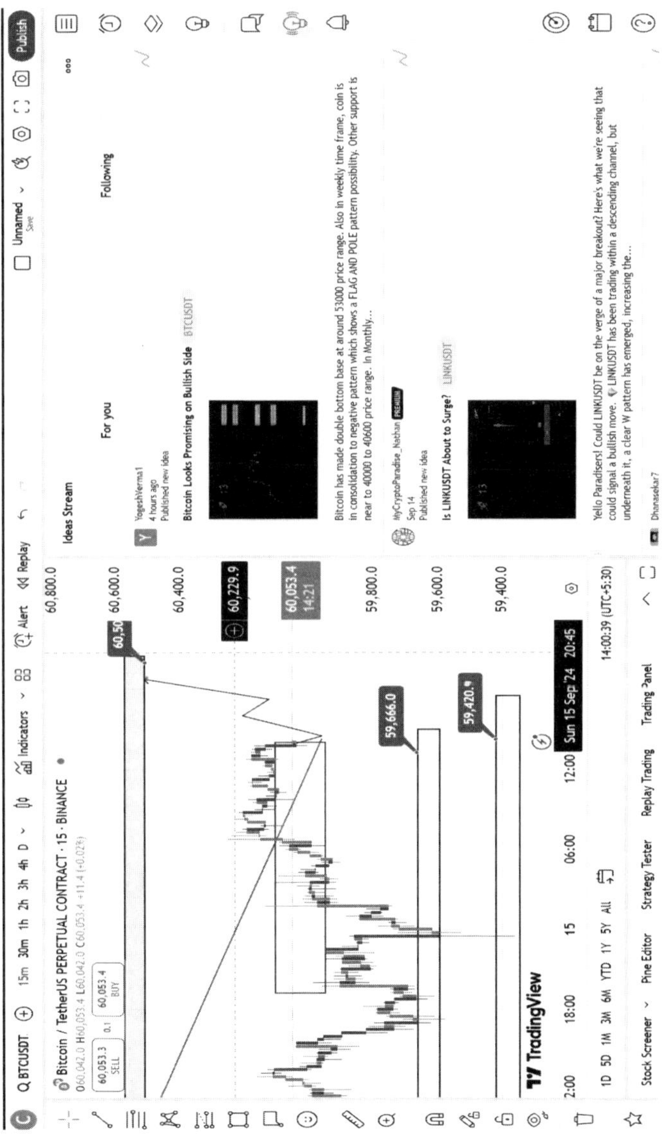

Trading Panel

At the bottom of the chart, you'll find the Trading Panel. This allows you to connect to brokers and exchanges so you can make real trades directly from TradingView. If you're not ready to trade with real money, you can switch to Paper Trading, which lets you practice using virtual funds in real-time market conditions. It's a useful way to test strategies without risking any money.

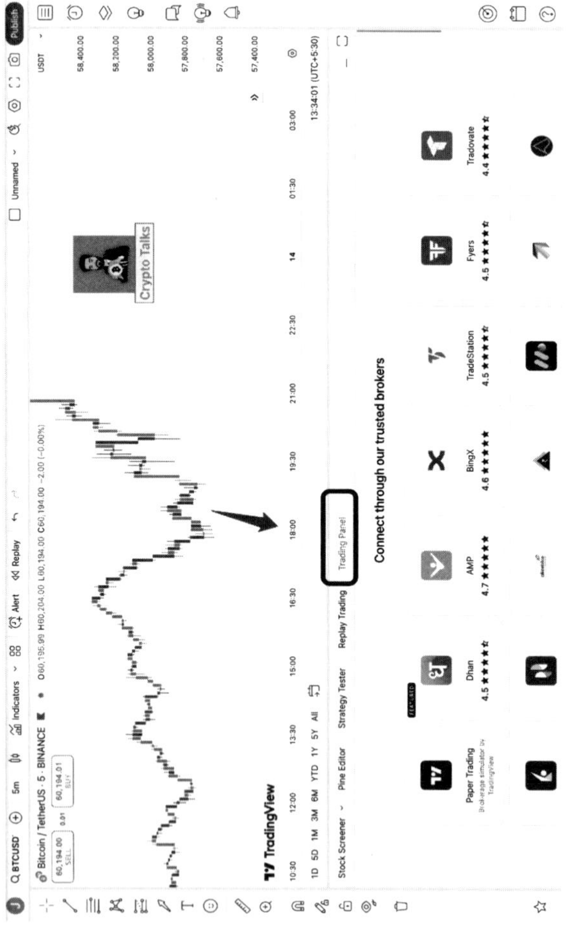

Adding Technical Indicators

As we learned in the previous chapter, technical indicators are important for trading, and TradingView makes it easy to add them to your charts. To do this, click the "Indicators" button at the top of your chart and choose from hundreds of available tools. Some popular indicators for crypto traders include:

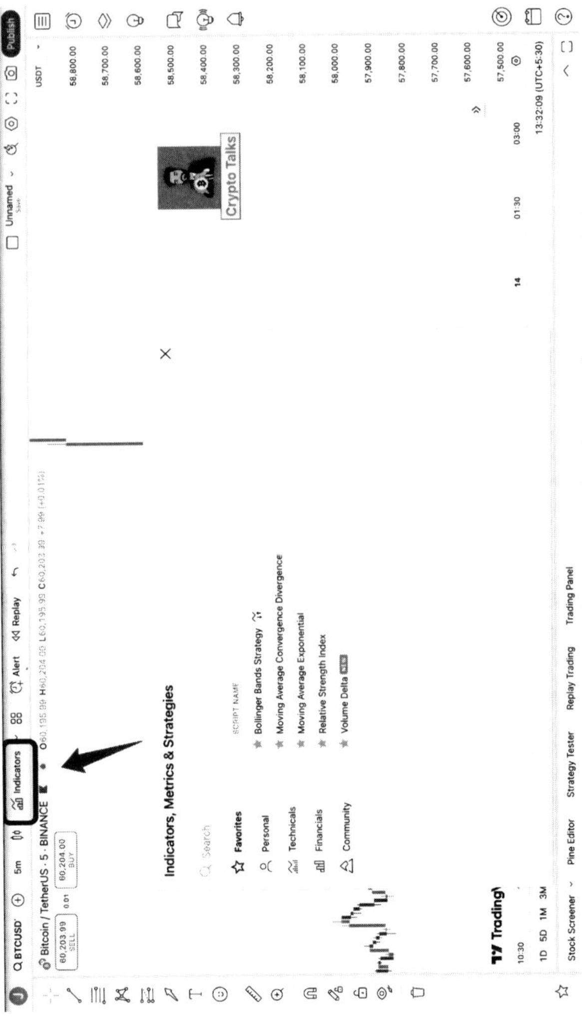

- **Moving Averages (MA, EMA):** Helps identify trends by smoothing out price movements.
- **Relative Strength Index (RSI):** Shows if an asset is overbought or oversold.
- **Bollinger Bands:** Indicates market volatility and possible trend reversals.
- **Volume:** Tracks the trading volume to confirm trends.
- **MACD (Moving Average Convergence Divergence):** Suggests possible trend reversals.

You can customize each indicator's settings, like changing the periods for moving averages or adjusting RSI levels. You can also add multiple indicators on the same chart or display them in separate panels to keep it organized.

Using Drawing Tools

TradingView's drawing tools let you mark important patterns, levels, and trends directly on your chart. On the left side of the screen, you'll find the toolbar with various drawing tools:

- **Trendlines:** To show trends and key support/resistance levels.
- **Fibonacci Retracement:** To find potential reversal points in the market.
- **Text and Shapes:** Add notes, arrows, boxes, or circles to highlight specific areas of interest.

One great feature is that TradingView automatically saves your drawings. Even if you switch charts or timeframes, your annotations will stay in place. You can also lock drawings to prevent accidental changes while analyzing.

If you like trading with specific colors, you can change the chart's color scheme. Right-click anywhere on the chart and choose "Settings." Here, you can adjust the color of:

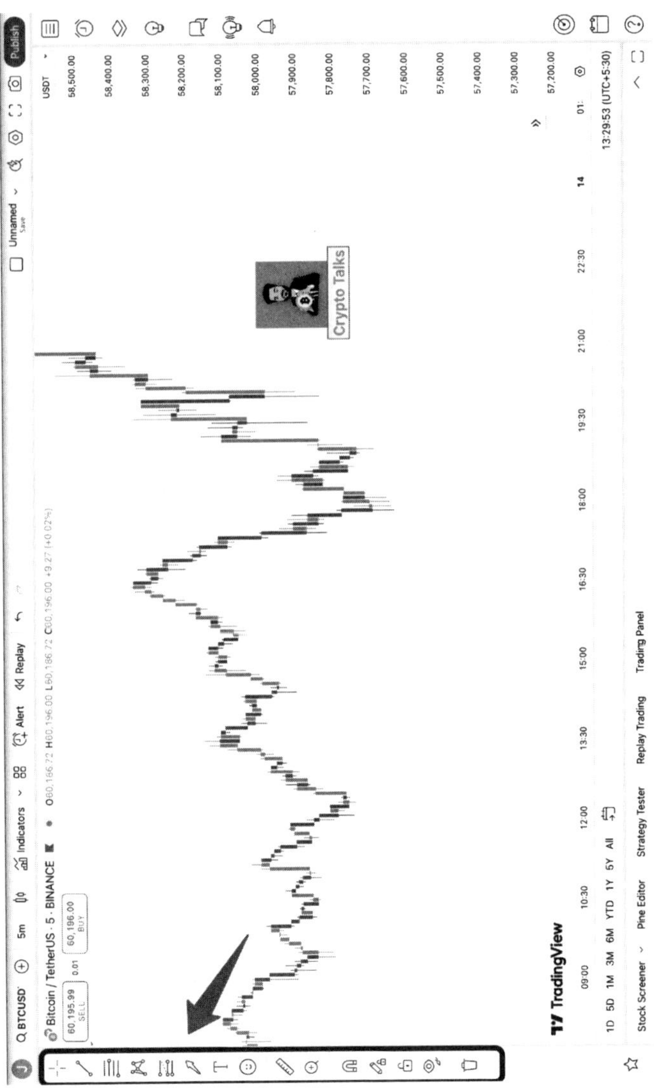

- **Candlesticks or Bars:** Choose different colors for bullish and bearish candles.
- **Background:** Make the background light or dark based on your preference.
- **Gridlines:** Change the color or visibility of gridlines for a cleaner look.

A customized color scheme can make your charts easier to read and more suited to your trading style. If you spend long hours trading, an eye-friendly color scheme can help prevent eye strain, keeping you comfortable while spotting trends.

Saving and Sharing Chart Layouts

Once you've customized your chart just the way you like, you can save it for future use. Just click the "Save" icon at the top of the chart and your layout will be stored. This is helpful if you use different strategies or indicators for various markets. You can easily switch between saved layouts, making it simple to adjust to different trading situations.

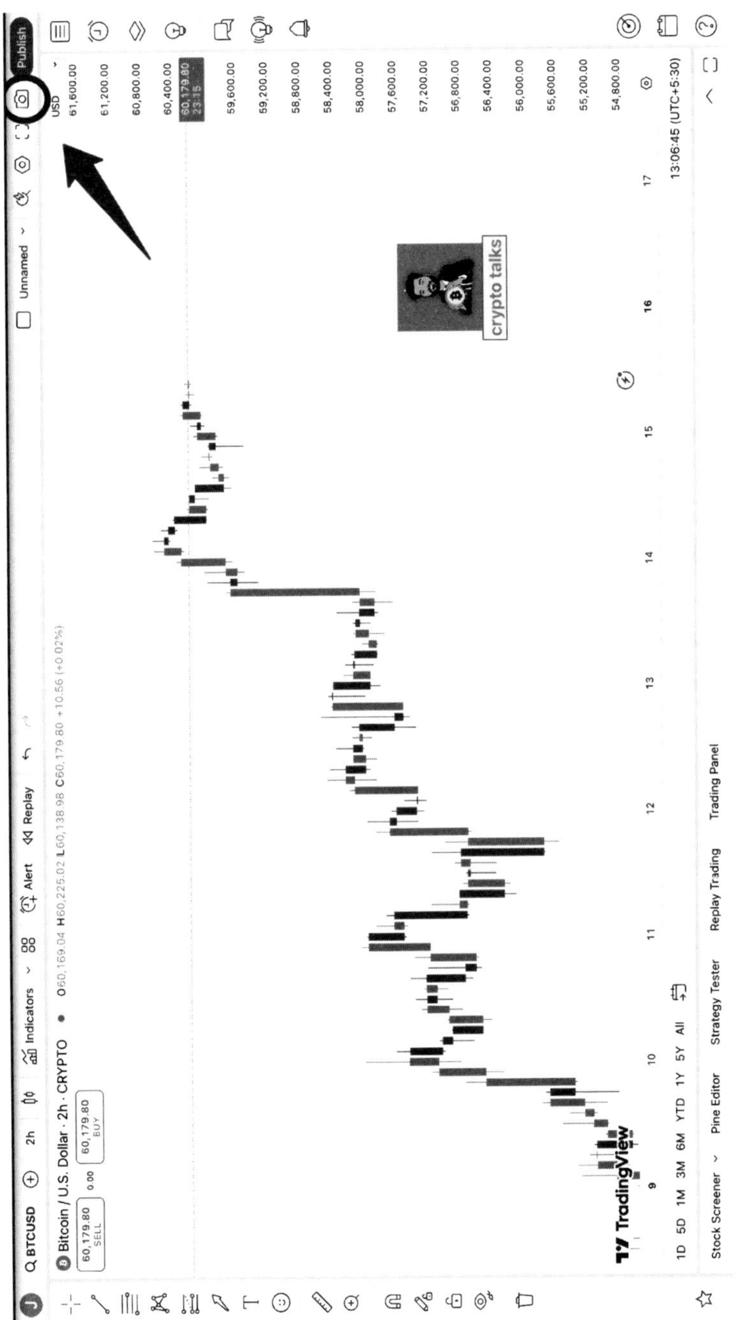
BTCUSD
2h
Indicators
Alert
Replay
Unnamed
Publish
Bitcoin / U.S. Dollar · 2h · CRYPTO
60,179.80
SELL
0.00
60,179.80
BUY
USD
61,600.00
61,200.00
60,800.00
60,400.00
59,600.00
59,200.00
58,800.00
58,400.00
58,000.00
57,600.00
57,200.00
56,800.00
56,400.00
56,000.00
55,600.00
55,200.00
54,800.00
crypto talks
9
10
11
12
13
14
15
16
17
13:06:45 (UTC+5:30)
1D 5D 1M 3M 6M YTD 1Y 5Y All
Stock Screener
Pine Editor
Strategy Tester
Replay Trading
Trading Panel

If you like to share your strategies or collaborate with others, TradingView allows you to share your custom layouts. You can create a shareable link or take a snapshot to post on social media or forums. This is especially useful for crypto traders who like to share their analysis or get feedback from the community.

Setting Alerts

One of the most useful features, especially for crypto traders, is the ability to set alerts. Since the cryptocurrency market runs 24/7, it's hard to always keep an eye on price changes. Alerts help by notifying you when important market conditions are met, so you don't have to constantly watch the charts. So, alerts act as your personal assistant, notifying you when something important happens, whether it's a price hitting a certain level or an indicator reaching a key value. For example, if you're waiting for Bitcoin to break a resistance level, you can set an alert to notify you right when it happens, so you can take action immediately. TradingView offers different types of alerts to help you track the market:

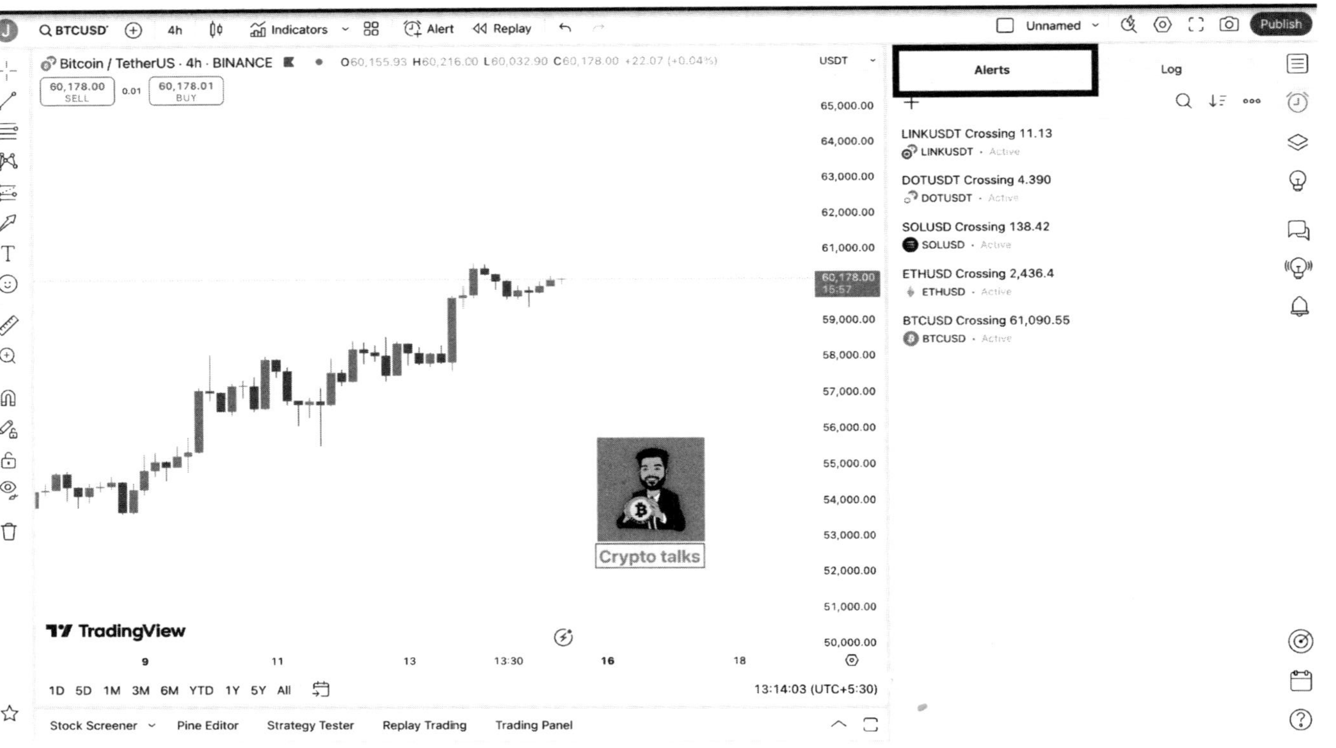
BTCUSD
4h
Indicators
Alert
Replay
Unnamed
Publish
Bitcoin / TetherUS · 4h · BINANCE
O60,155.93 H60,216.00 L60,032.90 C60,178.00 +22.07 (+0.04%)
60,178.00 SELL
0.01
60,178.01 BUY
USDT
Alerts
Log
LINKUSDT Crossing 11.13
LINKUSDT · Active
DOTUSDT Crossing 4.390
DOTUSDT · Active
SOLUSD Crossing 138.42
SOLUSD · Active
ETHUSD Crossing 2,436.4
ETHUSD · Active
BTCUSD Crossing 61,090.55
BTCUSD · Active
65,000.00
64,000.00
63,000.00
62,000.00
61,000.00
60,178.00
15:57
59,000.00
58,000.00
57,000.00
56,000.00
55,000.00
54,000.00
53,000.00
52,000.00
51,000.00
50,000.00
Crypto talks
TradingView
9
11
13
13:30
16
18
1D 5D 1M 3M 6M YTD 1Y 5Y All
13:14:03 (UTC+5:30)
Stock Screener
Pine Editor
Strategy Tester
Replay Trading
Trading Panel

- **Price Alerts:** Set alerts when a cryptocurrency reaches a specific price, useful for tracking support, resistance, and trading opportunities.
- **Indicator Alerts:** You can set alerts based on indicators like Moving Averages, RSI, or MACD. For example, get notified when RSI enters overbought or oversold zones.
- **Trendline Alerts:** If you've drawn trendlines on your chart, you can set alerts for when the price crosses them, helping you spot breakout opportunities.
- **Crossing Alerts:** Set alerts for when the price crosses a certain level or when two indicators (like Moving Averages) cross each other, signaling potential buy or sell points.
- **Time Alerts:** You can set alerts for specific times to remind yourself to check the market or review trades at certain intervals.

Setting an alert on TradingView is easy and can be customized to your needs. Here's how:

1. **Right-click on the Chart:** To set a price-based alert, right-click on the price axis or the chart at the level you want. Then, choose "Add Alert" from the menu.

2. **Define the Condition:** A pop-up will appear where you can set the alert conditions. For example, you might choose "price crosses" a certain value or "RSI crosses above 70."

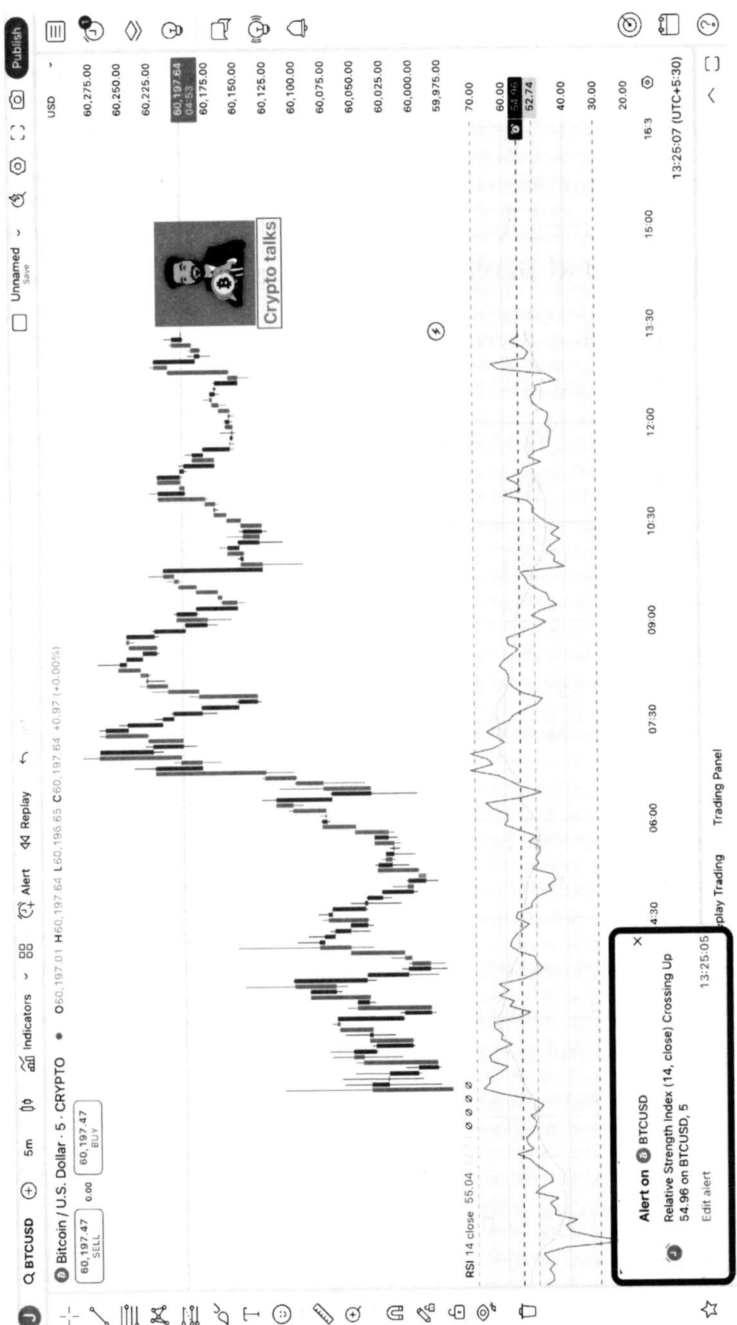
BTCUSD
5m
Indicators
Alert
Replay
Unnamed
Save
Publish
Bitcoin / U.S. Dollar · 5 · CRYPTO
60,197.47 SELL
0.00
60,197.47 BUY
USD
Crypto talks
RSI 14 close 55.04
Alert on BTCUSD
Relative Strength Index (14, close) Crossing Up 54.96 on BTCUSD, 5
Edit alert
13:25:05
Trading Panel
13:25:07 (UTC+5:30)

3. Customize the Alert: You can decide how long the alert will stay active (e.g., until it's triggered or for a few days), how often it should trigger (every time or just once), and how you want to be notified (e.g., pop-up, email, SMS, or app notification).

4. Review and Save: Once your conditions are set, click "Create" to activate the alert. To manage your alerts, click on the Alert Manager at the bottom of the screen.

TradingView offers several ways to notify you when an alert triggers. It includes Pop-up Notifications that will show up on your TradingView screen, Email Alerts, SMS Alerts or Push Notifications. If you use the TradingView mobile app, you can get all these notifications on your phone, great for staying informed on the go.

Managing and Modifying Alerts

Once you've set an alert, you can easily manage it. The Alerts Manager at the bottom of your screen lets you view, edit, pause, or delete alerts. For instance, if you originally set an alert for Bitcoin to cross $30,000 but now want to adjust it to $32,000, simply click on the alert in the Alerts Manager and modify it. You can also pause alerts if you don't want notifications for a while but plan to reactivate them later. There are a few good practices you should keep for Setting Alerts:

Be Specific: Focus on important price levels and indicators that match your trading strategy, instead of setting alerts for every small price move. For example, set alerts for key resistance or support levels or when an indicator suggests a strong buy or sell signal.

Don't Overload with Alerts: Setting too many alerts can lead to alert fatigue, where you might start ignoring them because there are too many. Stick to the most important levels and conditions to avoid feeling overburdened.

Use Alerts to Support Your Strategy: Alerts aren't a trading strategy by themselves, but they can help you stick to your plan. For example, if your strategy is to buy when Bitcoin breaks a key resistance level, an alert can notify you quickly so you can take action.

Practicing with Paper Trading

One of the best ways to sharpen your trading skills without risking real money is by using paper trading. TradingView offers a built-in paper trading feature that allows you to practice making trades, experiment with strategies, and understand market dynamics in real-time—all without the fear of losing any money.

In simple terms, Paper trading is simulated trading. Instead of using real money, you trade with virtual funds in a risk-free environment. The prices and charts are live, just like in real markets, but the money is fictional. This gives you a chance to experience the ups and downs of trading, try out different strategies, and understand how the market behaves, all without the worry of financial losses. It's like having a practice round before entering the real game. You can make mistakes, learn from them, and improve your skills without any real consequences. For beginners or traders testing new strategies, paper trading is an excellent way to get comfortable before trading with real money.

For beginners, paper trading helps build confidence. Over time, this reduces the fear and anxiety that can come with real trading. Finally, paper trading allows you to learn from mistakes, whether it's placing a trade too early or forgetting to set a stop-loss. These valuable lessons come without the cost of losing real money.

Here's a simple guide to help you get started:

1. **Open the Trading Panel:** At the bottom of the TradingView screen, you'll see the Trading Panel. Click on it and a list of brokers and platforms will appear. Look for the "Paper Trading by TradingView" option.

2. **Connect to Paper Trading:** Click on "Paper Trading" and then hit the "Connect" button. This will link your account to TradingView's paper trading platform. You'll start with a virtual balance (usually $100,000, but you can adjust it).

3. **Start Trading:** Once connected, you can start placing trades just like you would with a real account. You can buy and sell cryptocurrencies, set stop-loss and take-profit orders, and track your performance in real time.

4. **Adjust Your Balance:** If you want to practice with a different amount, you can adjust your virtual balance. For example, you can lower it to match the amount you plan to use in your live trading account.

Best Practices for Paper Trading

Paper trading is a valuable way to practice trading without risking real money, but to get the most out of it, you need to approach it with seriousness and care. Here's how to make the most of your paper trading:

Follow a Realistic Strategy: Treat paper trading like the real thing. Use the same strategies, rules and risk management techniques you would apply with real money. Avoid making reckless trades just because you're using virtual money—this won't prepare you for actual trading.

Set Goals and Track Your Progress: Use paper trading to test specific strategies or reach particular goals. Keep a record of your trades, noting your wins and losses. Reflect on what's working and what isn't. This helps in refining your trading plan and improving discipline.

Simulate Real Market Conditions: Resist the urge to take huge positions or make trades you wouldn't normally make with real money. Instead, simulate real trading conditions—use your actual starting capital, position sizes, and risk management practices.

Test Different Market Scenarios: Cryptocurrency markets can be very volatile. Use paper trading to see how your strategy performs in various market conditions, like bull markets, bear markets, and periods of consolidation.

Once you feel confident with paper trading, it's time to move on to live trading, but do it carefully:

Start Small: Even if your paper trading has been successful, begin with small amounts of real money. Trading with real money affects you emotionally in ways that virtual money does not. Small positions help manage emotions like fear and greed.

Review and Adapt: Continue reviewing your trades, adapting your strategies and learning from your experiences. Real trading involves more emotional factors, which should be considered in your trading plan.

Keep Practicing: Even after you start live trading, keep using paper trading to test new strategies or refine your approach. It's a risk-free way to hone your skills and stay sharp in a fast-moving market.

Chapter 10

Risk Management

Risk management isn't the most glamorous part of trading, but it is absolutely essential. It is what separates the experienced traders from the ones who are not able to survive. Similar to how one requires good brakes in a sports car, in trading, especially in the wild world of cryptocurrencies, risk management acts like your braking system. It keeps you from losing your calm when things go wrong, which, let's face it, happens more often than we'd like to admit. A good risk management strategy helps you protect your capital, survive the rough patches, and keep you in the game long enough to capitalize on profitable opportunities. By focusing on the principles of capital preservation, emotional control, and setting smart stop-loss and take-profit levels, you can protect yourself from the market's unpredictability. And remember, trading is a marathon, not a sprint—your goal is to stay in the game long enough to win it. So, keep your head cool, manage your risks wisely and let the profits take care of themselves.

Risk management is mainly to deal with the effects of volatility. But volatility is both a blessing and a curse in the crypto market. It's what makes trading exciting but also what makes it so dangerous. As explained earlier, volatility refers to how much and how quickly the price of a cryptocurrency can change. High volatility means big price swings in a short amount of time. For traders, this means there's potential for big gains—but also big losses. The key to dealing with volatility is preparation. You need to be ready for sudden price changes and that means having a solid plan in place to manage those inevitable swings. There are few things that if you get a grip on, you will be able to make it through the crypto market.

Capital Preservation

Ever heard the saying, "It's not about how much you make, but how much you keep"? That's the essence of capital preservation. In the crypto world, it's easy to get caught up in chasing big returns, but the truth is, your primary goal should be to protect the money you have invested. Think of your capital as your trading lifeline. The more you protect it, the longer you can stay in the game. This doesn't mean you won't take risks—trading is all about taking calculated risks—but it does mean you should avoid careless risks. By focusing on capital preservation, you ensure that a single bad trade doesn't knock you out of the market entirely.

Emotional Control

Let's be honest—trading can be an emotional rollercoaster. One minute you're euphoric because your trade is up 20% and the next, you're in a panic because it's down 15%. The key to surviving this ride is emotional control. Emotions like fear and greed are natural, but they can lead to poor decision-making if you let them take the wheel. How many times have you heard a trader say, "I knew I shouldn't have done that, but I just couldn't help myself"? Probably too many times. Successful traders learn to manage their emotions by sticking to their trading plan, setting clear rules and not letting short-term market fluctuations cloud their judgment. Remember, your brain is your best trading tool, not your heart.

Survivability

You might think that trading is all about making big profits, but ask any experienced trader and they'll tell you that it's really about staying in the game long enough to reap those rewards. The goal isn't to make a fortune in a week (though that's nice if it happens) but to steadily grow your portfolio over time. To do this, you need to manage your risk so that you can weather the inevitable storms that come with trading. The market can be brutal, but if you're smart about your risk, you can survive—and even thrive—when others are throwing in the towel.

Setting Stop-Loss and Take-Profit Levels

Setting stop-loss and take-profit levels is like installing a safety net. As explained in the earlier chapters as well, stop-loss levels are designed to limit your losses, while take-profit levels ensure you lock in gains before the market turns against you. The idea is to plan your exit before you even enter the trade. Why? Because it's much easier to make rational decisions before you're caught up in the heat of the moment. Think of it this way: Would you rather make a plan in a calm, collected state or when you're panicking because your trade is tanking? By setting these levels in advance, you take some of the emotion out of trading and stick to a more disciplined approach.

Portfolio Diversification

Portfolio diversification is like not putting all your eggs in one basket. Instead of betting everything on a single cryptocurrency, you spread your investments across different assets. This way, if one coin takes a nosedive, your entire portfolio doesn't crash with it. In the crypto world, diversification might mean investing in a mix of well-known coins like Bitcoin and Ethereum, along with some promising altcoins. Diversifying your portfolio helps smooth out the ups and downs, making your overall returns more stable.

Asset Allocation

Asset allocation is about deciding how much of your money goes into different types of assets. In your crypto portfolio, you might put a larger chunk into safer, more established coins, while dedicating smaller portions to riskier, but potentially more rewarding, investments. The idea is to balance your portfolio in a way that matches your comfort with risk. If you're cautious, you might lean towards safer assets; if you're more daring, you might allocate more to high-risk, high-reward options. It's all about finding the right mix for you.

Correlation

Correlation is about how different assets in your portfolio move in relation to each other. Ideally, you want to pick assets that don't all move in the same direction at the same time. For example, if Bitcoin and Ethereum tend to rise and fall together, holding both doesn't give you much protection against market swings. Instead, you might include assets that behave differently, like stable coins or tokens tied to other sectors. Managing correlation helps you avoid situations where everything in your portfolio drops at once, keeping your investments a bit safer from market surprises.

Risk Assessment

Risk assessment is all about knowing what you're getting into before you jump in. This means looking at how volatile a cryptocurrency is, its past performance and current market trends. By assessing the risks, you can make smarter decisions about where to put your money and how much risk you're willing to take. It's like checking the weather before going for a hike—you want to know if there's a storm coming so you can plan accordingly. Regular risk assessment helps you stay prepared and adjust your strategy as needed to minimize losses and maximize gains.

Rebalancing

Rebalancing is like giving your portfolio a regular tune-up. Over time, the value of your investments will change and your portfolio might drift away from your original plan. Rebalancing involves selling some assets that have performed well and buying more of those that haven't, bringing your portfolio back in line with your target allocation. This keeps your risk level consistent and helps you lock in profits.

Managing Leverage and Margin

Leverage and margin are tools that can supercharge your profits—or your losses—depending on how you use them. Leverage lets you control a larger position with a smaller amount of money, while margin involves borrowing money to trade with leverage. While these tools can boost your returns, they also increase your risk. If the market moves against you, even a small drop can lead to big losses. Managing leverage and margin is crucial to avoid getting in over your head.

Leverage Ratios

Leverage ratios tell you how much leverage you're using in a trade. A higher ratio means more borrowed money is involved, which can lead to bigger gains or bigger losses. Common leverage ratios in crypto trading might be 2:1, 5:1, or even higher. While high leverage can make you rich fast, it can also leave you broke just as quickly. It's important to choose a leverage ratio that matches your experience and risk tolerance. For beginners, sticking with lower leverage is usually a smarter move.

Margin Calls

A margin call happens when the value of your leveraged position drops too much, and your broker demands that you add more funds to your account to cover the potential losses. If you can't meet the margin call, your broker might close your position automatically to prevent further losses. Margin calls are every trader's worst nightmare, as they can force you to take a loss at the worst possible time. To avoid margin calls, keep a close eye on your positions and maintain enough funds in your account to cover any potential losses. Setting stop-loss orders on leveraged trades can also help protect you from getting a dreaded margin call.

Position Sizing

Position sizing is about deciding how much of your money to put into a single trade. It's a crucial part of risk management because it determines how much you could lose if the trade goes against you. A good rule of thumb is to never risk more than a small percentage of your trading capital on any one trade—often suggested at 1-2%. For example, if you have $10,000 in your account, you might risk only $100 to $200 on a trade. This way, even if the trade goes south, your overall portfolio remains largely intact. Position sizing helps you manage risk by ensuring you're not putting too much on the line with any single trade.

Risk Limits

Risk limits are predefined levels of risk that you're willing to accept in your trading. These limits can apply to individual trades, daily losses or your entire portfolio. For example, you might decide that you're not willing to lose more than 5% of your total portfolio in a single day. If your losses approach this limit, you should stop trading for the day to avoid further losses. Setting risk limits helps you stay disciplined and prevents you from making emotional decisions that could lead to significant losses. It's like setting boundaries for yourself—knowing when to step back can save you from chasing losses and making things worse.

By applying the above risk management strategies, you can better protect yourself in the unpredictable world of cryptocurrency trading. Diversifying your portfolio, allocating assets wisely, and understanding correlations help spread out and reduce your risk. Regular risk assessment and rebalancing keep your portfolio in line with your goals. Managing leverage and margin responsibly ensures you don't get in over your head, while position sizing and risk limits protect your capital. Remember, in trading, it's not just about how much you can make—it's also about how much you can keep.

Chapter 11

Psychology of Trading

Understanding the psychology of trading is just as important as understanding the technical aspects of the market. In fact, some might say that mastering your own mind is the real key to becoming a successful trader. In this chapter, we'll dive into the concept of market sentiment—how it influences price movements, the dangers of herd behavior, and how shifts in sentiment can turn the market on its head.

Understanding Market Sentiment

Market sentiment is essentially the overall mood or feeling of investors and traders about a particular market or asset. It's like the market's collective attitude—are people feeling optimistic (bullish) or pessimistic (bearish)? Market sentiment is driven by a combination of factors, including news events, economic data, and even social media buzz. It's not always rational, but it's powerful. In fact, market sentiment can sometimes drive prices more than the actual fundamentals of an asset. Think of it as the market's emotional temperature, and just like with people, emotions can lead to unpredictable behavior.

Market sentiment has a huge influence on price movements. When sentiment is bullish, traders and investors are generally optimistic, leading to increased buying and rising prices. On the flip side, when sentiment is bearish, fear and negativity take over, resulting in selling pressure and falling prices. The tricky part is that market sentiment can change quickly, often based on rumors, news, or unexpected events. Understanding how sentiment influences the market can help you anticipate price movements and make more informed trading decisions.

Price Movements

Price movements in the crypto market are often a reflection of market sentiment. When sentiment is positive, you might see prices climbing as more people want to buy in, thinking that prices will go even higher. Conversely, when sentiment turns negative, prices can drop quickly as people rush to sell before things get worse. This creates a feedback loop—rising prices fuel more optimism, leading to even higher prices, and falling prices fuel more fear, leading to even lower prices.

Herd Behavior

Herd behavior is when traders and investors start following what everyone else is doing, often without much thought. In the crypto market, herd behavior can lead to extreme price movements. For example, when a coin starts to pump (rise rapidly in price), more and more traders jump in, fearing they'll miss out on the gains. This can drive prices up even further, often beyond what's justified by the asset's actual value. But beware—what goes up can come down just as fast. When the herd turns, it can lead to a sharp crash as everyone rushes to sell at the same time.

Sentiment Shifts

Sentiment shifts occur when the overall mood of the market changes direction. These shifts can happen gradually or suddenly, and they're often triggered by new information, such as major news events, regulatory changes, or technological developments in the crypto space. For example, positive news about Bitcoin being adopted by a major company might shift sentiment from bearish to bullish, sparking a rally. On the other hand, a security breach on a popular exchange could quickly shift sentiment from bullish to bearish, causing prices to plummet. As a trader, it's crucial to stay aware of these sentiment shifts and be ready to adapt your strategy accordingly.

Dealing with FOMO (Fear of Missing Out)

If there's one thing that can make even the most seasoned trader break a sweat, it's FOMO—the Fear of Missing Out. This sneaky little feeling creeps in when you see a cryptocurrency skyrocketing and you're not on board. But here's the catch - FOMO is one of the biggest traps in trading, often leading to poor decisions and painful losses. Let's break down what FOMO is, how it impacts your trading, and how you can keep it under control.

In the crypto world, FOMO can hit hard—especially when you see a coin shooting up in price and feel like you're missing the opportunity of a lifetime. The impact of FOMO can be devastating. It pushes you to jump into trades without proper analysis, chase after price spikes, and buy at the top, only to watch the price crash soon after. FOMO can also lead to overtrading, where you make too many trades, often with little thought, just to avoid missing out.

The good news is that FOMO doesn't have to control your trading decisions. There are strategies you can use to keep it in check:

1. Developing Discipline

Discipline is your best defense against FOMO. Developing discipline in trading means sticking to your rules, even when it's tempting to break them. It's about making decisions based on logic and analysis, rather than emotion. One way to build discipline is by keeping a trading journal where you record your trades, along with the reasons behind them. This helps you stay accountable and learn from your mistakes. Over time, as you see the benefits of disciplined trading, it becomes easier to resist the pull of FOMO.

2. Avoiding Overtrading

Overtrading is a common consequence of FOMO. When you're afraid of missing out, you might find yourself making too many trades, often without a solid reason. This not only increases your transaction costs but also exposes you to unnecessary risk. To avoid overtrading, set a limit on the number of trades you'll make in a day or week, and stick to it. Focus on quality over quantity—sometimes, less really is more. If you find yourself itching to trade just for the sake of it, remind yourself that patience is a virtue in trading. It's better to wait for a high-probability setup than to jump into every little price movement.

3. Setting Limits

Setting limits is another effective way to manage FOMO. These limits can be related to the amount of capital you're willing to risk on a single trade, the number of trades you make, or even the time you spend watching the market. By setting these boundaries, you create a safety net that keeps your trading in check. For example, you might decide that you won't risk more than 2% of your total capital on any one trade. Or you might set a rule that you'll take a break after two consecutive losses to avoid making emotional decisions. Limits help you maintain control, even when the market gets crazy.

4. Real-Life Examples

Let's look at some real-life examples of FOMO in action. During the 2017 crypto boom, many traders jumped into Bitcoin and other altcoins as prices soared, fearing they'd miss out on huge gains. Some bought Bitcoin at its peak around $20,000, only to see it crash to below $10,000 within weeks. The result? Massive losses that could have been avoided with a bit more patience and discipline. On the flip side, traders who avoided FOMO and waited for the price to settle found better entry points, eventually profiting when the market recovered.

5. Case Studies

Case studies can provide valuable lessons in managing FOMO. Take the example of a trader who, during a sudden bull run, feels the urge to buy into a fast-rising altcoin. Instead of giving in to FOMO, the trader checks the coin's fundamentals, looks at the technical indicators, and realizes that the price has already moved too far, too fast. They decide to wait for a pullback, which eventually comes. By entering the trade at a lower, more reasonable price, they avoid the losses that hit those who bought in at the top. This case shows the importance of patience and sticking to your plan, even when everyone else seems to be rushing in.

Coping with Losses

No matter how experienced or skilled you are as a trader, losses are an inevitable part of the game. It's not a matter of if you'll face losses, but when and how you'll deal with them. Coping with losses effectively is crucial to your long-term success in trading.

Let's face it: losses do hurt, a lot. Whether it's a small dip or a significant downturn, losing money in the market can take a serious toll on your mental and emotional well-being. The psychological impact of losses can be profound, often leading to feelings of frustration, disappointment, and even self-doubt. You might start questioning your strategy, your decision-making, or your ability to succeed as a trader. The key is to recognize that losses are a normal part of the trading process. Every successful trader has faced losses, sometimes significant ones, but what sets them apart is how they respond to these setbacks.

1. Emotional Responses

When you experience a loss, it's natural to feel a surge of emotions. Anger, frustration, sadness, and anxiety are common reactions. You might feel angry at yourself for making a mistake, frustrated that the market didn't go your way, or anxious about what this loss means for your future. These emotional responses can cloud your judgment and lead to impulsive decisions, like trying to immediately recover your losses through risky trades. This emotional turbulence can create a cycle where one bad decision leads to another, making it harder to regain your footing. It's crucial to acknowledge these emotions but not let them control your actions.

2. Long-Term Effects

If not managed properly, the psychological impact of losses can have long-term effects on your trading career. Repeated losses can erode your confidence, making you hesitant to take risks or follow your trading plan. In some cases, traders may become overly cautious, missing out on profitable opportunities because they're too afraid of losing again. On the flip side, some traders might swing to the other extreme, taking on too much risk in an attempt to "make up" for their losses—a strategy that often leads to even bigger setbacks. Understanding the long-term effects of losses can help you take proactive steps to mitigate their impact.

3. Strategies for Managing Losses

Fortunately, there are strategies you can use to manage and recover from losses effectively:

- **Reflect and Learn:** Every loss is an opportunity to learn. Instead of beating yourself up, take a step back and analyze what went wrong. Was it a flaw in your strategy? Did you let emotions drive your decisions? Reflecting on your losses helps you identify areas for improvement and prevents you from repeating the same mistakes.

- **Stick to Your Plan:** One of the best ways to manage losses is to have a solid trading plan in place and stick to it, even when things go wrong. Your plan should include risk management strategies, such as setting stop-loss orders and position sizing. By following your plan, you minimize the chances of making impulsive decisions in the heat of the moment.

- **Take a Break:** After a significant loss, it's often a good idea to take a step back and give yourself some time to cool off. Trading while you're still reeling from a loss can lead to poor decision-making. Taking a break allows you to reset mentally and come back to the market with a clear head.

4. Avoiding Revenge Trading

Revenge trading is when you try to immediately recover your losses by making more trades, often with higher risk. It's like trying to win back your money at a casino by doubling down after a bad hand—rarely a good idea. Revenge trading is driven by emotion, not logic, and it often leads to even bigger losses. The best way to avoid revenge trading is to recognize when you're feeling the urge to "get back at the market" and resist it. Remember, the market doesn't care about your losses, and trying to force a win usually backfires.

5. Support Systems

Having a support system in place can make a big difference in how you cope with losses. Trading can be a lonely endeavor, especially when things aren't going well, so it's important to have people you can talk to who understand what you're going through.

6. Mentorship

A mentor who has been through the ups and downs of trading can provide invaluable guidance and support. They can help you navigate the emotional challenges of trading, offer perspective on your losses, and share strategies that have worked for them. A good mentor won't just teach you about trading—they'll also help you develop the mindset you need to handle the inevitable setbacks.

7. Professional Help

If you find that your losses are having a serious impact on your mental health, it might be worth seeking professional help. There's no shame in talking to a therapist or counselor, especially if trading is causing you significant stress or anxiety. Professional help can provide you with tools and strategies to manage your emotions, improve your mental resilience, and ensure that your trading doesn't take a toll on your overall well-being.

Developing a Trading Plan

In the world of cryptocurrency trading, having a well-thought-out trading plan is like having a map and a compass when navigating through uncharted territory. Without it, you're just wandering aimlessly, hoping to stumble upon success. A trading plan isn't just a nice-to-have—it's an essential tool that guides your decisions, keeps you focused, and helps you manage risk. Let's explore why a trading plan is so important, how to structure it, and what key components it should include.

Imagine trying to build a house without a blueprint. You might get the job done eventually, but the process would be chaotic, and the end result probably wouldn't be very stable. The same goes for trading. A trading plan is your blueprint—it outlines your goals, strategies, and rules for entering and exiting trades. It helps you stay disciplined, avoid emotional decisions, and focus on long-term success rather than short-term gains. Without a plan, you're more likely to make impulsive trades, take unnecessary risks, and ultimately, lose money. With a plan, you have a clear path to follow, which can make all the difference between success and failure in the volatile world of crypto trading.

1. Structure

A well-structured trading plan provides clarity and direction. Think of it as the framework that holds everything together. Your plan should be organized, easy to follow, and tailored to your individual trading style and goals. While every trader's plan will look a little different, it should cover key areas like your trading strategies, risk management rules, and performance goals. The structure of your plan helps ensure that you don't overlook any important details and that you're prepared for different scenarios in the market. It's like building a strong foundation before you start constructing the rest of the house—get the basics right, and everything else falls into place more easily.

2. Consistency

One of the biggest advantages of having a trading plan is that it promotes consistency. When you have a set of rules and guidelines to follow, you're more likely to stick to a consistent approach, which is key to long-term success. Consistency means making trades based on your plan, not on your emotions or a whim. It helps you avoid the common pitfall of jumping from one strategy to another whenever things don't go as planned. By being consistent, you can better evaluate what's working and what's not, making it easier to fine-tune your approach over time. Remember, in trading, it's not about getting lucky once—it's about being consistently good.

3. Components of a Trading Plan

A solid trading plan includes several key components that work together to guide your trading decisions. Let's break down these components:

- **Goals and Objectives:** Start by defining your goals and objectives. What do you want to achieve through trading? Are you looking to make a certain amount of profit each month, or are you focused on growing your portfolio over the long term? Your goals should be specific, measurable, achievable, relevant, and time-bound (SMART). Clear goals give you something to aim for and help keep you motivated, especially during challenging times.

- **Risk Management:** Risk management is the cornerstone of your trading plan. This includes setting rules for how much of your capital you're willing to risk on each trade, where you'll place your stop-loss orders, and how you'll manage leverage. The goal is to protect your capital and ensure that a few bad trades don't wipe you out. A good risk management strategy will keep you in the game long enough to see your trading plan bear fruit.

- **Trading Strategies:** Your trading plan should outline the strategies you'll use to enter and exit trades. This could include technical analysis methods like chart patterns, indicators, and moving averages, or fundamental analysis techniques like following news and market trends. Whatever strategies you choose, make sure they align with your goals and risk tolerance. It's also important to test your strategies in a demo account or backtest them using historical data to see how they perform before you put real money on the line.

- **Review and Adjust:** Markets are constantly changing, and your trading plan should be flexible enough to adapt. Regularly reviewing and adjusting your plan is crucial to staying on top of market conditions and improving your performance. This might involve tweaking your strategies, adjusting your risk management rules, or setting new goals. Think of it as a continuous improvement process—each review helps you refine your approach and get closer to your objectives.

5. Goals and Objectives

Your goals and objectives are the foundation of your trading plan. They give you a clear target to aim for and help you stay focused on what you want to achieve. When setting your goals, be realistic and specific. Instead of saying, "I want to make money trading," try something like, "I want to achieve a 10% return on my portfolio over the next 12 months." Clear goals help you track your progress and make adjustments as needed. They also keep you motivated, especially when the market isn't moving in your favor. After all, it's easier to stay on course when you know exactly where you're headed.

6. Risk Management

Risk management is all about protecting your capital and ensuring that you can continue trading even after a few losses. In your trading plan, risk management should include rules for how much you're willing to risk on each trade, where you'll set your stop-loss orders, and how you'll use leverage. The idea is to limit your downside while giving yourself room to profit when things go well. For example, you might decide never to risk more than 2% of your trading capital on a single trade. This way, even if the trade goes against you, your overall portfolio remains largely intact. Remember, in trading, it's not about avoiding risk entirely—it's about managing it wisely.

7. Trading Strategies

Your trading strategies are the specific methods you'll use to decide when to buy and sell. These could include technical analysis techniques like identifying chart patterns, using indicators, or following trends, or they might involve fundamental analysis, where you make decisions based on news, events, and the overall health of the cryptocurrency market. Whatever strategies you choose, make sure they align with your goals and risk tolerance. Testing your strategies before using them in a live market is crucial. You wouldn't want to jump into a new diet without knowing how it might affect your health—treat your trading strategies the same way.

8. Review and Adjust

No trading plan is set in stone. As the market evolves, so should your plan. Regularly reviewing and adjusting your plan ensures that it stays relevant and effective. Maybe a strategy that worked well in a bull market isn't performing as expected in a bear market—that's okay, as long as you recognize it and make the necessary adjustments. Review your performance regularly, look at what's working and what isn't, and be willing to tweak your plan to improve your results.

Overcoming Psychological Biases

In the world of trading, your biggest challenge isn't just the market—it's your own mind. Psychological biases can cloud your judgment, leading you to make decisions that aren't in your best interest. The tricky part is that these biases often operate under the radar, influencing your choices without you even realizing

Psychological biases are like mental shortcuts that help us make decisions quickly, but they can lead us astray, especially in the high-stakes world of trading. Here are some of the most common biases that traders face:

1. Confirmation Bias

Confirmation bias is the tendency to seek out information that confirms what you already believe while ignoring or dismissing information that contradicts it. In trading, this might mean focusing only on news or data that supports your existing position while disregarding signs that suggest you should reconsider. For example, if you're bullish on Bitcoin, you might only pay attention to positive news and overlook warning signs that the price could drop. The danger with confirmation bias is that it can lead you to hold onto losing trades for too long or enter trades that aren't well-supported by the data.

2. Overconfidence

Overconfidence is exactly what it sounds like—having too much faith in your own abilities or judgment. In trading, overconfidence can make you take on too much risk, trade too frequently, or ignore the possibility that you might be wrong. Overconfident traders might believe they have a special insight into the market, leading them to dismiss advice, ignore warning signs, or take on leverage that's too high. The problem with overconfidence is that it can lead to big losses when the market doesn't behave as expected. Remember, the market doesn't care how confident you are—it only cares about the facts.

3. Anchoring

Anchoring is the tendency to rely too heavily on the first piece of information you receive (the "anchor") when making decisions. In trading, this might mean fixating on the price at which you bought a cryptocurrency and letting that anchor influence your decisions, rather than focusing on the current market conditions. For example, if you bought Ethereum at $1,000, you might anchor to that price and hold onto it even as it drops, believing it will return to that level. Anchoring can prevent you from adapting to new information and making objective decisions based on what's happening in the market right now.

4. Recency Bias

Recency bias is the tendency to give more weight to recent events or information than to earlier data. In trading, this can lead to overreacting to short-term market movements while ignoring the bigger picture. For example, if the price of Bitcoin has been rising steadily over the past few days, recency bias might lead you to believe that the trend will continue indefinitely, causing you to buy in at a peak. The danger of recency bias is that it can make you overly optimistic (or pessimistic) based on short-term trends, rather than considering the long-term view.

Strategies to Mitigate Biases

The good news is that psychological biases aren't insurmountable. By being aware of them and using specific strategies, you can mitigate their impact on your trading decisions.

1. Awareness

The first step in overcoming psychological biases is to be aware that they exist. Recognizing that your mind can play tricks on you is crucial. Take time to reflect on your past trading decisions and identify any patterns where biases might have influenced you. For example, did you hold onto a losing trade for too long because of confirmation bias? Did overconfidence lead you to take on too much risk? By acknowledging these tendencies, you can start to catch yourself before you fall into the same traps.

2. Diversified Information Sources

To combat confirmation bias, make a habit of seeking out diverse sources of information. Don't just read articles or watch videos that align with your current beliefs—actively look for perspectives that challenge your views. For example, if you're bullish on a particular coin, read what the bears have to say. This doesn't mean you have to agree with them, but considering different viewpoints can help you make more balanced, informed decisions. Think of it like getting a second opinion before making a big decision—you want to make sure you're seeing the whole picture.

3. Objective Analysis

One of the best ways to overcome biases like anchoring and recency bias is to rely on objective analysis. Use data, charts, and indicators to guide your decisions rather than gut feelings or initial impressions. For example, if you're tempted to hold onto a coin because you are anchored to your purchase price, look at the current market conditions, technical indicators, and trends. Is the trade still valid based on this objective analysis? If not, it might be time to adjust your strategy. By focusing on facts rather than emotions, you can make more rational decisions that align with your overall trading plan.

4. Regular Review

Regularly reviewing your trades is another effective way to mitigate psychological biases. After you close a trade, take time to analyze what went well and what didn't. Did any biases influence your decisions? If so, how can you avoid them in the future? Keeping a trading journal where you document your trades, your thought process, and the outcomes can be incredibly valuable. Over time, you'll start to see patterns in your behavior, and you can work on improving your decision-making process. Think of it like a performance review at work—except you're the boss, and the goal is to become a better trader.

In conclusion, psychological biases are a natural part of the human experience, but they can be detrimental to your trading success if left unchecked. By understanding common biases like confirmation bias, overconfidence, anchoring, and recency bias, you can start to recognize when they're influencing your decisions. Using strategies like awareness, seeking diversified information, relying on objective analysis, and regularly reviewing your trades can help you overcome these biases and make better, more rational trading decisions. Remember, the mind is a powerful tool—but like any tool, it's important to use it wisely. In trading, overcoming your own biases might just be the edge you need to stay ahead of the market. And who doesn't want that kind of edge?

Building Emotional Resilience

In the high-pressure world of trading, emotional resilience is your secret weapon. It's the ability to stay calm, focused, and rational, even when the market is throwing curveballs at you. Emotional resilience isn't something you're born with—it's something you can build over time, like a muscle. The stronger your emotional resilience, the better equipped you are to handle the inevitable ups and downs of trading without letting your emotions take over. Let's explore why emotional resilience is so important in trading and how you can develop it for long-term success.

1. Importance of Emotional Resilience in Trading

Emotional resilience is crucial in trading because the market is unpredictable, and it can be a rollercoaster of emotions. One minute, you're on top of the world because your trade is up 20%, and the next, you're questioning your life choices because the market just wiped out those gains in a heartbeat. Without emotional resilience, these swings can lead to stress, anxiety, and, ultimately, poor decision-making. Traders who lack emotional resilience are more likely to panic-sell during a dip, overtrade out of frustration, or hold onto losing positions out of fear. On the other hand, emotionally resilient traders can stay calm, stick to their plans, and make rational decisions, even when the market is in chaos. Simply put, emotional resilience is the difference between reacting impulsively and responding strategically.

2. Long-Term Resilience

Building emotional resilience isn't just about surviving the day-to-day fluctuations of the market—it's about thriving in the long term. Long-term resilience means developing the mental toughness to keep going, even when things aren't going your way. It's about learning from your losses, bouncing back from setbacks, and maintaining your focus on your long-term goals. Over time, long-term resilience helps you build a strong foundation for your trading career, enabling you to weather the storms and come out stronger on the other side. One way to build long-term resilience is by setting realistic expectations. Understand that losses are part of the game and that every trader, no matter how successful, faces challenges. By accepting this reality and focusing on continuous improvement, you can develop the resilience needed to sustain your trading journey over the long haul.

Conclusion

As we wrap up this book on crypto trading, let's take a moment to go through the key points and leave you with some final tips for success.

1. **Stay Disciplined:** Discipline is the cornerstone of successful trading. Stick to your trading plan, follow your rules, and avoid letting emotions drive your decisions. Consistency is key to long-term success.

2. **Keep Learning:** The market is always changing, and so should your knowledge and skills. Stay curious, keep learning, and be open to new strategies and approaches. The more you know, the better equipped you'll be to navigate the market.

3. **Take Care of Yourself:** Trading can be mentally and emotionally taxing, so it's important to take care of your overall well-being. Make time for rest, relaxation, and activities outside of trading to maintain a healthy balance.

4. **Have a Support System:** Don't go it alone. Whether it's a mentor, a trading group, or professional help, having a support system can make a big difference in your trading

journey. Sharing your experiences and learning from others can help you stay motivated and focused.

5. **Be Patient:** Success in trading doesn't happen overnight. It takes time, practice, and persistence. Be patient with yourself and the process, and remember that every setback is an opportunity to learn and grow, so keep calm and keep moving forward one step at a time.